D0696878

POVERTY AND PRISON

FOLLOW-UP TO
FRUSTRATIONS OF MY PAST

Jennifer —
Thanks for the support
Champ!
9-7-18

CHRIS "CHAMP" NAPIER

CHRIS "CHAMP" NAPIER

Copyright Information
© Copyright 2017 Chris "Champ" Napier.
All rights reserved. No part of this publication may be
reproduced, stored in a retrieval system, or transmitted, in
any form or by any means, electronic, mechanical,
photocopying, recording, or otherwise, without the written
prior permission of the author.
PP-FV4

ISBN: 978-1542983396

DEDICATION

TO MY FAVORITE person, my beautiful grandmother Ella Mae Bonner, who made her transition from this life just nine months after my incarceration. To my family for their prayers and lack of support, you all really made me stronger. To my good friend Sister Esther Gales who encouraged me to write like John when he was on the Isle of Patmos. Brother Fateem for giving me a Holy Quran and introducing me to true Islam, and helping me understand that Islam is counterproductive to the recidivism rate.

CHRIS "CHAMP" NAPIER

MAN! WHAT A MAN!!

I write to acknowledge a person, Christopher "Champ" Napier. Champ, grew up in Prichard, AL, where I was Mayor from 1972 to 1980. Prichard then had a population of some 45,000. It was half Black and half white, and strictly segregated. Prichard was the third poorest city in the United States, after Laredo and Brownsville, Texas. Champ's memories are from growing up on Omega Street, behind Shepard's Lounge. By the time Champ was growing up, Shepherd's Lounge was a place where, if you asked every one to put their guns on the table, each table would fill up with weapons. The surrounding neighborhoods, where Champ learned to fight, to make a living on the streets, getting the finest girls and becoming a threat to his rivals, were Prichard's "Killing Grounds". Champ's memories reveal a riveting recollection of life which persists to this day.

When you read about neighborhoods like Alabama Village, Snug Harbor and the projects in Prichard, it is useful to know that these neighborhoods and projects were built for white workers at the Mobile shipyards and returning white veterans. These neighborhoods, over time, due to white fight, absentee landlords, joblessness and rampant drug use became home to the poorest African Americans in Prichard.

Champ's story tells about life, how it was truly lived by the underclass of African Americans. His story belies the hundreds upon hundreds of young people who navigated their way through Blount and Vigor High Schools to graduate from Bishop State Junior College, Alabama State, Tuskegee and Talladega colleges. Blount and Vigor produced star athletes were recruited by Alabama and Auburn and even some out-of-state colleges. Some of these Prichard natives went on to play in the NFL. Many of these young people received advanced degrees becoming doctors, lawyers and teachers. Very few returned home. Most of them understood how fortunate they were to be able to leave. But Champ's life tells a very different story.

What Champ has written raises the blinds for all to see the real life in for poor, destitute, angry and hopeless young men, found not only in Prichard, but in every city in the nation. Mandatory minimum sentences were filing Alabama's prisons. Champ details how fortunate he was to escape with his life. He was not, however, able to escape being sent to prison. It was a shock to him. It was mind bending for him. At the age of 19, Champ thought he was invincible, until the Judge told him that he was to go to prison for the rest of his life. For year after year, Champ was unrepentant, angry but strong enough to survive the assaults and overwhelming homosexual advances by other inmates.

Related to the reader with clarity and detail, Champ's story is arresting and reads like a novel. But, Champ never gave in and he never gave up. He became anti-social and remained a rebel. Over time he was introduced to the Muslim religion. Like so many prison converts, it took time for this convict, now a man, to submit to the Muslim religion and the teachings of the Holy Quran. The Muslim religion teaches a very conservative life style, different form Champ's history. Champ's change did not go unnoticed by prison authorities. He became one of law enforcements favorite advertisement for where an evil life leads. Champ was trotted out to school and churches to tell his story of redemption. The jailers finally became convinced Champ had made a conversion and, after serving almost 15 years in prison, Champ was paroled.

He shares with the reader the pain of freedom, the mistreatment of former felons, and the cost of paying the justice industry for freedom. Finally, Champ tells us about the collateral consequences of being a former felon. Champ also shares what it means to have a Parole Officer who gets to know you as a person, not just as felon. This newly born Muslim convert so impressed his Parole Officer that Champ eventually secured a Pardon from the Alabama Board of Pardons and Parole.

Champ's story, unlike so many whose life began like his, while still not yet complete, has an ending the reader cannot wait to come He is the epitome of the saying, "Be broke, but don't be broken". But, most of all, it shows the resilience needed to stay true to the tenets of the Holy Qumran, which teaches Protestants, Jews, Muslims, people of faith and of no faith alike, that there is always the possibility of forgiveness, even if forgetting is not in the deal. Rehabilitation is a reality that prevents recidivism. It is a truism that a society cannot have a justice system without punishment for crimes. What Christopher "Champ" Napier's, *Poverty and Prison Frustration of My Past*", leaves, with those who are fortunate enough to read, is a riveting review of poverty, young criminals, broken homes and no belief in a future. It implicitly asks what it is that we individually and as a society, can do to change that which is described in this important book.

A.J. Cooper, Esq.
Mayor, Prichard, Alabama
1972-1980

CONTENTS

1. Dysfunctional Family - Page 3

2. The Ghetto - Page 5

3. Hostile Environment - Page 13

4. Rebellious - Page 29

5. I Quit!! - Page 57

6. Don Juan - Page 89

7. Crack Cocaine - Page 109

8. Trigger Happy - Page 123

9. Incarceration - Page 137

10. Plantation - Page 161

11. THE BOTTOM - Page 171

12. Sexual Mischief - Page 179

13. Consciousness - Page 195

14. Madhouse - Page 211

15. Intellectual Giant! - Page 241

16. Political Prisoner - Page 257

157061 - Page 269

CHRIS "CHAMP" NAPIER

POVERTY AND PRISON

FOLLOW-UP TO
FRUSTRATIONS OF MY PAST

CHRIS "CHAMP" NAPIER

CHRIS "CHAMP" NAPIER

CHAPTER 1
DYSFUNCTIONAL FAMILY

THE ESSENTIAL INGREDIENTS for a dysfunctional family and community are genocide, fratricide, and menocide. Dysfunctional families are something that existed within the black family structure well before slavery. It began during the biblical days of Cain and Abel because of jealousy. Look how Joseph's brothers sold him into slavery. Somewhere along this process we were truly disconnected from God and have been catching hell ever since.

Black people are the only people who came to America by malicious and forceful means, which was a very dehumanizing act. It was never planned for us to be productive for ourselves. During slavery the black man was never allowed the opportunity to spend quality time with the black woman. He had to work in the fields from dusk to dawn. The only time he spent with a woman was for producing children. Therefore, the family bond was trained out. That is why hit-and-run is so common today. There are many social dysfunctions keeping us unstable such as racism, poverty, drugs, and murder. The lack of unity has killed us, fear and ignorance has imprisoned us.

The social injustices have affected my family greatly. All are poverty-stricken, drug users, or high school dropouts. Before I was thirteen years old we lived in seven different locations and that is seven different ghettos. The majority of my family is unemployed or underemployed. It is a proven fact that education is the most important factor that determines whether a person is poor. Poverty is hell.

This confusion has played us against one another. The vast majority of people who are hooked on drugs are from poverty. Most American prisoners are also from poverty. It's been more black people who have gotten killed by blacks in the last ten years for drugs or some form of petty hustling.

I have been victimized by this, as well as a victim. Before I was four years old my father was killed by a black man. When I was eighteen years old I murdered a black man. I have four uncles who have been to prison. Becoming a product of this type of environment can make you unstable.

CHAPTER 2
THE GHETTO

MY LIFE BEGAN on March 30, 1971. I was born somewhere in Mississippi to Alice Napier and Willie James Bonner; both of my parents were high school dropouts. My mother had her first child at sixteen years old. I have a brother named Ricky eighteen months older than me.

My father was a construction worker and, as far as I can remember being told, a big fan of boxing. Due to his enjoyment of boxing, he nicknamed me "Champ." Champ is a very big part of my life; basically because that is all I have to remember my father by. We all lived with my grandmother in the heart of the ghetto (Queens Court Projects). It was probably three or four bedrooms for the ten of us: my grandmother, my two uncles (Larry and Freddie), my aunt Jean, her husband Warren, my favorite cousin Tiffany, my mother, my father, my brother Ricky, and me. Things were tight, but we were happy.

There was a playground not too far from where we lived. Often Ricky, Tiffany, and I would play out there. Sometimes it would be a few older bullies hanging around out in the playground. My father would always instruct us that there's no fair fighting, hit them with something and run.

One day I was playing on the playground and two little boys jumped me and I ran home, only for my father to make me go back outside to fight. He wanted me to get a stick or something to hit the bigger one with. After I hit the older one, my father came behind me and took the stick and encouraged me to beat the youngest one's butt. I did just that. I can remember my father holding me up in the air hollering, "The Champ! The Champ!" The name Champ has stuck with me until this day. Often my father would make me fight my cousins and whenever I beat them up, he would hold me up and say, "You're the Champ!"

Nevertheless, I was traumatized by living in Queens Court; it was hell. My uncle Larry was always getting off into trouble. Larry had gotten into a fight with an older man named Sammy Campbell. Sammy must have won. My father ended up taking the fight up and shooting Sammy in the leg.

One day Ricky, Tiffany, and I were sitting on the front porch; there came a man limping across the parking lot hollering for my uncle Larry. Larry wasn't there, so my father came to the front door. By both of them being light-complexioned, Sammy mistook my father for Larry or probably didn't care. Anyhow, Sammy pulled out a sawed-off shotgun and shot through the front door; the buckshot from the gun ripped my father's chest into parts.

All alone, Ricky, Tiffany, and I were frozen, not aware of what really happened, until a loud outburst of cries and screaming was heard. I went inside and my father was lying on the living room floor—dead. My grandmother, my aunt, and mother were lying around begging him not to die. But it was too late. My mind went blank for a few years. I was too young to realize that this was the beginning of a downward-spiraling life for me. Every time I went inside of Queens Court Project, I would feel very uncomfortable. The smell of my father's death is still floating through the air.

After my father died we moved to several more ghetto hoods. I mainly stayed with my grandmother, until my mother hooked up with Richard. He told her that my grandmother

6

was getting a social security check and that if my mother had me she could be getting a check as well.

By now my mother had two more children, Miranda and my little brother Damien. Richard is Damien's father. We don't know who Miranda's father is.

I never got along with Richard. Richard used to say he didn't like my father because he thought that he was a gangster. Richard didn't have a stable job and my mother didn't work. Therefore, we moved around mainly to different rat-infested ghettos.

One of the most decent places we lived was on 1415 Omega Street in Prichard, Alabama. I remember this place because this is where I've chilled at the majority of my life. Today I still visit this hood. The house we had on Omega St. was really nice with central air and heat. Finally we felt rich, although it was Section Eight. We had it made. It was three bedrooms and all had tile floors. The only negative factor was that there was a nasty wooded area next to where we lived and a pathway. On the other side of the woods was a hole-in-the-wall nightclub.

The name of the club was Shepherds Lounge. At night, we could hear the music from the club and when shootouts took place at the club we could hear gunshots. A lot of times we were home alone and around midnight someone would burglarize our home. Ricky would always tell me to play like we were asleep; this happened on many occasions. We only lost a black-and-white television and radio. We couldn't afford jewelry. Events like this make you angry for life.

Normally, they'd end up in our back yard half-dead or stabbed and shot up pretty bad. One morning, my uncle's old partner, Pony Head, ended up on our front porch damn near dead. This was caused due to a fight he had gotten into at the club. He claimed he was trying to run for help and collapsed on our front porch.

Other than that, it was okay living on Omega Street. The neighborhood was full of kids our age. Bruce, Willie Jones, Pat, and my favorite homie Temo all lived on Omega Street. Next door from our house lived the Dunns.

Terry was about seven years older than me. Real cool player type. Fighting dogs and getting high was his main thing. Terry had one of the baddest dogs in the hood named Killer. I hated that dog. Killer was a full-blooded German Shepherd dog that would chase the hell out of you.

Sometimes they would let the dogs chase you for no reason. We would all go to the big field and watch the dog fights. People from surrounding neighborhoods would bring their dogs to let them fight: Grant Circle, Alexander Court, and Bessemer Projects.

On the other end of Omega Street lived Terry Austin and the rest of the bad dudes. Terry Austin had a dog named Bandit. Terry Austin and Terry Dunn would never let their dogs fight each other out of respect for each other or simply out of fear of embarrassment, because dog fighting was a big thing to them. They would get together and steal dogs from the dog pound to let their dogs practice with. Normally they would let their dogs kill the other dogs.

I just stood around and watched the action. I've always had a strong dislike for dogs and it just increased after we moved on Omega Street. You couldn't walk or ride your bike down the street without getting chased by a dog. Their dogs were so crazy they would even chase cars.

Every time Terry Austin got drunk he would chase behind you with his dog or a pump shotgun. This took place all while we lived in this hood, until one day he got drunk and forgot he had tied his dog to the car bumper and dragged his dog down the street full speed. I was glad this happened, less problems.

The majority of the children on Omega St. attended Chickasaw Elementary or K. J. Clark Middle School; both are located in Chickasaw, an all-white, redneck city. Every time a black person got caught doing any type of wrong, he would be found hanged.

We were bused to and from school and weren't allowed to go any farther. I was now in the first grade and my brother was in the third. The bus picked us up on the corner so it wasn't a problem until we headed towards this slum-ass hood, Alabama Village—nothing but poor white trash lived in the Village.

On the way to school through the Village we would be victims of so many verbal racial attacks that you couldn't keep up with them with a computer. These dirty white folks would pull up next to the bus in their car, with their hippie dog-type hair, and shoot the bird at us and call us all kinds of nasty niggers.

This was real strange to me since we had on clean clothes and were on our way to school to be educated. But these people were driving raggedy cars, living in houses that weren't up to living standards, looking like they hadn't used a toothbrush since they had been invented, and would be insulting us.

I just didn't understand the racial aspect of life.

At every red light, white folk would insult us, even the little kids. It was only about eighty-five blacks at the entire school. When the bus entered the school parking lot, the racist shit continued; white parents who were dropping their kids off would be sitting in their cars giving us dirty looks.

The racial overtone was very high at Chickasaw Elementary, not just among the students, among the staff as well. It was only three black teachers, no more than four: Mrs. Cunningham, Ms. Hill, the P.E. teacher, and another fat lady. The majority of the cooks in the cafeteria were black. This must have resulted from the effect of slavery—we were good enough to cook white folks' food but not smart enough to educate their children.

I was in Mrs. Cunningham's class my first-grade year. All of us were in love with this beautiful sister. She understood us well, although with her teaching position, I believe she knew that she was out of place.

My mother had already attempted to teach me how to read, write, and count, but I had a slight problem with my ABCs and controlling my temper. Playing games was cool to me. Whenever it came to playing the dozen, I had no understanding. Every time someone would say something like your mother such-and-such and your father this, I would go upside their head. I normally got away with it because my father had been killed while I was young and the teachers and staff at school tried to sympathize with me. Sometimes, whenever I would get mad with somebody, I'd hit them and claim that they said something about my father.

My mother was always whipping me for something that I had supposedly done wrong. She would tell me not to fight or curse but I would always do the opposite. I thought she was trying to make a sissy out of me. I rebelled and she whipped me some more. I received so many whippings that I was under the impression that I was an adopted child.

I've always had a psychological repercussion about eating rice. Rice reminds me of nasty maggots. The way we were living in the projects, I was forced to take out the garbage with maggots all over the bags.

One day my mom had cooked chicken and rice. I wanted hot dogs and french fries, I had told her earlier, but she didn't listen. So she started her complaining, "My daddy told me not to laugh at those retarded children when I was pregnant with you, I wish I had listened. Look how you turned out." She was always indirectly trying to tell me that I was mentally retarded. My brother found the shit funny.

While we were sitting down eating, I ate the chicken but I refused to even touch the rice. When I would ask for more chicken, I was denied because I didn't eat the rice. My mother would say, "Eat the rice!" When I refused, my mother would jump up and shove a few spoons in my mouth. I refused to swallow; she kept telling me to swallow. I would shake my head no. My mother would jump up and slap me and rice would go everywhere. I would start crying and she would tell me to eat the rice again. I just couldn't eat the rice. She would grab the broom and hit me a couple of times with it. I still didn't eat the rice; she made me go to my room. My chump brother would laugh. It wasn't all that funny to me.

So as I walked from the kitchen table, I would grab him by the neck with my left arm and hit him in the face with my right fist. He was stronger than me; he broke out of my headlock and we went head-on for a while, until my mother broke us up. Then I got another whipping for jumping on my brother. I felt as if I was treated unfair. I would get two whippings from my mother, and he would only get one.

I didn't appreciate the way I was being treated. Inside of my home had become a hostile environment to me. Every day when we got from school, if my mother had rice cooked, I'd say I guess I will be getting a whipping again today. These whippings didn't affect me at all, because I would simply go outside and fight someone down the street.

If I wasn't getting a whipping from my mother, I'd get one from my sorry-ass stepfather, Richard. He never did like my father for some reason, so he probably was trying to take it out on me. Everyone I've ever met always said that I was a reflection of my father, and I knew Richard disliked me. Once we were at Prichard pool and this chump (Richard) knew I couldn't swim so he threw me off into the deep end of the pool (12 ft). He was probably hoping that I would drown.

Black men do suffer from a misdirected source of anger. They'll be angry at white folks for the way they are treated on the job, but be too big of a slave to direct it to the supervisor; so they'll come home and beat the hell out of whoever is closer to them—wife or children. It didn't matter as long as the person is black. So every time this sorry-ass nigger hit me, I hit him back. My father had never beaten me, so I felt no one ever should. I lost a lot of fights between me and Richard, but I promised myself I would get him back whenever I got bigger and older. I did.

CHAPTER 3
HOSTILE ENVIRONMENT

ALONG WITH ALL the abuse and neglectful treatment I received at school, inside of the house had become a hostile environment for me as well. I was constantly fighting in the hood.

Willie Jones lived across the street from us. Willie and I would fight every day, sometimes two or three times a day. The older guys in the hood were boosting us up: "Get him Champ, get him Willie." As I think of it now, they did us exactly the way they did their dogs. Sometimes I would beat him and sometimes he would win. If I won, I would bring hell to him because I would start the fight back on the next day.

Willie was one of the fortunate ones in the hood. His family supported him. He had everything he wanted when he was seven or eight years old. He had a Go-Kart and mini bike, when most of us were only blessed to get a cheap bicycle from the dollar store.

I should have had everything since my mom was getting social security on my behalf or supposed to have been. I never received any of it. Every time the issue came up she would argue that the check was in her name and she did what she wanted to do with it. I never had anything I wanted. My mother had everything she wanted and needed—cheap jeans, perm, and money to buy cigarettes and beer—and I almost starved to death.

Most of the time, my mother and Richard would go to the club and spend unnecessary money. Ricky and I would have to stay home to watch Miranda and Damien by ourselves. Ricky was probably nine or ten and I was six or seven years old. Ricky would cook rice intentionally to get back at me. Sometimes I would have to boil eggs to eat. We were so broke I had to eat dry saltine crackers or ketchup sandwiches with the end parts of the bread, and drink sugar water when we didn't have Kool-Aid. These times were hard for us.

Sometimes throughout the night one of my mother's sorry brothers would come and stay with us. I can recall a lot of times on the weekend that someone from the club or from somewhere would burglarize our house and we would have to play like we were asleep until they left. The only thing they could steal was a small black-and-white TV and portable radio. They got that like our life was most important to us.

My uncle Redbird and uncle Freddie were always trying to avoid Jean, although they lived right next door to each other; probably because they owed her some money or because of something that my grandmother told her they did. How did a woman get so much power?

One day Redbird had his girlfriend, Pat, came over to the house and he beat her up. My grandmother tried to break it up, but he wouldn't quit. My grandmother ran out of the house and called Jean. Here comes superwoman running to her mother's rescue with a glass in her hand.

Redbird must have heard the call also, because he was dragging Pat out of the front door. Jean caught him on the front porch and beat him half to death, all over the front yard. Pat was crying, therefore Jean made her go inside of the house and continued to beat him. I don't know what the fighting started over, but Jean stopped it and won it. This helped me get in compliance with her. From that day forward she was my favorite auntie.

I remember one time Jean came home from work and someone was in her backyard trying to break in her garage. Jean went in her purse and pulled out a thirty-eight and chased whomever it was down the street while shooting at them. I don't think anyone ever went into her backyard again.

One evening Redbird and Lil Pop ran into my grandmother's house with a lot of money. He gave Tiffany and me two bags of change to have; we counted it and divided it. We didn't ask where the money came from and didn't care. We just were glad to have it and spend it well.

Later, Prichard police came and busted my grandmother's front door down looking for Redbird for first-degree robbery. Redbird and Lil Pop had robbed a laundry mat on Main Street in broad daylight. One of his old partner's aunts saw who it was and said she would tell if they didn't give her a hundred dollars. I assumed they didn't give her the money, therefore she told.

Redbird and Lil Pop left and went to New Orleans for a while until they got tired of running and hiding. They eventually got caught and were sentenced to ten years in prison. This traumatic experience had a very big effect on my grandmother's life. For the rest of her life she would have to deal with one of her children being in prison, including me.

I was constantly back and forth between the two, my mother and grandmother, when I was a child. My mother thought it was a good idea for me to spend as much time as possible with my grandmother, since I was my father's only child. I couldn't get along with my stepfather or anyone else in the neighborhood.

I wish I had been the only child. I could've had everything that I wanted. I always wanted a Go-Kart. I wanted a Go-Kart because everyone on Omega Street my age had something to ride with a motor it. On Christmas day almost everyone would be showing off their new Go-Karts, mini bikes and motorcycles.

The only thing I was infatuated with was BB guns. The majority of the time and whatever money I received went to shooting my BB gun. Every dime or quarter I got, I ran to the corner store to buy me a pack of BBs. I would shoot birds all day long in the wood next to our house. I had gotten so straight, that I had started to brag.

My uncle Big Bro had taught me how to shoot a gun. Sometimes we would be in the backyard lining up bottles to have target practice; he would always instruct me to aim a little lower than your target because the gun has an automatic kick to it. Sometimes I would shoot his twenty-two rifle.

If I wasn't shooting birds, I was running with the dudes down the street. I was at a disadvantage because they already had pellet guns. I only had a cheap Daisy. I just enjoyed the opportunity of shooting a gun.

Later, when my mother bought me a pellet gun, I was shooting everything on Omega Street. Omega Street was full of dogs. Every dog that barked at me, I shot. The sorry neighbors would come to my mother's house complaining.

"Your son Champ was shooting at my dog this morning" or "He shot my child." I would lie and tell my mother that the dogs were chasing me. Majority of the time the dogs were barking at me. I would shoot the kids because they offered themselves as good targets. Normally, I would shoot the girls because they would have no chance in beating me up in a fist fight. The only girl I spared was Hermonica Bullard, only because she was special to me.

Broderick, Temo, and I were on the rock pile hanging and Broderick was winning, so we double-teamed him and got the best of him. This sissy ran in the house to his older brother Head, and me and Temo started to shoot his ass up.

The same way, none of us ever got along until it was time for us to go fight against someone else. But we had plenty of mischievous activities.

Sometimes we would all get together and go up inside of an empty house and kick a hole in the wall and kick doors open. Our most mischievous act was to buy firecrackers and smoke bombs from the corner store. We would go off in Alexander Court and throw firecrackers in people's houses and run; or we would find a house with an open window and we would throw smoke bombs in and make them run out.

Everybody in the hood was really impressed with wrestling. We used to wrestle all day in school and out in the field on an old mattress when we came home from school. Every time someone moved out we would pull their mattresses out in the front yard and make us a ring. This kept us bruised up. Sometimes it would be so many of us that we would have to tag team or have to build two rings. I was the champion in the hood for wrestling.

When it came to karate, I would get my butt kicked. Ricky once kicked my two front teeth out while we were outside kicking at each other.

My mother was one of the first ones to get a floor model TV. Every Saturday morning all of us would be in the living room watching wrestling. She would tell us not to watch that fake stuff because my little brother Damien was always crying whenever he saw blood on TV. We were really hyped and believed in Bob Armstrong. We watched this man get beat for thirty minutes, then come back with a karate blow and win. We were young and didn't know any better. Bruce Lee would come on and win. I can't ever recall him losing a fight. This little man would beat up the whole Chinatown by himself.

Whenever this went off of TV, we would go and give our version of it in the backyard. Ours would always end up in a real fight. We would have sticks, bats, chains and anything to hit someone with.

Most of the time, we would go up to Prichard Stadium to fight the boys from Bessemer Projects. It would be so many of them in our hood that they would get chased from Prichard Stadium. We all would go around the back side of the stadium to get a piece of cardboard. We would walk on the side of the interstate and pretend the hillside was a large mountain. It would be about twenty-five children or more on the side of the interstate playing on the hill.

Every Saturday morning this was our routine. After the Friday night football games there would be leftover sodas and sometimes food.

During the very first part of my second-grade year, a hurricane by the name of Fredric came. This hurricane nearly destroyed Mobile County and most of the southern part of the state.

They had been teaching us in school what to do if a hurricane appeared or a tornado arrived during a school day. No one took it serious. They would blow the whistle and rush everyone into the hallway. We had to go through this silly practice. We had to get on the floor and put your head between your legs. I kind of liked this activity because it interfered with our boring school work. We ran into the hallway saying put your head between your legs and kiss your ass good-bye.

Hurricane Fredric did appear but it wasn't during school hours. We were at home when it started to get really dark. It seemed like the world was coming to an end. It was raining as well. People in the hood were taping up windows, heading to nearby shelters, and running to the store to collect last-minute items.

My mother said that we were not going to a shelter because the hurricane wasn't going to blow down a brick house. That was true, but trees started to fall and windows were breaking out. She decided to leave as soon as my stepfather came home. We went over to Blount High School for shelter. This was as far as we could make it.

On the way to Blount, trees were flying everywhere. We passed by three or four houses that were crushed by trees. The streets were flooded.

Once we entered the school it was filled to capacity. People were everywhere, trying to find a comfortable place inside the gym. It seemed like the entire city of Prichard was there. People were laying their blankets up and down the hallway. Blount High School was so raggedy that we probably could have found a safer place in the middle of the football field.

We survived the ordeal of the hurricane. The worst part came when everyone was settled in, trying to go to sleep. Then the roof was blown off of the gym. Everyone inside had to head for the hallway. People were running around like they were going to outrun the hurricane.

The next morning, things were messed up pretty bad. We got in the car and rode around to check to see how much damage was done to the city. There were many streets that we could not even drive down.

Trees were blocking the streets, along with light poles. Somehow we made it to our house and we just experienced flood damage. Willie Jones' grandmother's house was destroyed completely. It was a big oak tree in the front yard and strong winds from the hurricane blew it over the top of the house.

As we were riding by Prichard Mall, we could see people running back and forth from the stores to put merchandise in their cars they had taken. They were robbing these people blind. Down the street it was Goodyear and Firestone. Brand new tires were rolling up and down the streets so fast. People were going crazy putting these tires in their cars. It looked as if they were having so much fun. If I had been grown, I probably would have done the same thing.

The living conditions were so bad that the National Guard was sent in and a curfew was placed. Everyone had to be off the street by dark. The power was out for months.

My only benefit from the hurricane was that school was delayed for a long time. The schools had to be cleaned and repaired due to the damages that occurred during the storm. I really enjoyed this.

Most of the time I would ride with my uncle Big Bro around the neighborhood, since school had not begun. He was in love with smoking weed. I never saw him without a sack of weed or a joint. We would ride, smoke weed, and listen to the latest jams on the radio. His favorite singers were Rick James and Prince. All Rick James talked about was getting high and freaking women. My favorite songs were *I'm in Love with Mary Jane* and *Mary Had a Pimp*.

My father, my father! These words affected me dearly and they still do to this very day. I hated it all throughout the school year. Everyone was talking about what their father did for them over the summer. I was jealous because I would never have the opportunity to see my father again. This had me crying a lot because I needed my father bad. I needed someone to teach me how to be a man, to ride a bike, and to furthermore kick my stepfather's sorry ass. If my biological father was never killed, my mother would have probably never ended up with Richard.

Every time I would be in the room crying, I was told that boys don't supposed to cry and that made me cold-blooded vindictive because I didn't want to show any weakness. That's a lie that men are not supposed to cry. Prophet David cried. I'll give some respect: my stepfather was okay sometimes. In my eyesight, stepfathers are only substitutes.

Most of the boys in our class were either a member of the Boy Scouts or playing little league football or baseball. I wanted to participate in some of these activities, but I couldn't because my family did not have the money to pay the fees. It was always next season, but that season never did come.

I was never able to buy books from the school's book fair to enhance my ability to read.

Once, I was fortunate enough to attend the fall festival. Absolutely nothing at the event excited me. There were just a bunch of kids running around with their faces painted like clowns. I did not want any of that on my face.

I did not even ride the mechanical bull. I wasn't a cowboy. I am a nigger from poverty. All I wanted was to eat hot dogs and cotton candy.

We eventually went inside the haunted house. We turned it out. There were people dressed like ghosts and monsters jumping out to scare us. Maybe they were teachers but we dealt with them. I made sure that when they came within swinging distance they were introduced to my left and right fist.

Rick and I walked down the long dark hallway; in the middle of the hallway sat a casket. There was someone in the casket playing dead. I turned the casket over and ran the hell out of there.

After that, we ran around the back of the third-grade hall and, deep in the woods, we saw some white people standing around a burning cross. This was my first time seeing the Ku

Klux Klan. I later learned that for the rest of my life I would have to deal with them, hooded or unhooded.

The best thing that happened to me that year was that I met Hermonica. She had moved on the other end of Omega Street. She became a true friend. She was real nice and someone to help keep me focused. We sat on the same seat on the bus and spent hours talking over the phone. This was the only girl in those days that I respected and still do.

Whenever a girl normally called our house for me, my mother used to curse them out and tell them that they needed to be cleaning up their mammy's nasty house instead of talking to boys on the phone.

Somehow, my mother would always let me talk to Hermonica. Every time that she called, I would ask her, "Girl, how in the world did you get my mother to let you talk to me?" She would state, "I asked 'May I please speak with Champ?' " I guess it is true that everyone is influenced by kindness.

Hermonica taught me how to be nice as well. Whenever I called her, she would always remind me to say "may I?" It was strange, but it worked.

I passed the second grade, barely. I took a variety of reading comprehension and math tests. I failed comprehension and did okay in reading. But I still had to take second grade reading.

They wanted to put me in special education classes. I was probably a little too smart for those classes. My attention span was low and my behavior was so negative that everyone was under the impression that I was crazy. So I played along with this so I'd be considered for the most simple work assignment, finish my work and had plenty of time to play around or draw.

During my third-grade year, I realized that the same people who were in the first- and second-grade class were now in the third grade with me. This made things a little bit easier for me because I always have had trouble trying to make new friends.

Even with this, it was a lot of social disturbances going on.

Some deranged guy was going around killing little children, so every day after school I would run from the bus stop and didn't stop until we hit the front door. Sometimes a few concerned adults would meet us at the bus stop. I preferred to run.

I didn't know exactly who the boogey man was. This took place for a few months until the Klan killed Michael Donald in downtown Mobile. This was retaliation because a black man was acquitted for killing a white police officer.

We didn't know why or when the attacker was going to appear. Therefore, everyone stayed close to the house and stayed inside at night. People would be in hallways saying, "You going to end up on brown paper bags or milk cartons."

They eventually arrested Wayne Williams in Atlanta for the children murdered. The killing stopped after he was arrested. I sincerely believe this was a fraud, being only white people became serial killers throughout history. Only one black, to my knowledge, has been convicted of such a crime.

My third-grade teacher was Mrs. Bryant; she was the ugliest racist white person I had ever encountered. She always made a conscious attempt to degrade black people.

During social studies, she would discuss the awful effect of slavery. She would gladly discuss how white people used to sic their dogs on black people for trying to march in Selma, Alabama, and then laugh until her face turned red. All year long she would put dusty white students before the decent black students. She was a true Klan without the hood, a real diabolic witch. I had already consciously and unconsciously developed ill feelings towards white people. This increased my hatred.

While in class, a nasty white girl called me a nigger. I pimp-slapped her and whipped her good. Mrs. Bryant broke up the fight and, instead of taking us to the principal's office, she attempted to settle the confrontation by paddling us. She gave the white girl three licks and tried to give me five, because I was a boy, black, and accused of aggression. After she tried to hit me the fourth time, I took the paddle from her and hit her back with it.

This was my first time being suspended from school. I enjoyed it and realized that it was the best way to avoid those barbarians at the school. Afterwards, I spent more time suspended or expelled.

On the fourth day of my suspension, my mother sent me to the corner store to buy her a pack of cigarettes. I went to Charlie Boys because this was the cheapest and the farthest away from the house. If I could get the cigarettes cheaper, I would have a quarter to keep to myself to buy me a pack of BBs and some candy.

As I was crossing the street on my bike, here comes a car approaching at full speed and hit me. I can't remember the accident in its totality but it was an undercover police officer who hit me and I kept telling him that I was alright and did not want to go to the hospital.

I passed out and the next thing that I remembered was waking up in General Hospital. The accident should have been our way out of poverty. My mother could have sued the officer and got paid. The only thing happened was I was X-rayed and sent home with a few bandages, some pills, and a lot of doctor appointments that kept me out of school.

The majority of my time was spent at my grandmother's house. She would always cook me anything I wanted. I would be over to her house every day. This was the only place that I felt safe, secure, and loved.

When my suspension was up, I only lasted a week before I was suspended again. This time for fighting a white boy named Kirk. He was making racial remarks, how poor black people in Prichard were compared to white people in Saraland and Satsuma. He was talking to my little cousin Al; by Al being real small he probably assumed that he could bully him. But I have always felt obligated to take up his fights. So I kicked his white butt well.

I later found out that Al had stolen one of his hot-wheel cars from under his desk. That's why he was joking with Al in that manner. I knew that Al was a kleptomaniac but it was also my duty to protect him.

I endured the racial harmony of Chickasaw Elementary until the last day of school. This was our day to get back at anyone who had disrespected you in anyway throughout the entire school year.

All the blacks who normally rode the bus would either walk to school or ride their bikes. Everybody from Omega Street and Grant Circle rode their bikes and made sure we had extra chain locks to fight with. Once the bell rang, it was war time. We would run all over the school grounds slapping and hitting every white person in sight, even if they were in kindergarten. We would even fight little white girls the same.

Ricky, Al, Pat, and I almost stomped one white boy to death on the playground before some teachers arrived. Then we jumped on our bikes and got the hell out of Chickasaw. It seemed like the entire white community was chasing behind us for this.

By the time we got close to Prichard, on the side of K.J. Clark Middle School, the drama started all over again because the middle school students were doing the same thing. I loved this type of stuff. This is the only type of freedom I experienced in my life.

Around the second week of summer vacation, Ricky went to live with his father in Florida. My mother let me spend the entire summer over to my grandmother's house. By this time she had moved off of Meaher Street because both of her sons had been sent off to prison. She could not afford a three-bedroom house with the small amount of money she was making. Therefore, she had to move to a one-bedroom apartment on Section Eight on Williams Street in Prichard, Alabama.

Living with my grandmother, I had it made. All I had to do was cut grass and take out the trash. I could easily convince my grandmother to let me do something whenever I felt like it. I would go off to Bessemer Projects to the recreational center to eat free lunch. This was only a hangout for all the gangsters.

About the third time I went to free lunch, someone stole my bike. I was mad as hell. This was the first time that this had happened to me. I later caught Dewayne riding my bike and beat him off of it with a stick. Therefore, I had to stop going to the recreational center.

About once a month my aunt Jean would take all of us, along with my grandmother, to visit my uncles in prison. Early on Saturday mornings we would load up in her Ford Pinto and head for Atmore. This was my first time visiting a prison; even as a visitor, I hated it. They treated visitors no better than they treated the inmates.

My uncles were in the same prison camp. They would come to the visiting area looking fresh. Redbird would always tell me these wild prison stories. Some, like I heard myself while I was in prison.

He would tell me how white people were working them on the farm and how people in prison were killing each other for packs of cookies. This was crazy.

One person named Soldier, who had already done thirty years, had come to prison riding a mule and a wagon. By the time they released him, they had invented cars. On the day he was released, a high-performance Z-28 passed by him and scared him to death. He went right back to prison and told the administration that he couldn't make it because there were flying space ships out there.

Jr. and I would laugh to death about this story. The sad thing about it was, less than ten years later, I was in the same prison talking with Soldier face to face and experiencing this madness myself.

From there we would go to Wilcox County, the hometown of my grandmother, to visit her family. This place was small. I believe everyone we saw in the town was a relative of ours. We would all stay over to Lil Momma's house; this was my great grandmother's house.

She was paralyzed on one side of her body and she was confined to a wheelchair, due to suffering from many strokes, which are a common killer among black people. It was nothing up there that impressed me. I hated the dirt roads and hearing the roosters crow early in the morning. Sometimes my cousins and I would sit on the porch and play spades, waiting to get back to Prichard.

My summer vacation passed very fast. Somehow, my grandmother talked my mother into letting me live with her (thank God). Living with my grandmother, I would attend W.D. Robbins Elementary School. This was my first time experiencing how blessed I actually was. The majority of the students at Robbins lived in Bessemer Projects.

The school was in worse condition than Chickasaw Elementary. I believe that was because the school was located in an all-black community. Roaches and rats were running throughout the cafeteria like they were in the Olympics. The ceilings leaked in the classrooms. Sometimes windows would be broken out. There were times when my home boys and I would break the windows out after school.

While attending W.D. Robbins, I met my partner for life Arthur McFadden. He was a few years older and knew every dirty trick in the book. After school, sometimes we would hang out and just do crazy things. Overall, the environment proved to have a negative influence on me. After that school year, I was transferred back to Chickasaw Elementary. I went back to live with my mother and passed to the fifth grade with very little enthusiasm.

CHAPTER 4
REBELLIOUS

BIOLOGICALLY AND SOCIOLOGICALLY I was raised in a pool of piranhas, barbarians, and sharks—all of these types of vicious predators. Therefore, it was no way possible for me to be a cute little goldfish.

I'll confess I'm not a very nice person and I've never tried to be. I don't believe in such things as turn the other cheek when it's used to defame and rob me. I can't and won't believe in mercy or forgiveness. I learned to be dirty at a very young age. I don't play fair nor do I fight fair. If a stick is available then that's my weapon of choice.

If I run, I'm running to get something to fight with. As I think about it, my entire family has been so badly oppressed that they are incapable of handling the smallest responsibility. Laziness is my family's tradition and welfare is a normal way of life. The people who you are surrounded by influence you, one way or the other. So, I simply refuse to let someone continue to profit off of my pain.

Prichard got to be one of the poorest cities in the state of Alabama. Where there are a lot of poor people, crime is a common factor. Integration has corrupted the city. Prichard Mall is now nearly all abandoned buildings. Black people are so anxious to be able to spend their money with white people that they've destroyed and neglected their community's economic stability.

There isn't a public swimming pool or decent park in the city of Prichard. The park is now a killing hill for anyone who is foolish enough to walk through it. I've heard of a lot of women being raped in that thing that we call a park.

All my life I regretted living in Prichard. Whenever my mother used to take me downtown shopping or to the mall in West Mobile, seeing how people there had well-manicured lawns opposed to ours, it didn't take a rocket scientist to realize that we were being deprived of the good of life.

It's a lot of negative stereotypical things associated with the residents of Prichard. The crime rate is excessive. It was once a joke or rumor floating around that Mobile was going to get a new zoo. It was said that all they had to do was put a fence around Prichard.

Even when you meet girls at the mall, if you tell them you are from Prichard they will either disrespect you or throw your phone number away. I've met plenty of girls who would tell me that I didn't fit the mold of someone who lived in Prichard. Sometimes this even made me regret the fact more.

One thing people in Prichard are highly respected for is fighting and killing. There is only one other community in Mobile that might just fight harder than Prichard and that's Happy Hill.

Prichard had a real popular and dangerous street gang called the Night Zoids. Bessemer Projects was home of the Night Zoids. The Night Zoids didn't play. They were famous for their sawed-off shotguns and robbing. Their girlfriends were called the Pink Ladies. All of the Night Zoids were overgrown juvenile delinquents that had been raised in the detention home, dropped out of school, and were shooting dope daily.

They made every event they attended a bloody affair. If you went to the skating rink or football game, it would end up as a shootout. Even at Mardi Gras you would see them blasting their sawed-off shotguns in the crowd. They should've been shooting the people on the floats. They were only some

30

rich white folks throwing some hungry niggers some candy. No one was ever able to figure out why they had so many shootings at Mardi Gras since they had so many police.

I was standing in front of McDonald's during Mardi Gras when Larry Bear, Arthur Franklin and some of the leaders of the Night Zoids came up with long black trench coats on and said, "Lil Champ, this isn't a good place to be standing tonight. We are fixing to turn it out." So I just moved on down Government Street.

Later I heard a whole lot of shooting. It seemed as if the army was down there shooting it out with them. It turned out that the Night Zoids got into it with someone out of Happy Hill. The Night Zoids made the news almost every night.

I was now going to K.J. Clark Middle School; the school was located in the outskirts of the white community. During my sixth- and seventh-grade year, I caused so much trouble that the entire staff at the school knew my mother, not just by face but by name as well, including the phone number by memory.

All my partners' interests ran along the same line as mine. We were all from dysfunctional families and frustrated with these miserable lives. So we refused to be abused or manipulated.

The most important thing on our mind was getting high, getting over, and getting some sex.

All the people who had attended W.D. Robbins with me were now going to K.J. Clark. They were much older and a little more rebellious. We fought all six periods; sometimes we would fight together and sometimes against each other.

Marcus, Tyrone, Marlo, and I were in the same homeroom class. Ms. Williams was just about as crazy as we were. Sometimes she would be half drunk herself. We used to tell her, "Girl, you need to hook up with us."

Willie's and Herman's fathers were selling reefer. They would steal a couple of bags and bring them to school. We all would go off into the gym bathroom and get high or smoke it at the bus stop. Smoking this weed really made me feel good. I'd be so high I thought I could sing and dance.

Big I.T. was already an alcoholic. I.T. would run across the street to Delchamps and steal a few bottles of Mad Dog 20/20. He would drink the wine with us. This wine really gave me a high.

Some mornings we would be in Mrs. Williams' homeroom class with our eyes barely open. As she called roll she would ask, "Why do you look so funny? Come up to the desk." I'd say something like, "I didn't get much sleep last night." Marcus and I.T. would say the same thing.

When she smelled our breath she would scream, "You thugs! I can't believe you all are drunk early in the morning." She'd just start preaching, telling us we were just messing our lives up at a young age. We would do nothing but shake our heads.

Before Mrs. Williams dismissed class she would always make a statement: "If you are not drunk in homeroom, don't be drunk in my third-period class; and if you are drunk in homeroom, please be sober by third-period class." She'd be pointing directly at us, and everyone in class would burst out in laughter. Marcus and I were in her third-period class; this became my favorite teacher.

I would see her years later, hug her neck and ask to take her out. She would tell me to stop being mannish and to take care of myself.

K.J. Clark was a fashion show. Everyone was competing against one another for the best dressed and who was the finest. We were never concerned about who was the smartest or who's going to study hard to make honor roll. They had me trapped in this.

I'd iron my duck head pants and button-down shirts for an hour, making sure I be sharp. Everybody wanted waves for them babes. So I would keep a fresh hair cut. Hair packed tight with Murray hair grease and I would brush it for hours before I placed my wave cap on it tight. Most of the time, I'd get one of my mother's stockings and tie it over my wave cap. My hair was so wavy; girls use to get seasick looking at my hair. Almost every morning my mother would curse me out for cutting up her stockings.

The sixth-grade students elected me as best dressed for the sixth-grade class. Hermonica and I were still really cool. She told me that they were considering choosing me for the cutest, until some girls said I was conceited and had a bad attitude. They didn't want it to go to my head. I told Hermonica thanks, but no. I didn't care about my picture being in a damn yearbook. I wasn't going to buy one anyway.

Over half of the school was sexually active. Young girls were already pregnant in the seventh and eighth grades.

All throughout the hallways girls were telling me how cute I was and making sexual comments about how bad they wanted to have sex with me. This was right up my alley because I was young and dumb, full of cum, and needed somebody to give me some.

My very first was Tracey. We had science class together. She was fairly unattractive in the face, but had a real nice shape.

While Mr. Thomas was teaching about the sexual reproduction system, we were ready to experience it.

Tracey and I were sitting at the table together one day in class. She told me that she was hot and reached under the table and massaged my penis. I got off right there in class. I had to go to the bathroom to clean myself up, so I asked Mr. Thomas if I could be dismissed. When I left class to go to the bathroom, Tracey followed me. We went off into the girls' bathroom and had sex in the stall. She was good to me although I didn't really know what I was doing. Tracey asked me to be her boyfriend. I said yeah. We kissed and went back to class.

Everybody at school was after those girls who were light, bright, damn-near white, and had Jeri curls. The word is redbones are really freaky as hell and got some good sex. I liked any girl who was willing to lie on her back. Some of my partners even settled for white girls, because they were so easy to have sex with.

My attraction was to dark-complexioned girls. Mainly because I was the exact opposite and dark girls' self-esteem had been crushed really badly according to the way society was.

If you were dark with a big nose, nappy hair, and a big ass you were considered ugly. It looked good to me because I wasn't stuck on the Jim Crow laws.

If you were white, you were right. If you were brown, you could stick around. But if you were black, get the hell back.

Valerie was superfine and pretty as hell. Mostly everyone was fighting over her. I never did entertain her that much. We would flirt from time to time or rub against one another in the hallway. She was really a big tease.

We still had to deal with the racial aspect of life. Every Monday morning the Klan would have been behind the school over the weekend burning crosses and hanging ropes from trees with a black dummy.

A few of us realized that we didn't have to tolerate this any longer. So we would hook up and cut off ax handles, put them in our book bags, and take them to school. We would walk from school that day and beat up on white folks.

Sometimes we had to run through Gulf Village because it was all white. While running through there, we would hit everyone on the streets; even if it was an old white lady, we would throw rocks or wine bottles at them while they be sitting on their front porches.

Once we caught a little white girl almost three or four years old riding on her tricycle. When she saw us running down the street with sticks and ax handles in our hands, she hollered, "Niggers! Niggers! Niggers!" I walked up to her and grabbed her by her hair and slapped her down.

Some fat white man ran out of the house. He didn't have anything in his hand so we stood there and beat him bloody, right there in the middle of the streets. We didn't beat him like we wanted to because some more white people ran outside of their houses to help this cracker. If God wasn't with this white man, I could have had my first murder case at the age of thirteen.

It was too many of them, so we ran down the street laughing until we got in the middle of Alabama Village. Then we just stood around Marvin's Package Store waiting on someone white to come up there so that we could whip them or snatch their pocketbooks. It seemed like every time a white person came, they would be holding their pocketbooks extra tight and looking at us out of the corner of their eyes. If no one came and offered themselves as a good victim, we would leave.

I would go inside of the house to let my mother see me get something to eat and ask her what she wanted me to do before I go down the street. My mother would tell me to wash dishes, clean up my room, or do anything besides run the streets. Whatever my mother told me to do, I did it quick and in a hurry. She never asked about homework because she knew I didn't even play about bringing books home from school. Everyone would meet back up in the big field on the end of Omega Street. Then we would head towards Alabama Village to terrorize.

The first stop would be the 7-Eleven Store. All of us would go off into the store, walk around the store, looking around to see who was inside. Whenever the cashiers turned their heads, that would be the sign for me to go through the door and hold it wide open. The four of us in the store would grab as much as we could and then turn and run out. I was always one of the ones who held the door because I was too scared of stealing.

Then we would go off into the park in the Village, drink the beer, get drunk, and wait for someone white to arrive. If it was baseball season, the little league teams would be up there practicing; therefore, it was always someone to beat up.

On this particular night, we ran across a white boy and girl in the dugout kissing. We surrounded them, "Hey, y'all must think y'all are grown." The white boy jumped up and said, "You bastard, don't mess with us." We didn't want her. We had come there for him. We slapped the shit out of him. She jumped up and got slapped right back down. Someone pulled her shirt off of her. Then everybody started grabbing on her. I picked up his bike and threw it on top of him. Keith said, "Champ, don't tear it up because we plan on keeping it." We beat them a little bit more, poured some beer on top of them, took the bike, and left.

The following day at school, Arthur and I were skipping class looking for some trouble to get off into. While running through the gym, Arthur suggested going to peep through the girls' locker room window, watching them change clothes.

Every girl we wanted to have sex with, we saw. Someone must have seen us and called the principal.

As soon as class changed, Mr. July was on the intercom telling Arthur and me to come to his office immediately. I grabbed my books and headed for the hallway. Arthur was waiting on me.

I asked Arthur, "What you want to do, man? You know Mr. July wants to paddle us bad." So we decided to go smoke us another joint before we went to the office. We went to the seventh-grade hallway and went inside of the bathroom and smoked a joint.

While we were in the bathroom, this white boy named Billy asked did we want to smoke an Alabama pin joint. He pulled out a joint the size of his thumb. All while we were in the bathroom smoking the joint, we heard our names being called over the intercom again. The bathroom was filled with smoke and Arthur and I were coughing. Billy was laughing at us. We were tripping hard, laughing our asses off while all the teachers were looking for us.

The school's guidance counselor, Mr. Covington, found us in the bathroom. Mr. Covington said, "I can't save you all this time, but I just stopped Mr. July from calling the truancy officer on you all. Now go to the office."

As we entered the hallway, everyone was looking out their classroom at us like we were fugitives on the run. We made our way to the office. Mr. July was sitting behind the desk with a mischievous smile on his face. He grabbed his paddle and turned on the intercom. His intentions were to humiliate us in front of the entire school, because everyone looked up to us. My ego stepped in the way of his plans.

Mr. July was talking about giving us five licks and a week of detention. Detention meant staying after school to do homework or extra school work. I told Mr. July that I get too many whippings at home, so it is no way possible that I was going to let him hit me. Arthur just busted out in laughter. I believe the whole school did the same. Mr. Covington said, "You are not going to let him paddle you?" I said, "No." The white boy accepted his paddling and Arthur and I were suspended for a week.

We enjoyed ourselves all during our suspension. We would get up and act like we were going to school and call the school and make bomb threats. This way everyone would be sent home early, and the girls who were scared to skip school we could pick up and run trains on them.

We picked up this Amazon girl. She lived close to the school; her mother ran the streets all the time, so we went to her house. Arthur and I argued about who was going to be first. She picked me first. I was glad because that was the only way I was going to accept it. Mine was a quick one and then I let Arthur have her.

While he was having sex with her, I ransacked the house looking for something valuable to steal. It wasn't anything in the house worth something so I went and hit her again. The girl was real good. She was giving everybody some that was taking off their clothes. Most of the time it would be so many of us surrounding her house like a soul train line.

Our mothers didn't find out we were suspended until it was time for us to go back to school and that's when Mr. July notified us that we had to have our parents to bring us back. We acted like we had just gotten suspended and told our mothers it was only for two days. They found out the truth when it was time for us to go back. Mrs. McFadden would always tell me to stop letting Arthur get me in so much trouble.

The teachers tried to convince everyone that I was the one influencing Arthur to act that way. This was my partner.

We took care of each other. If he had five dollars, half of it was mine. Whenever I was skipping school to go to Burger King, if I only had enough money to buy one Whopper I'd get it cut in half and we would split it. Whenever all the guys got together and bought reefer together, Arthur would always steal a few joints out of the bag for us to have something to smoke later on.

When we got back in school I didn't stay that long.

One of my teachers, a funny-looking white lady, asked me to put my legs in front of my desk. I tried to explain to her that I was too tall for the little desk. She didn't listen, she insisted on making me put my legs in front of the desk. So she tried to bump my legs with her leg and I jumped up and kicked her down.

She ran to the principal's office, faking like she was hurt bad. When I explained to them what had happened, they tried to make me apologize. I wouldn't because I hadn't done anything wrong. They expelled me for good.

Mr. July called my mother and informed her of what had happened and told her he was in the process of calling the juvenile authorities, so it's whoever comes to get me first because that's who would have me. My mother didn't have a car at this particular time. So I left school running. This was my biggest fear, of being locked up.

Since school was officially over with for me that year, I went to stay at my grandmother's house. Most of my time was spent there anyway, especially on weekends and summer vacations. I hated staying with my mother.

By now my grandmother had moved to Snug Harbor on West Drive. This was a real ghetto; the living conditions were so poor. I almost cried when my grandmother had to live there. Snug Harbor was drug infested and crimes were excessive. More people have gotten killed in Snug Harbor than in the Vietnam War.

My grandmother was very understanding towards my situation. She would only say that I'm just like my father. This was good because this was the only time someone ever mentioned anything about my father. When people saw me fight on the street, it would bring my father's name up.

My uncles, Freddie and Redbird, had both been released from prison. Neither one of them ever stayed out any longer than Pat stayed in the army. They were already on the run from the police.

Every morning before the sun rose, the sheriff would bust down the front door looking for them. Their compulsive drug habit that they had developed was kicking their asses hard. Cocaine and shooting dope was their inner confidence. It gave them the drive to get up and do things they wanted. Both of them stayed robbing and stealing.

It seemed like almost every time one of them came off into the house, they would be on their way back from hitting a lick at a store. I would be in the room right behind them and grab me a radio or a watch, or get me some clothes to wear. I'd hang around until they pulled out their needles to shoot up with. I would leave because needles scared the shit out of me. My grandmother was a diabetic. When she took her shots I'd turn my head.

When rap music arrived on the scene, everyone went buck wild. Everybody wanted to dress like the rappers. Run DMC, Fat Boys, and LL Cool J, all these rappers were wearing tennis shoes, sweat suits, and gold chains. My speculation is that their appearance helped increase the sales of tennis shoes and sweat suits. Everyone in the hood started trading in their three-piece suits for sweat suits. All the modern-day players dressed like them as well.

The Fat Boys had a jam called *All You Can Eat*. Seeing the three fat brothers on video weighing over 300 pounds, talking about how hungry they were, and that they needed food, made people start living off of fast food. It fashioned my lifestyle in many ways.

Obesity became normal. Big women started walking around with super-tight miniskirts on, exposing cellulite, saying this is what's in and fat is where it's at.

Break dancing and popping became famous. All the teenagers were imitating the rappers and trying to learn break dancing. Cardboard boxes were spread all throughout the hood. People were standing in line to get down and spin on their heads. You better not slip and tear the box up. If you did, it would automatically get you a good ass whipping. The little children would still be flipping on pissy mattresses and spray painting their names on all the walls.

My mother and stepfather had both started going to church. Before this, they held such nonchalant attitudes towards church. I hadn't been on the inside of a church since I was five years old.

My stepfather would be up early in the morning listening to loud church music and sprinkling olive oil everywhere. I would tell my mother that he's putting a curse on all of us and that this shit didn't work for real.

Ricky and I hated church and my mother because she made us go. The worst thing any parent can do is force a child to attend church. If you are going to make your child go to church, train them up in it while they are young and when they are older it shouldn't be a problem.

Sometimes I would be hoping that the church burned down so I wouldn't have to go or the preacher got sick and the congregation would have to rush him to the hospital. I was happy if anything would prevent me from being involved with the church.

Even in their religious faith they displayed disunity. My stepfather went to one church and my mother, along with us, went to Central Baptist Church. Sometimes Damien went to church with his father. We all never went together. I'm glad for that. The entire Christian doctrine was instrumental in enslaving the black minds.

We were in a black church with all black people praying to a white Jesus. This helped maintain an inferiority complex. Every time a white man stepped off into a black church, I know he smiled and said to himself "I still got me some niggers."

I would go stay at my grandmother's so I wouldn't have to attend church sometimes. I'd even contemplated running away from home. My grandmother would tell me to stay because things will eventually get better. But, they didn't. The only other place I had to stay was with Arthur's mother. Mrs. McFadden said, "You can stay here, but we go to church in this house on Sunday." So my suffering would continue.

Mrs. Davis was my Sunday school teacher. Her teaching ability was very effective. She always taught us about setting goals and ambition.

Mrs. Davis was teaching me about a manipulative snake in the Garden of Eden. Satan had already captured my attention and imprisoned my inspiration. The things Mrs. Davis taught me didn't actually register in my mind until three years off into my prison sentence.

It was fifteen people in our Sunday school class; we had nothing in common with these people. Their parents had good jobs and their mothers and fathers were living together, probably married.

They even believed in the things they were being taught. None of this applied to me. Someone was already dealing with me wisely.

My only benefit was that the girls were constantly flirting with me. They sensed that I wasn't pleased by being in church. So after Sunday school class, they'd encourage me to keep the faith that God was going to bless me, when I got familiar with some of them. I would let them know that I wanted them to bless me; all they had to do was go back upstairs during church service so we could have sex in one of the classrooms; that's the type of blessing I wanted.

My mother had another child, Ingrid. She was so pretty I thought my mother had picked up the wrong child at the hospital.

Soon after Ingrid was born, we moved to Caledonia Street near Prichard Stadium. This was one of the smallest places we had lived. It was a real quiet neighborhood. There were plenty of young and pretty girls.

I still was hanging out on Omega Street most of the time. I had gotten used to that environment. The people on Caledonia Street seemed strange to me. Gary lived right next door. Sometimes we'd get together and pump weights and drink beer. This put a little weight on me. We didn't stay cool for long because he liked to drink beer and I loved to smoke reefer.

When school started, it was my eighth-grade year. I stayed suspended from school for being involved in so many foolish activities.

My mother was trying to do everything to save me. Whenever they had prayer meeting over to our house, she and Sister Gales and some more old ladies with old-fashioned dresses on would come out of the room to pray for me. They'd have this so-called bless oil, shouting in the air, jumping up and down with their fat asses, these people would have the whole house rocking.

"Sit on down, Champ. We are fixing to cast out them evil spirits out of you." I'd go to school the next day, get into a fight and get kicked out. I'd tell my mother, "Those people are working Voodoo or something on me." Prayer does not do any good if the person you are praying for don't have faith.

My mother forced me to get baptized. This didn't help either. No one explained to me what this foolishness meant. The preacher just recited a short prayer and dumped my head under water. One time he held me under water so long that I actually thought he was trying to drown me.

The wine and crackers were a blessing to me. Ricky and I got baptized on the same day. So we bet on what type of wine they were giving us. Ricky would say Mad Dog and I would say Wild Irish Rose. I had seen the preacher a few days before buying it at the store.

Ricky didn't believe me, so we went behind the church and looked off into the garbage can. It proved that I was right; besides, Arthur and I were drinking Mad Dog every day. Therefore, I would have known if it was that.

One of the reasons we drank 20/20 every day was because the bottles were flat, which made it easy to steal. Arthur would skip class and run to Delchamps, put a few bottles inside of his pants and walk out of the store.

Sometimes, when I'd try to be good, trouble just seemed to always be waiting on me. I would question God. When God didn't answer me, I would turn my back on him and the devil would beat the hell out of me.

1986 was a year I will never forget. Crack cocaine, commonly known as rocks, had demised the black community. Everybody who had been broke all their lives had nice cars, plenty of money, and gold around their necks like Mr. T.

Big Buck and Montgomery had more traffic behind King and Mary's Club than the World Series. Arthur, Marlo, and I and a few more would stand around and watch in amazement. Crackheads would be walking the streets like zombies.

Smoking crack is just like slow dancing with self-destruction. Crack smokers will do anything for a hit of crack. They will sell their wedding rings and cars. Their most common saying was "I just got to suck that devil's dick." That is what crackheads call hitting the pipe. I purchased my first pistol from a smoker. It was a chrome twenty-two for twelve dollars.

We eventually lost a lot of friends. Crack didn't discriminate, neither did we. Crack destroyed many lives, including ours. Most of the Night Zoids became smokers. Some of our own teachers and NFL players that we used to admire even started sucking that devil's dick and went all the way down.

When they let me back in school, I was trying to stay out of trouble. Mr. Covington just kept messing with me and Arthur for some reason. He called us to his office because he had heard that I was messing with a white girl. "You know these white folks are going to do you just like they did that boy Michael Donald."

Arthur jumped up and said to him, "Sissy, we don't want to hear that shit. Give me your car keys." He said no and Arthur went off into his pockets, grabbing for the keys. Mr. Covington hit him. I then hit Mr. Covington and we wrestled him down to the floor. Arthur went off into his pockets and got a ten-dollar bill. He grabbed a chain and ran us out of his office. We ran to Burger King to get something to eat.

He didn't tell on us because a lot of people at school were doing him this way. He would always try to frame us and tell us we would be going to CLC riding on that little yellow bus. I had to be crazy for trying to stay in school because the education I was receiving was so inferior that I was making passing grades and barely studying.

My stepfather had gotten a better job at a chemical company and told me that he was going to give us ten dollars for every A and five dollars for every B that we made on our report cards. Money was always my motivation, so I did real well for the next two quarters, until he reneged on the deal. He has multiple personalities.

There was a Black Muslim who always dressed in all-white and had just been released from prison after doing eighteen-and-a-half years. He had a distorted version of Islam; he carried a big oak stick, so we called him Moses. Everybody was telling us not to listen to him because he was crazy. This made us listen to him even more. We'd go buy us some reefer and a forty-ounce and smoke with him. He would not drink. He said, "Alcohol is only the devil in a bottle." We just laughed.

When Marcus got him a good high, he would say, "Moses, turn that stick into a snake." He would ask the question, "You think I can't?" We would laugh at him like a fool. He would run down some deep racist slurs to us about how the white man has produced AIDS to kill off black people and how the whites want all black men in prison or on drugs. This made us rebel harder against the white man and his laws.

We would go off into the Village singing, "We going to whoop us some white folks and it's going to be real soon." We all had guns by now, so we didn't give a damn about anyone. We shot up white folks' cars. Their cars looked like Swiss cheese when we got finished.

We listened to this fool, until he told us that every black person who went to Fat Tuesday in 1986 would not come back alive. He prophesied this all throughout the city of Prichard;

basically, he had a lot of people afraid to go to Fat Tuesday. They went anyway because they had been conditioned to never, ever believe what a black man says when he is a predator, for some reason.

Ricky, Marquail, and I ended up riding our bikes down there. The only thing that happened on that Tuesday was the Baltimore Warriors got into a shootout because they had put the word out that they wanted to be the only people on Government Street with a flat-top haircut. The Warriors had enough members so they could regulate like that. Government Street was like the Wild Wild West.

We eventually lost a lot of respect for the Muslim brother. If he would've been telling us the truth he could've had a lot of followers. So, after that, whenever we saw him walking down the railroad tracks, we would throw rocks at his freeloading ass and run him off.

On my fifteenth birthday, Arthur, Marcus, C.B., and I got together and spent all of our money on getting high. We walked up and down Alexander Court like we owned it. We were lying under the trees, smoking on a joint and drinking Colt 45. A lady came outside and said, "This is a nice day to barbeque." We responded, "Yes, it is." She put a small grill in her backyard and started to barbeque.

We had saved just enough money to get a family box of Church's Chicken, so I told them to get something for us to get high with, and we would just steal her meat off the grill. Everyone agreed.

We went and got us a couple more forties and waited until the meat was ready. By the time we got back, she had went in the house, so we grabbed the hot meat off her grill and ran. The meat was half-done but we didn't have time to finish cooking it because if one of our mothers would have seen us like that, they would've made us stay in the house, and our fun had just begun. We ate the meat half raw and headed to Bessemer Projects to get a sack of reefer.

In Bessemer Projects, we surely got us a good high. I was so drunk they had to walk me home. When I entered the front door, I fell out on the living room couch. My mother came and asked why I came in the house late. I was too drunk to understand what she was saying to me so I would just smile. "Champ, have you been drinking? I thought I told you not to come off into this house drunk again while you are 14." I said "Momma, I'm 15, today is my birthday," and I went to sleep on the couch.

When spring break was over, someone was going around the school taking white boys' money. My name came up because white folks think all of us look alike.

Mr. July came through the gym looking for me and Arthur. As Marcus and I were going through the locker room doorway, he called out my name. I tried to hand my knife over to Marcus; he would not take it because Mr. July was too close to us. So I had to face Mr. July with it. I was for sure that I hadn't done any wrong. When my partner Arthur didn't come to school that day, I knew I was safe.

When I got to Mr. July's office he asked, "How much do you have?" I knew what this was about, so I emptied my pockets on his desk. He said to empty the other one. I gave him the knife. He said, "I know you just can't stay out of trouble."

I proved him wrong because my mother gave me three hundred and twenty-five dollars to go on a field trip to NASA Space Center in Huntsville, Alabama. Mr. July called my mother to verify where I got the money from. After she explained it to him, he hung up the phone and apologized to me and asked, "Do you know who is taking the white kids' money?" I knew but there was no way I was going to tell him, so he suspended me for having a nine-inch knife in school.

Since this was only my second time getting suspended that year, my mother considered me to be doing real good. They wouldn't allow me to go on the field trip. So, my mother let me have the money to go to a LL Cool J concert at Ladd Stadium. Ricky, Marquail, and I attended. I kept the other half of the money just in case I didn't get expelled for the remainder of the school year and I could go to the prom.

Marquail was one of our fortunate partners—he was an only child and lived in a good neighborhood.

He was impressed with the ghetto, so he spent a lot of time at his grandmother's house in order to hang out with us. Most of the time, he would tell us that he hated being the only child and didn't like where he lived. Most of us hated living in Prichard and wished daily to be in his shoes because he had everything he wanted and didn't realize it. Marquail drove his mother's car whenever he wanted.

Good luck did shine on me and I was able to attend the prom. My mother really was proud; she rented me a white tux with a penguin tail, with a red bow tie, and cummerbund to match. We stood in my mother's front yard for a half-hour taking pictures.

My uncle Big Bro let me and Ricky use his car so we had transportation to do whatever afterwards. We went by my grandmother's house to let her see me and to pick up some spending money.

Rick and I bought a half-gallon of gin. I couldn't find any weed to smoke; I had to damn-near make Ricky drink. I regretted it later on because he didn't drink regularly and almost wrecked the car twice before we even got to the prom. Drinking gin straight without orange juice really got to me. I was so drunk when I got to the Admiral Semmes Hotel I could barely walk.

When I entered the hotel's ballroom, everyone was shocked to see me because no one actually knew that I was coming to the prom. They had already labeled me as a thug. A few girls approached me, wanting to dance with me. I ignored them and walked away. The girls we were hoping to win we didn't win.

To top off the school year, we planned to tear the school down. We all skipped school the day before the last day. We had to find some bullets and a good way to sneak the guns into school without getting caught because Mr. July was going to be suspecting us of something.

Someone suggested that we leave the guns on the bus and we would just skip the last class of the day. We had a forty-four on a bulldog frame. We could not find any forty-four bullets, so we used some thirty-eight hollow points and stuffed paper off into the side to make the bullets fit. We also had two sawed-off shotguns and a thirty-eight.

When the bell rang, we went into action. We grabbed the guns and headed for the back side of the school. This was the direction where all the white students lived. It was this big white boy we wanted and had plans to get, because he thought he was tough and some of the black girls liked him. He was known for having a lot of reefer and we wanted it. That punk didn't even come to school. So we took all the rest of their watches and left.

As we made our way to Burger King, it was two carloads of Chickasaw police officers sitting in the parking lot waiting to shoot the first black person in sight. We didn't even go thataway.

I.T. was carrying a book bag full of wine. Everybody had a bottle of Mad Dog and a piece. As a crowd was departing

Burger King, Arthur, Marcus, and I stood in front of them and unloaded our guns. People were hollering, screaming, and running for their lives. We took off running in case the police heard the shots.

We hit Alabama Village, running through it while shooting up cars that were parked along the street. Some Night Zoids arrived; they wanted to try to take our guns, but they didn't know whether or not we would shoot them. They followed us until we got behind Vigor High School. From there, we all eased into Michael's house and threw a small party.

My partners bragged about being in the youth center for the weekend. Before the summer was over, everyone I hung out with had been in the youth center at least once or twice, except for Marcus and me.

When I received my report card in the mail, I had three As, two Bs, and a C for physical education. My mother was so happy; she gave me fifty dollars and made me promise that I would not buy anything to drink with it. When my partners and I got together, we bought reefer to smoke instead.

My entire summer vacation was spent doing what I wanted to do—nothing. My mother normally made me stay n the house until the sun went down because she didn't want me to get too black.

Mr. Sanders lived a street over from us on Whistler Street; he had a swimming pool in his backyard, and he was one of those fortunate black people. Mr. Sanders was a school teacher, businessman, and a gambler. I would tell mother that I was about to go swim over to Mr. Sanders' house. He most likely was at work somewhere. So I would go ring the doorbell to make sure no one was at home; if no one answered, I would jump the fence and swim.

When this became a bore, I would invite other people over. One time, it was about nine o' clock in the morning, there were about ten of us in his backyard swimming. Sometimes we would tell the girls that this was my uncle's house and he was at work. This was our way of tricking them over there.

One Friday Mr. Sanders got off at twelve noon. I didn't know his work schedule; therefore, he caught us in the pool. We were about to run. But he just wanted to know whose idea it was. Everyone said, "Champ, of course." Mr. Sanders asked, "Who in the hell is Champ?!" I jumped out the pool and talked with him. He was real understandable, and said, "The next time, wait until I get home before having a party." I said, "Okay" and jumped back in the pool. When I realized that girls will basically go for anything, it was time for me to take advantage of it.

Around the fourth of July, Temo and I were just hanging around kicking it. One of his uncles was off into the dope game pretty heavy by this time. Temo pulled out a gram of cocaine he had stolen from his uncle. This was my first time seeing pure cocaine. I had seen crack cocaine before. I've seen plenty of cocaine on television. One of our favorite movies was *Scarface*.

Temo said, "Come on, let's get high." He spread it out along the table and made a few lines like they did on TV. Temo pulled out his house key and took a snort, then passed the key to me. I snorted about half of a line. The cocaine immediately rushed to my head. My feet got cold, I felt my toes curl up, and my mouth got numb. We jumped up, ran, and looked in the mirror to look at ourselves. We were under the impression that our faces had changed.

It is a true fact that once you start getting high you will spend the rest of your life doing it, because right then me and him had made a pledge that we would get high forever; well, at least until I went to prison, and I believe he stayed getting high until he got killed.

We finished the rest of the lines off. We were sitting in my mother's living room listening to Run DMC "King of Rock." The cocaine would not let me sit still, I was anxious as hell. I jumped up and said, "Come on, Fat Timmy, we going to see the city."

We walked to my grandmother's house in Snug Harbor. I talked with her for a little while, then she gave me ten dollars. We went and bought a nickel bag of reefer from this lady around the corner and went to the bus stop on Prichard Lane. We smoked a few joints at the bus stop while waiting on the bus. When the bus arrived, it seemed as if everybody in Prichard was catching the bus to go to the mall. The bus was jam-packed. Everyone on the bus was laughing and joking with one another.

The only thing that was really funny was that all of us were probably going to the mall to do some wishful window shopping.

An old lady got on the bus and took a seat in the front of the bus. Temo's fat ass hollered, "Come on to the back of the bus." Everyone on the bus busted out in laughter, even the old lady laughed. When the bus pulled up to the Bel-Air Mall parking lot, there were so many black people jumping off the bus that you could hear the sound of white people's car doors locking (Click, Click).

The inside of Bel-Air Mall was full of teenagers; girls were everywhere. We were exchanging phone numbers like we were celebrities. If we came across an ugly girl, we would give her the number to the police station.

T.J. Maxx was a new store that had just recently opened. So everybody was going there to see what was on sale. We entered the store, it was filled to capacity. There was not a security guard anywhere in sight and there were only a few cashiers. So this was a golden opportunity to steal.

Stealing was not my thing, but if an opportunity presented itself correctly, I would take a little something.

So Temo and I cuffed a few pairs of shorts and some T-shirts real neatly, and went off into the dressing room and placed them in a large shopping bag and headed for the door. As we were walking out the exit door, there was a glass case of watches just sitting like they wanted someone to take them. Temo gave me the bag.

I continued for the exit door in case someone noticed what was going on I could be in a position to hold the door open for him to run out of it. Temo grabbed the watches and walked behind me. Things went smooth.

From there we went to the other side of the mall. Once we got into the main part of the mall, I suggested to go inside McDonald's. There, we divided the watches in the bathroom and got something to eat. Temo saw some girls he knew, so we sat with them. He immediately started putting his game down.

One of the girls was Charlene; she seemed to be about five months pregnant. She was flirting with me hard. She told me that every time she saw me walk today she got wet between the legs. (She had good reasons to have these feelings.) As the rest of the young men were focused on adding a gangster walk to their style, I had incorporated a real slow walk into my character like time was waiting on me. I thought I was an ugly girl's dream and a pretty girl's nightmare. This girl tried to follow me all throughout the mall.

Temo and I got on the bus to go home. We got off the bus on Prichard Lane, walked back to our hood, and sold the watches to some drug dealers. The clothes I stole, I took them home and told my mother that Redbird gave them to me.

54

She didn't ask any questions. Temo and I chilled around the house until dark and then we went looking for Marcus and Arthur. We couldn't find them, so we went and got something to get high with and stood in Alexander Court.

Temo kept instigating that we walk through Bessemer Projects. I knew what time it was so I said, "Hell no, nigger." Temo was kind of fat and thought he was a true player. He stayed desperate for some pussy. So when I told him that I was getting more on accident than he was getting on purpose, he got fighting mad. He pulled out his ragged sawed-off and said, "Nigger, I haven't forgot about the time we was shooting marbles in the front yard and you hit me with a stick and ran."

Every time he gets mad with me he always brings this up, so I didn't pay him any attention. I drank the rest of the forty-ounce and threw the bottle up against the brick wall. As I turned and walked away, Temo blasted the sawed-off in the air. He scared the shit out of me. I stopped and called him a fat-ass bitch. He laughed, we laughed, and then I left to get with Tonya.

Temo and I stayed cool, until his mother moved up the country and forced him to leave with her. Whenever he came over to his grandmother's house, he would stop by and kick it with me and Ricky. When we would get together, we stayed high and tried whatever came to our minds.

The rest of the summer was spent with my old partners, Willie and Arthur. They both had gotten summer jobs, so money wasn't a problem. I am about the only one of the crew who never had a summer job, but they'd always look out for me. We would ride around in Willie's father's brand new Riviera, smoking that good reefer, drinking gin and orange juice, and listening to 2 Live Crew.

CHAPTER 5
I QUIT!!

RIGHT BEFORE MY ninth grade school year was about to begin, Marcus and I were standing in our favorite alley in Alexander Court drinking on a forty-ounce of Colt 45 and smoking on some reefer. It was our plan to go to Blount High School that night for a bonfire and pep rally. When we got close to the railroad track, we could see the blaze from the fire—it had to be about nine feet tall.

The cheerleaders and majorettes were running around in their tight shorts. I knew right then high school was going to be fun. Tracey came up to me and informed me that one of her friends was going to have a quiet house party afterwards and that she would appreciate it if I came. There wasn't anything on my agenda, so I decided to check it out. I told Marcus I knew where a lot of girls were going to be at tonight so just hang with me. The bonfire didn't last long. It ended up being a shootout and some fights. Everyone jumped in their cars and left.

Marcus and I walked to the party. It looked as if we had made it to heaven. We were two of the four males there and the rest were females.

As we were standing in the backyard smoking on reefer and joking, Tracey approached me and we hugged. She wanted to know if I was going to be with her for the night. I said, "Sure!" She was still a freak for me. Eventually, we became one for one another. We sat around the living room joking around.

Marcus pulled this big-booty girl. I went to him and said, "Damn, chump, I bring you to a party and you get the best pick." He just laughed.

The party was boring to me. There were many women sitting around gossiping about how they were going to have sex whenever they got a chance. Tracey suggested that we go around to her house, so we did. She only lived two streets over from where the party was being held.

When we entered her house she let me know what she wanted off the top. She was bold and didn't play games. She knew how I liked it. Tracey told me that she had been watching some sex movies. She wanted to try out some new positions.

We went into her bedroom and took off our clothes. She had a gap between her legs that would make you think you were looking in a tunnel. We got in the bed and did everything that came to her mind and more. Since it was just the two of us there, we went into the living room, turned on the VCR, and put the movie in to make sure we didn't leave anything out.

She had a snapper—the best sex I had engaged in. We stayed busy until around one o'clock in the morning. I missed my curfew, which was midnight. I knew my mother was going to kill me, but Tracey was so good to me that I didn't care. If I would've left earlier, I would have probably killed myself. As Tracey walked me halfway home, she asked me not to get rid of her so soon. I kissed her and told her I enjoyed her and would be back for some more.

When I walked into the house I prepared myself for the argument with my mother, but to my surprise she was already asleep.

The next morning when my mother woke me up I had prepared for the argument in my sleep. She only said to get up and go register for school and if I wanted to sleep I should've been in the house earlier like she had told me.

I got up, took a bath right fast, got dressed, and headed for Blount.

Blount High School should've been condemned years before I attended it; well over half of the school's windows were knocked out. The school was located so close to the railroad tracks, people threw rocks while standing on the tracks and knocked out windows. The rest of the building looked as if it hadn't been maintained since Hurricane Fredric.

The staff was unprofessional and the principal was an alcoholic. Most of the time, the principal was intoxicated. His nickname was Ned the Wino.

The Night Zoids made it their business to rob the trains daily. The day of registration, the Night Zoids hit the train. It was full of Thunderbird wine. The principal ran out of his office onto the train tracks and grabbed him a couple of cases of wine and put them in the trunk of his car.

Even the teachers had problems. Some of them were homosexuals and the rest of them were child molesters. Many of the girls ended up fornicating for passing grades. Some got pregnant and had abortions because the father of their child was a teacher. The female teachers ended up having affairs with students, especially the white women. They were curious about the black males' sexual organs.

Although these school teachers had a college degree, they conducted themselves like thugs. I'm not holding them totally responsible for their negative and unprofessional ways. College degrees only make teachers certified fools. There were about five good teachers at the school, and they acted as though they graduated from an F.B.I. Academy; they were really strict.

The education at Blount High School was so devalued that any nigger who could hold a pencil could graduate from there.

My class schedule was very hectic. I had mostly advanced classes, when I barely passed regular classes during my middle school years.

Ricky was in the eleventh grade and didn't have the type of classes that I had. None of my middle school partners were in my advanced level courses. I revised my schedule to basic classes so I would know everyone. I requested that my schedule reflect regular classes, but the counselor informed me that my placement was based on my eighth grade test scores. We argued for about 15 minutes. Her attitude was so sluggish. I should have slapped the hell out of her.

I went home and showed the schedule to my mother; she went to the school to try and get my schedule changed. The secretary refused to change my schedule. My mother got into an argument with this old witch. They insisted that I take advanced classes.

After what I encountered during registration day, I knew that it would be impossible for me to make it at Blount.

Besides the advanced courses mix-up, all the people who had kept me motivated during my eighth-grade year were attending Vigor. That left me hanging out with all of my hell-raising associates at Blount. Peer pressure was one of the strongest influences around, next to drugs.

My mother went to the school board to try to get me a transfer to Vigor High School, but the school board didn't approve the transfer.

The very first day of school, I attended all the classes to see how things looked and were operating. Just as I had expected, I was the only male freshman in biology. There was a fat, nerdy, four-eyed girl who was a freshman. There were a lot of girls in advanced classes with big asses, but I still regretted it.

When people heard my last name they'd ask if Ricky was my brother and was Nikki my cousin. These students were stupid. If Ricky and Nikki were cousins and Ricky is my brother, common sense would tell them that Nikki is my cousin also. Really, it wasn't any of their business.

I hated that socializing shit; everybody at school would always try to make a comparison between Ricky and me. We were just like night and day—not only in skin complexion. Ricky was off into school and friendly, and I hated the foundation all schools were built on. I became more and more stubborn as time passed.

On the first lunch wave, Arthur, I.T, Marcus, Willie, Stanley, and I met up under the pine trees outside by the cafeteria, talking about how much we hated school. We all chipped in on some reefer, then we had to decide who was going to make a run to get something to get high with.

Arthur and Stanley were the only two who had cars. Arthur's father gave him a beat-up Ford Pinto, and Stanley's grandmother bought him a raggedy Chevy Nova. Those cars really served us well; with transportation, you could easily get girls to skip school and we ended up skipping more classes than we attended.

Arthur made the run to get reefer because Stanley really didn't care about getting high, he was just off into chasing chicken heads. I preferred it this way, because I knew that Arthur was going to go off into the sack so we could have a few joints for us later on.

As we were under the trees getting our heads straight, my cousin Nikki approached me, "Champ, what are you doing?" She really didn't know me because we barely saw each other.

Nikki was about two years older than me, so she assumed she was going to be my babysitter or something. Before my first day of school, she had already pitched me a girl. I just laughed because from what I saw, girls were not going to be a problem. All her friends wanted to know if she was my sister. If they were fine, I would say yes. Some of them had some sex; most of them should have stayed out of my face. They tried to get me to choose one of them. I wouldn't choose any of them. I didn't have girlfriends.

When I was in high school, girls would run to me and tell me to slow down before I hooked up on the wrong thing. Their concern was sincere because a lot of people at Blount High School were already smoking crack.

The big thing in high school, during the first week of freshman orientation, is when the sophomores, juniors, and the seniors dog out the freshman class. Our freshman group proved to be a little bit different from the ordinary freshman class.

When one of them approached us, we cliqued up and beat their asses. Rockhead was a newcomer among us; he lived in Bessemer Projects. He had never attended school with any of us. He proved to be solid. A junior approached us and said something stupid. He said, "You all might as well get ready."

Rockhead said, "Weak-ass nigger, I'm ready now." He then slapped the junior down before any of us were able to help him; he had already jumped up in the air and kicked down, stomped, and beat the shit out of him. I never saw anyone fight like that. He became our partner.

Rockhead's Coca-Cola shirt got ripped doing the fight so Rockhead beat the boy's ass again after school.

From that day forward, Rockhead started bringing a sawed-off shotgun to school in his book bag. A sawed-off shotgun was the popular thing at school. Rockhead was already selling weed, so we stayed high.

Arthur, Marcus, and I were light-complexioned and slim; we could have easily passed for brothers. Light-complexioned brothers were perceived as weak or soft, but when it came down to us we cleared up that psychological misconception. We weren't anything to be messed with.

We tricked a freak out of the Trinity Gardens area to come over to Arthur's house so we could run a train on her. She did, and we trained her. Her boyfriend found out about it and couldn't accept the fact that his girl had been trained by someone much younger. This chump confronted us about it. Arthur slapped him, and we kicked him from one end of the hallway to the other.

He caught Marcus coming out of the gym one night by himself and shot Marcus in the arm. Marcus was mistaken for Arthur. So every time we caught somebody out of Trinity Gardens, we cliqued up and whipped them and the same happened to us if we got caught over there. We didn't have any reason to go through Trinity Gardens except to pick up females. They had to come through Prichard in order to get to school.

We were all standing on the railroad tracks around the third day of school. We were drinking on a half-gallon of Thunderbird. Somebody brought their boom box and it was blasting. The disc jockey, Mad in the Morning Time, would be hollering, "Get up outta that bed, it's school time I said. When you are getting up, Mad is getting down."

The last thing on our minds was going to school. Arthur suggested that we ride over to K.J. Clark. We piled into a car and raced towards the school.

When we walked through the hallway, the students that were now attending Clark were much wilder than us. When the first period bell rung, there were more students standing around than going to class. Some of the girls were so hot in the ass they acted if they were reading our minds. We suggested that they skip school; they agreed. We hopped into the car and headed to Arthur's house. Marcus stopped to steal some wine. Arthur and I went for the reefer.

We went to Arthur's house and had a ball. We took turns running trains on the three girls. I was in the den; Arthur was in the back bedroom. A car pulled up; I jumped and grabbed my clothes and told the girls to get in the closet. When Arthur's mother blew the horn I knew we were in trouble. I ran to the back room and told Arthur his mother was out there. He thought I was playing games, trying to get the girl he was with, until he heard the door open and his mother said, "Who's in the house?" We climbed out of the bedroom window. I fell out of the window because I was so drunk. Arthur laughed and climbed out behind me; we couldn't even jump across the fence. Arthur jumped across the fence and helped me across. The girls and Marcus got caught in the house.

We stayed behind the church to see what Arthur's mother was going to do. We felt sorry for them because we knew she was going to preach to them. My white jeans had dirt stains in them. I was mad as hell; it was against my belief to get dirty. As I complained about my clothes, Arthur said, "Nigger, stop crying." "How are we going to talk our way out of this?" "Nigger, that's your mother. You got to come up with something. I need to get my clothes clean."

We stayed behind the church until Arthur's mother kicked them out the house. Marcus and the girls came around the corner to meet us. Marcus said, "She know it was you, Champ. She said you all might as well come on to the house."

We tried to take the girls to Arthur's sister's house, but she wouldn't let us in unless we would babysit for her. Since it was absolutely nowhere for us to take the girls, we just hung in the alley the entire day. Arthur knew his mother was waiting on him to come home. He tried to convince me to face her with him, but he had to face this one alone.

We had so much fun during our first week of high school that when the staff passed out school books, I didn't even go to pick any books up. At fifteen I decided that I wasn't going to be like most people I've known in the past. Some people I knew struggled for two or three years of high school and still were in the ninth grade. I considered myself smarter than the rest of those fools. My partners had the same thing on their minds.

Willie quit right after football season. Arthur tried to hang on so he would have an opportunity to play basketball. Rockhead quit along with the rest of us. Big I.T. quit right after the first lunch wave. Stanley quit during the first quarter. Marcus quit a week before his sixteenth birthday. Before the second semester of the official school year, approximately a hundred or more freshmen dropped out of school. A large percentage of us quit to sell crack, to smoke, to go to prison for trying to sell drugs, or to get killed.

Quitting school was the first of my many mistakes. It just didn't make any damn sense to me to complete twelve years of school and the only job available was frying french fries at a fast food restaurant.

One of our teachers had a genuine interest in our future. Whenever we skipped her class she would come look for us. Normally we would be on the railroad track. She was heavy-set, with a real pretty face and filled with sympathy for us. She would walk us to class holding our hands and telling us that we both were good-looking men.

We started attending her class on a regular basis. We would go up to her desk and flirt with her. Once she told me I had pretty bedroom eyes and told Arthur he had some pretty brown eyes. We went for this shit. Arthur was getting more girls than brothers with money and cars because he had light brown eyes.

We immediately worked out a plan on how we were going to run a train on the teacher. We had never trained a teacher before. We wrote her a note and had this girl rewrite it for us so she wouldn't recognize the handwriting. We dropped the letter in her desk drawer. The next morning we went to class she wrote a big sign on the chalkboard, "I'm happily married," with a big smiling face next to it.

After this event, we started back skipping her class. I still remember when she told us a black man from age eighteen to twenty years old is more likely to get killed or get hooked on drugs than to have a job making thirty-thousand dollars a year. I thought she was just talking crazy until I got older.

Some way I hooked up with Tracey for awhile. Every time I wanted some sex, she would make herself available for me. I would sneak over to her house late at night or we would skip school together and go off. Stanley and I shared her; we passed her around just like we passed around our Thunderbird. He had her during school hours most of the time, and then I would go over to her house that night. She really thought she was playing us, but we had been cool since the fourth grade.

Tracey's mother hated Stanley because he would beat her like she was an adopted child. Therefore, he could never go over to her house. Tracey's mom thought I was friendly and innocent. Therefore, I could come see her daughter (if she only knew). This was funny to me.

Tracey tried to get too close to me. She started talking that love talk, so I started pulling away from her. She tried this same shit on Stanley. Stanley and I got together and laughed about it. I told them how her mother responded to me when we picked up the girls, so I would be the one to go knock on the door and it would always work.

They started shooting ball; the girl and I sat inside the dug out. See how your friends talk. I can't stand them. Your language has changed. It's no longer how you doing. It's what up my nigger. I called girls bitches and whores behind their backs and sometime in their faces if they didn't give me what I wanted. First I play the good boy role. Some older women tried to warn me. I wished I would have listened.

We hooked up with Willie. He got his father's car; we pitched in about ten dollars apiece and got a half-gallon of gin and a quarter bag of reefer. We were riding getting high.

Arthur had about two hundred dollars because he was seriously applying his get-rich-quick scheme. Arthur snatched pocketbooks and used stolen credit cards to get money. He wanted to go through Trinity Gardens to buy some crack to sell. We rode through Trinity Gardens by the old middle school. Some smokers were out there trying to beat so we kept on going.

We went on Esau Street; traffic was jam-packed. It took us fifteen minutes to get down a small street. Hustlers were running back and forth to cars asking what you need. I'm on. Arthur jumped out of the car; I jumped in the front seat and we turned a corner while he made the transaction.

As we hit the block, some more crack zombies were walking in that direction. We picked Arthur up. He jumped in the backseat. He showed us the crack. I said, "Man, you paid a hundred dollars for that?"

"Nigger, I'm fixing to make two hundred and twenty-five dollars off this." Arthur started cutting the crack up and putting it in a match box. Put the crumbs in a joint. I asked, "Man, what you doing?" Arthur responded, "Fixing to smoke me a primo, a laced joint." "Champ, you don't need none of this—you already crazy." This was Willie and Marcus talking now. I knew Willie was smoking but Arthur and Marcus surprised me. I asked Marcus, "Man, you smoke that shit too?" He said, "Sometimes."

Well, damn, this is what the people in the projects were trying to tell me; my partners were becoming baby crackheads. The reefer along with the crack had an awful smell. As they were smoking, I rolled the window down. They said, "Man, you letting the smoke out."

I went off. "Y'all crackheads. Y'all will be running around sucking dicks in a few months." They said, "Man, you can't get hooked this way; you don't know what you are talking about."

A song came on the radio. "Crack killed Apple Jack." I turned the radio up loud. They started complaining that I was blowing their high with this crazy shit. We rode around cursing each other out until Willie decided to kick me out of the car. He pulled in front of my mother's house and said, "Momma boy, go home."

As I got out the car, I said, "You crackheads take care, don't go turn tricks for crack." Willie pulled off kicking wheels and cursing.

Their advice really helped me out because as time progressed, every time I saw people smoking laced joints I thought about what my gang said. Because everyone starts smoking laced joints and then graduate to sucking on the devil's dick. I really can't say if they were trying to save me or was it that they wanted more for themselves. I took it to heart.

Later that evening, I explained what happened to my brother Ricky. My little cousin Al had already joined in. Ricky and I went to stand down the street waiting for our folks to go to church so we could sneak this girl into the house.

As we stood on the corner talking, this crazy-ass lady who lived in the hood came out of her house and started spreading all of her personal possessions on the grass. She took almost everything out of her house. I asked the girl, "Why is she doing that?" The girl responded, "Oh, that bitch is just crazy; she has spells and does crazy shit from time to time."

Everyone else in the hood was used to her acting crazy. This was shocking to me. Sometimes the crazy lady took her trash out in the nude. I would be right there watching her crazy ass, too.

Ricky said, "Champ, if she leave that TV and radio outside when it get dark we are going to get it." This sounded good to me. We stood around flirting with the girls until it was dust dark; our folks had not left yet. Our only option was to go ahead and get the TV. We dismissed the girls, walked around the corner so everyone would think that we had left the hood, went behind some houses, jumped the fence, got on the crazy lady's blind side of the house so she couldn't see us, and grabbed the TV and radio.

We went around the corner to a crack house trying to sell the stuff to the crack dealers. Crack dealers were so used to crackheads coming around selling stuff for such a cheap price that they offered us ten dollars apiece for the TV and radio. We sold the radio for ten dollars and took the TV to Big Bro. Big Bro told us that one of our uncles needed a TV real bad and had been asking about one. We jumped into his car and went to our uncle's house and sold him the TV for forty dollars. We wanted sixty dollars for it, that was our original plan, but his cheap ass talked us down.

Around nine-thirty at night Ricky and I were sitting in our bedroom contemplating on whether or not we were going back over to the crazy lady's house to see what else was outside in the yard that was valuable. Time we stepped out the back door, we saw a police car in her front yard. We said "Oh, shit," went back inside and immediately worked out an alibi just in case the police came for us; we also hid the money.

A few minutes later, someone knocked on the front door. My heart started beating fast. Ricky's heart was beating so fast his shirt rose several times. We peeped out the bedroom door; the police was standing in the living room doorway asking my stepfather does Ricky live here. My stepfather called Ricky out of the room. The police asked him about the TV and radio. Ricky was real calm and said, "I've been on the streets all day. I haven't seen anything. I came in just before dark." My stepfather supported Ricky's lie. "He's been in that room listening to the radio for the last two hours."

The police said, "I'll do an investigation and I'll get back with y'all." When the police left, my stepfather called us out of the room.

"Champ!!! Did you get that TV?"

I responded, "No!!!"

He started bitching like an old irritable woman, "One of y'all got it. That police didn't come here for nothing. When you go to jail, don't call here."

This nigger was so scared to death of white folks and the law; they had him trained so good that he thinks that whenever the police suspect you of anything you are guilty. According to white folks, we are guilty of something once you start walking.

That night I told Ricky, "Man, we are too big and old now for that chump to be talking to us like that. We need to get together and jump him tonight." Ricky dismissed my notion, but my mind was made up.

Arthur, Marcus, C.B, Willie, and I were standing on the railroad track just chilling out. We went to Arthur's house to chill out when the homeroom bell rang. I said," Let me treat you all to a couple half-gallons of Thunderbird for breakfast."

Arthur said, "Nah, let's go to the house and have two joints and a cup of coffee for breakfast." Arthur pulled out two fat joints.

I had to convince them to go get the wine because the last time we had two joints for breakfast, the reefer along with the caffeine affected my nerves greatly. We couldn't control our arms; they were jerking out of control. The nerves in my neck were jerking the same way. My partner found this shit to be amusing. So that was my last time wanting a breakfast like that.

Marcus said, "Champ, you buy the wine; I'll get a dime bag and a family box of chicken." I'm glad someone else beside me had some sense, because right then Arthur was overruled. We walked down the railroad track and headed to the store. Some stupid-ass girl hollered out the school window, "Y'all need to come back to school."

Instantaneously, we picked up a hand full of rocks and threw them in the classroom and knocked the rest of the windows out. This happened so fast, I don't believe none of us realized what we had done. When we were alone we always bust the windows out, but not during school hours. We took off running before anyone saw us. We got the wine and stood on the far end of the railroad track, out of sight of the school.

While standing on the track getting high, we saw two Prichard police cars fly by; none of us paid the cars any attention because it was an everyday thing in the area we were hanging around.

As we walked in the direction of the school, we saw the principal and the truancy officers, and Prichard police standing on the back hallway where we had just busted the window. We kept on down the track and ran inside of the projects next to the school.

The police attempted to catch us. One was on foot; the other two cars tried to circle us off. It was no way possible for those potbelly pigs to catch us in our own hood. Besides, they were running for a paycheck, we were running for our freedom.

The truancy officer and the principal tried to block us off on the other side of the projects. We had to jump gates to run through Grant Circle. We stood in the middle of Grant Circle while the police came flying through there. We ran and jumped a fence. Lo and behold, there was a bulldog in the yard so we jumped right back across the fence, jumped another fence and ran to Arthur's house.

When we got inside we were all out of breath. We kicked back trying to catch our breath. Arthur jumped up and said, "Man, it isn't worth it. I'm quitting school." He got up and started making coffee.

We heard a knock on the door and knew it was a stranger because no one uses the front door. I jumped up and peeked out of the window. The police and truancy officer surrounded the house. Then somebody knocked at the side door. We all got down on the floor. We were scared as hell; then the phone rang. We just ignored it. The pigs peeked through the windows, and we were crawling through the house trying to stay out of their eyesight. After a minute of this the pigs left.

We went back to the kitchen. Arthur started drinking coffee with a joint. I sent Marcus to the hit house to buy two forty ounces of Colt 45.

The nosey-ass old lady next door who always watched Arthur's house like a hawk, called Arthur's mom at work. Arthur said, "I bet that nosey bitch done called my mother. Let's go stand in Alexander Court." We left and sure enough Arthur's mother pulled up.

While we were standing in the alley the nosey lady called her to the fence and pointed in the direction of the alleyway where we were watching them. They couldn't see us. The nosey lady saw the police and assumed someone broke in the house.

We couldn't go back to school to eat lunch so we went to Church's Chicken to eat and hang out for the rest of the day.

My mother had a friend who was a school teacher, Mrs. Cooley, whom I didn't know anything about. Mrs. Cooley called my mother and explained to her what had happened at school. My mother rode around looking for me. Arthur's mother looked for us, along with the truancy officer, and we continued to run our ass off. We hid in some bushes, the truancy officer's car passed by, we threw wine bottles at him and ran, and we had plenty of fun playing around with this clown.

Around 2:45 p.m. I walked home; my mother was waiting on me. "Champ! Everybody at school has called here. Are you crazy?" She immediately took me back over to the school. I denied every bit of the things they accused me of.

Arthur's mother came to withdraw him from school. Marcus' grandmother came and did the same. They wanted to know who threw the rocks. I swore up and down I didn't know because I wasn't there. They suspended Marcus and me for a week. Before we were able to go back to school our family had to go down to Barton Academy School Board in order to get us back in school.

The principal, Mr. Knight, talked to my mother to see if I was in a gang. He thought that I was the one who was influencing the crew. This damn wino should have been hanging in the alley with us getting drunk, then he would have had some inside information on who was calling the shot.

My mother had gone to my grandmother's house and explained to my grandmother what she thought supposedly happened.

As they were telling me to take school and life more serious, I told them, "Y'all don't have to worry about me because I am sick of school, and when my sixteenth birthday come I'm quitting."

My mother said, "If you quit school you aren't going to live with me, you are going to get a job." She used to say, "Without a diploma you will end up digging ditches all your life." I would rather sleep under a bridge and eat meals out of a local Salvation Army than to dig ditches. When I told her that, she said, "That's your problem—you think you are too smart and too good to work."

My baby sister was just barely walking. So I would play with her so I would not have to listen to my mother's big mouth. I was the first one to hold Ingrid up in the mirror and tell her that she was pretty. She would just smile. Whenever I would put her down she would start crying. Then I would tell her she looked like her father's side of the family and that I hoped she would hurry up and grow out of it.

While reading through the newspaper, I came up with a trick. I'd always read through the classified section. So I told my mother I was looking for a part-time job. She would smile; she knew I was on to something. She gave me money to catch the bus.

Marcus and I went to the mall. I filled out a few applications at Wendy's, Shoney's, and McDonald's. Mostly everywhere I saw a bunch of pretty girls. I even took a few home to show my mother. My intentions were sincere.

While in the mall, we were walking through a few clothing stores. We saw a store that was half empty. Therefore, we stole us something to wear. This was so easy. We started stealing on a regular basis after this experience.

Whenever my mother gave me money to buy something to wear, we would steal it and keep the money to have a good time with. When she got suspicious I would buy one item to show her a receipt. Stealing was so easy to do. It was almost impossible to resist.

We would all go into a store where young women were the cashiers. Especially if we knew she just started the job. We would then ask her if she had a boyfriend. If she would smile, we knew we had her. One of us would talk to her, while the other one would go put the things we wanted into a shopping bag and walk out of the store.

My mother took me down to the school board to talk with my counselor. This fool asked me a lot of stupid questions, "How old were you when you started sleeping by yourself? When you turn the lights off at night, do you get in the bed before the room gets dark?" I laughed and wondered if he asked his mother those same types of questions.

On top of this, he gave me a four-piece puzzle of a car and asked would it be complicated for you to put the car together for me. I told him I didn't know, it looked hard but I would give it a try. My intention was to play with him for awhile. I tried to put the puzzle upside down. My mother said, "Boy, stop playing; these people are serious."

This punk smiled; his gay-ass smile was enough to convince me that he wanted to write me off as crazy. Be any chance of me obtaining a crazy check, I would have had to come into the office crying and shitting on myself.

When they approved me to go back to school, I was so far behind the teachers had taken my name off their roster. All of them made sarcastic remarks like "Who are you? Oh, you're one of those that the cold winter ran back into class."

I had already missed the first two months. They wouldn't give me a lunch ticket and that was always my favorite subject in school. So this forced me to go to Arthur's house to eat. Arthur had it made. All he was doing was sitting around getting high and watching white people cry on TV. Their TV had cable but he would rather watch soap operas.

I'd tell him, "Nigga, watching that shit on TV is going to make you a sissy." "Man, all real players watch the stories. That's all we do: get high, mess with hoes, and make fast money. See? Look how that bitch is crying, she playing for money." That's was Arthur highlight of the day.

I'd go straight to the refrigerator and make me a couple of sandwiches. Arthur and I would argue back and forth while I was eating. We would be back to school because he wanted to trick a girl to skip school with him. I was tempted to do the same.

There was a fine redbone in math class I wanted. So I went on to class to try my luck with her. Arthur couldn't find his girl. Someone had beaten him to her. All the sex we was getting was on first-come first-serve basis.

Marcus came down the hallway with this little chicken head girl with him. The thought of crabs came to mind. They suggested that we go run a train on her. I said, "Shhhhittt!!" Arthur pulled me aside and I explained to him what happened the last time Marcus turned me on. He said, "Man, I just like letting him use the house. Let me get a dollar to buy me a pack of cigarettes." I said, "You my partner and all, but if you smoke you must buy."

The bell rang, so I went upstairs and went to class. About five minutes off into class the principal and the truancy officer came and got me. They accused me of starting a fire. Arthur and Marcus had burned down a bulletin board in the hallway and they suspected me of it.

I told him, "NO, you got me all wrong this time. If I would've done something, you think I would be stupid enough to go to class? I would be running right now." The principal said, "Call his teacher and see how long he has been in class." I said, "Call all of them. I've been going to class all day." The teachers came and spoke up on my behalf. One of them said yeah he came to class and wasn't high. I had to look out of the window to see if it was raining or something.

My big pretty teacher walked me out of the principal's office. We walked holding hands. She said, "See, you can do better if you continue to try; we're not going to let anything happen to you; just break away from your negative associates."

That particular day I had swallowed my pride and forced myself to attend five classes and these fools are still messing with me. After experiencing this, it forced me to go further away. I would hang around the gym and shoot dice. During second period it always was a big dice game going on. The only thing I learned at Blount was to shoot dice and how to outsmart the police.

My mother's friend notified her of what I was doing. So she just started dropping me off at school. I would get out of the car on the railroad track and stay between the tracks, the gym, or go to Arthur's mother's house. She would circle the block and I would still be on the track, until she would holler out the window and tell me, "Champ, please don't stay on the track all day." This went in one ear and out the other. School was not for me. School is for fools and faggots.

The battle of Prichard is Blount vs. Vigor, the most popular football game in the city of Prichard. Although Blount never won, everybody that can walk would be at this game even if it rained. Prichard Stadium would be filled to the capacity. We had spent all afternoon at Arthur's mother's house getting high. Earlier that day, Arthur and I had broke in some drug dealer's house and we only got $500 and an ounce of reefer and a quarter bag of cocaine.

We threatened everyone with much love. Arthur and I snorted most of the cocaine, but the rest of them were afraid to try it. They wanted to suck on that devil's dick (crack pipe).

When we got to the game I was so high I was on cloud two thousand seventy-nine. I was tripping hard and paranoia set in. I was so scared to stay still, I felt like someone, everybody, was out to get me. When the football teams ran on the field I thought they were coming to get me. When they went into a huddle, I was under the impression that they was talking about me.

I took off my sweater because I wanted to be ready. Sweat was dripping from my body like I had run a marathon. Arthur knew how paranoid I became whenever I got high, so he started messing with me. "Here they come, Champ. Watch out, my nigger." They all thought it was funny, laughing their asses off. I would tell them to stop acting like bitches. Damn crackheads.

As I was walking around the field to get a better view of the half-time show, I bumped into Candy. She was a super-fine redbone. She earned her name because she was so sweet. Candy grabbed me by the hand and said, "Come on, Champ. I got something for you." I was hoping it was her, but it didn't matter, I was so blasted. I would have settled for a pig in a wig.

Candy took me to Charlene, which was a nightmare for me. Charlene had recently just dropped her baby. She was dark as night, plain-looking, tall, and knock-kneed. There was absolutely nothing attractive about her. She was just a female.

I walked her home to Bessemer Projects. We had sex. The only thing we knew about each other was that I had a quick temper, I was fifteen years old, and she was nineteen years old. I can't even recall seeing her baby; I probably heard it cry.

It was getting too cold to stand around the gym to shoot dice or on the railroad track. The truancy officers and police had started riding around all of our hiding spots daily. We hadn't attended classes in months. It was useless to even attempt to go towards the school, so we would just go over to Charlene's house and hang out until school was out.

Marcus and Arthur would go over there first and tell them if she give them ten dollars they'll bring me back over to her house. She would go for it. When she would give them the money, I would send them to go get some reefer while Charlene and I had sex.

When they would come back, we would get high. She didn't even smoke, and we all would just be tripping hard. I would make Marcus talk about Charlene. When Marcus get high, he gets real stupid. He always says Charlene was bowlegged to the inside. If she walked fast, her legs would catch on fire. We would all laugh our asses off.

Marcus eventually hooked up with one of her friends. Arthur had a project ho as well. Charlene had a lot of freaky friends. Her family would also tell her that I was too young for her.

Those comments made them curious about me. They would sneak behind her back and get with me and I would satisfy their curiosity. Her stupid friends would always go back and tell her, "Yeah, girl, you are so right about that nigga,

Champ!" Once I got tired of playing around and tried to get three of them in the bed with me at the same time. Charlene disapproved of it. Some girls even had the audacity to call me whorish. That was foolish of them because they were the ones who were giving it up.

Life is real strange. If a girl gets trained by two or more people she is considered as a freak, but when it is reversed we simply call it having fun.

Charlene let her sex drive and emotions get in the way of all rationale. She couldn't or didn't realize she wasn't my girl. She would try to have sex with my partner to make me jealous. I tell them get it, it's good. I would be glad. Willie Jones fell in love with her. Since that was my boy, I would try to respect him as much as possible. But she kept coming around and I would do what she asked for.

My mother and stepfather had gone out of town for the weekend. Ricky and I had the house to ourselves. Marquail had come to hang out with us. We was sitting around kicking it. Charlene kept calling me, begging for me to get with her. I would hang the phone up in her face. Her stupid ass would call right back. Ricky answered the phone and was talking to her. When he passed me the phone, I asked her to meet me at Prichard Stadium.

"Y'all want to run a train on that black bitch?" They said, "Yeah, Champ, set it out for us." I had them to hide in my mother's room while I went and met her at Prichard Stadium. When Charlene and I made it to the house, I immediately got undressed and took her into our room. Before she was able to take off her clothes, Ricky and Marquail busted through the door. These chumps ruined my plans. I got mad.

"Y'all weak-ass niggers, I told you chumps to wait for thirty minutes." I slapped her upside the head and told that bitch to get naked. She wouldn't, so I beat her ass. Ricky and Marquail changed their minds by the time I got finished.

Some women are so crazy they actually believe if a man beat up on them, the man loves them. That's some stupid shit. Bitches be walking around with black eyes and teeth knocked out saying, "He did it because he loves me."

That's so foolish but we didn't know any better. Therefore, I kept cracking my ankle in one of their asses. This was only a few of the negative behaviors young black men and women adopt growing up in the ghetto. Our slave master did it to us to keep us in check during slavery; now we use that same fear to chastise our women. Damn, I hate that evil slave master for what he has done to corrupt black people's minds.

My life was becoming more and more frustrated. It seems as if frustration was ordinary for me. My mother woke me up and asked me why I hadn't gone to school. My response was that I have been trying to get her to understand for the longest. "Momma, it is too cold out to be hanging around in the projects. You know I have been skipping class for months now. I will turn 16 in about five months, so I quit."

She went off, "Boy, you better get up and out of that bed and go somewhere and don't come back until three o'clock. Go find a job or something." My mother keep telling me to go to school, that's just like the police telling a black man to go to jail and stay. School confined you mentally and jail confined you physically. It's no big difference.

All the constant complaining from my mother was making me sick. So I left the house. As I was riding my bike, the cold wind was kicking my ass. The wind was blowing so hard it was almost about to throw me off the bike. This made me ride over to Vigor High School. This white boy was sitting on top of a Camaro, smoking a cigarette, listening to loud rock music.

I jumped off the bike and laid it up against the fence and walked behind him. I then busted him upside the head with the pistol and snatched his jean jacket off of him before the blood from his head got on it. The sight of blood and the pistol sent him in a state of total shock. Just by chance the jacket was just my size. He had a nice gold chain on with a cancer symbol on it. I figured he didn't need it, so I took it as well. Righteously, the gold was taken from my people so I was only getting some get-back.

I left Vigor and rode toward Arthur's mother's house. Arthur was out hanging out behind the King and Mary Club. We stood back there for a second. We were waiting on a lame to come buy some dope so that we could beat him out of it. Business was slow, so I left Arthur.

A few nights later I wore the jacket to the basketball game. Everyone was jocking hard. Marcus and I was standing in the gym bathroom fixing to smoke a joint when Charlene and Candy walked up. Their presence disgusted me, so I just walked away; they tried to stop me.

Charlene, stupid ass, grabbed my hand. I pushed her away; the crazy girl insisted on me being with her. So I slapped her across the head. During this altercation she scratched my face; that's the worst thing a bitch can do to me. This made me very vengeful.

After the game, she and some of her friends were walking home. I ran behind her and kicked her down and stomped her. I was blinded by anger. Marcus and C.B. attempted to stop me. As I struggled with them, I heard a bottle break, but it didn't register fully. So I picked up a pair of old bike handlebars and started swinging, hitting Marcus first for stopping me, then Charlene. Somebody came from behind me and grabbed me and overpowered me. This is what saved them. They got away. I wished I would have had my gun; then justice would have taken its course.

Marcus, C.B., and I were walking through the Bay Shore, going to get some weed. I kept telling them when I get my gun I'm going to shoot the hell out of them for holding me.

C.B. went and got the weed, while Marcus and I went over this girl named Tee's house. Tee was one of my good friends. She grew up and hung with me. When she stepped back, it was blood on her arm.

Tee said," Champ, baby, you been fighting 'cause you bleeding badly."

I took off my jacket; it was a six- to seven-inch cut on my left side. I didn't even know I had been cut. The reefer, wine, and anger had me in another world. Tee tried to call an ambulance. I told her not to worry about it because it was only a little cut. The cut didn't even affect me then, as much as it does now. Tee insisted on helping me.

She took me to the bathroom and washed the wound out with some peroxide and neatly placed a towel on it. While Tee was playing doctor, I was busy trying to undress her. She would stop me and say, "Champ, get your mind out of the gutter while I am trying to help you. You need to let me call an ambulance for you."

Girls like Tee meant me all the good in the world. I would reject them and their advice for those super-fast girls. It was all part of being a young and immature man.

She tried to get me to stay at her house so she could fix me up, but I couldn't. I had a bitch to kill. So I kissed her on the jaw, left, and went looking for Charlene. They must have made their way to Bessemer Projects.

We went to Church's Chicken to get something to eat on Highway 45. While in Church's Chicken a dizzy spell hit me. So I went to the bathroom and wet my face. When I looked in the mirror I saw the scratches on my face. The anger just amplified. My anger made me lose my appetite. All that was on my mind was shooting Charlene. We left Church's Fried Chicken and went and got a half-gallon of Thunderbird and a fifth of T.J. Swan; this helped control my temper.

The next morning I was lying in the bed, nursing my wound, and fantasizing about how good Charlene would look after she had been shot in both of her legs. It took me approximately a week to catch her. By that time I had already dismissed the idea of shooting her on that occasion. I dogged her good though.

Ricky told my mother I had been cut. She was in shock. "Champ, what's wrong with you boy?" When she told my stepfather, he started preaching about Jesus. Jesus couldn't save me. Why did they keep telling me about him? Even today they are still on Jesus. I was almost tired of my stepfather's shit anyway. My mother was in the kitchen cooking. I went and told her I was about to go hang out for a while.

My stepfather said, "Champ, don't go anywhere. If you leave, don't come back." I ignored him as I was walking toward the front door; he then pushed me from behind into the couch. I would say to myself, "This nigger got to be crazy, he just pushed me."

My mind reflected back to all the times he had beaten me for nothing when I was young. Now it was time to teach him a lesson about putting his hands on Champ. I immediately went and got a slat from under the bunk bed and went into the room where he was. While he was bending down looking in the dresser drawer, I gripped the slat tight in my hand and hit him upside the head and across the back. With every lick, I felt better and better.

I remembered how long I had been waiting to do this. I said to him, "This is for the time you hit me with a big belt.

This is for kicking me in the stomach. This is for hitting my momma, and this is for being a sorry-ass nigger." Around the sixth hit, the slat cracked; then my momma came and jumped between us. I would have liked to beat him unconscious. Then I got mad at my mother, because all of these years he had beaten me she would never attempt to stop him.

Now I am standing up, getting some get-back, and now all of a sudden she want to be a hero for him. If I was as messed up in the head as she was, I would have given her a few hits upside her head.

She disappointed me so bad, I had wanted to cry. I felt a deep sense of betrayal, a lack of love, negligence; all my life I had these feelings that my mother didn't care for me. This day she proved to me where her true feelings were at. The only thing that kept us connected was a social security check that she was getting for me because my biological father had been killed.

They pushed me out of their house. I just left crying and I didn't go back. I would rather be dead than live with those crazy people.

My grandmother's health had started failing so she was no longer able to clean up white folks' houses anymore. The only source of income she had was selling needles to the junkies. They would pay her a dollar apiece for them. If my grandmother would be gone, I would hold out on them junkies until they got desperate and they would then pay from two to five dollars for a set of works.

Staying with my grandmother, I got firsthand experience of how the ghetto was run. The slums, the whores, the junkies, and the artificial pimps would all stop by to purchase needles, so they could shoot dope with them.

It's common in Snug Harbor to find a junkie dead on the back porch or in the pathway from a gunshot. The crime rate in Snug Harbor is incredible. This must be a cursed ghetto section of town where there are constant deaths, stabbings, and shootings.

Prichard Police Station is located right on the corner, within walking distance, but no one would pay it any attention because Prichard Police only had five police cars, two of them were not even running. One needed a transmission and the other one's battery was dead in it. If you want to get away with crime, then come to Prichard.

Both of my uncles, Redbird and Freddie, was now back in prison. My grandmother had accepted prison as their second home, because in the last ten years of their life they both had spent more time in prison than living with her.

My grandmother had gotten legal custody of my little cousin Duke, which was Freddie's son. Duke's mother was a junkie as well; since Freddie had been in prison ever since Duke was born, my grandmother had been raising him. She had him ever since he was two weeks old.

My Uncle Pee-Wee was living with my grandmother as well. He was her third oldest son. Pee-Wee's wife had left him for another man and he had nowhere else to go because he had been living off of her and welfare the majority of his life. He stayed unemployed due to being an alcoholic. After the separation from his wife, he even drank heavier.

The doctor had warned him on several different occasions that if he didn't stop drinking it would kill him. Sure enough, he continued to drink and shortly after I moved in with my grandmother he was found dead on some of his wino partner's front porch. His liver had rotted on him.

I didn't even attend my uncle's funeral; I had absolutely no respect for a nigger who drank himself to death because of a woman. This was a valuable lesson in his death for me; this made me slack off drinking for a while. Whenever I drink, serious trouble always came to whoever was with me or against me.

I would smoke me a fat joint the size of my thumb; sit in a chair in the corner in my grandmother's living room, a pondered life. My grandmother would catch me sometimes when I'd be off into deep thoughts and ask why I was sitting in the dark room by myself. "Are you alright?" I would always say I was okay. She would go on to say, "Champ, you are just like your father. If you miss your family, it is okay to swallow your pride and go back home to your mother." I couldn't swallow my pride because that's all I had ever had, and my ego was so big I would choke if I even attempted to swift motion for a second.

Every weekend my auntie Jean would bring her three children over to my grandmother's house to spend the weekend. This became my family.

They knew I would stay high and when I had a serious case of the munchies I would get a chair and the telephone and sit by the refrigerator and eat and talk on the phone until I was full. My grandmother would always tell me, "Boy, open your god damn eyes." They'd just laugh.

Most of the time I would tell them jokes and make them laugh. They enjoyed my company as much as I enjoyed them. Every Sunday night they would hate to go home or to go to school. I would tell them, "Don't worry about Mondays. It has been canceled this week, so it's no school tomorrow." They would fall for it and call their mother and tell her what I told them. She would curse all of us out.

Sometimes I would sneak over to my mother's house and visit my little sister and brothers while my mother's and stepfather's sorry asses were gone. Not being around them was affecting me dearly. I had missed them and loved them more than I realized. Whenever I got ready to leave my baby sister Ingrid, she would holler and scream because she didn't want me to leave. She would be waiting to try and go with me every time.

I couldn't stay unless I killed her father, then what would Ingrid think of me when she grew up knowing I robbed her of the pleasure of having a father. She would probably feel the same way I felt toward the nigger who killed my father, pure hatred.

Miranda would grab Ingrid and take her in the room while I left the house. On nights like these, I would walk the streets with tears in my eyes, frustrated, fighting with the pain of being trapped in this cold-ass world alone. Getting high and quick sex became escape mechanisms for me. Within no time at all, I had crabs again and this time I wouldn't point the finger at anyone because I was with several different females.

I needed someone to inflict my pain on, therefore I would stand on the corners or the railroad track waiting on people to come buy crack. I would then take their money and beat their ass. Arthur had got caught stealing out the mall so he was in the youth center doing sixty days.

I was by myself one night as I was standing around; I heard Larry Bear got shot in the head with a three-fifty-seven. A lady caught him crawling through her window on Meaher Street and killed him. The Night Zoids didn't attempt to retaliate. They all were too busy smoking crack. All of a sudden I didn't want this life anymore.

Older folks would always tell us when we be hanging out that if we keep on living the way we were living, we would not live to be eighteen years old. I was a few months shy of my sixteenth birthday, and if the next two years was anything like what I had been experiencing in the last two years, they can keep them; I don't need this horrible experience. I grew up on the rough side of the mountain.

CHAPTER 6
DON JUAN

PSYCHOLOGISTS, PSYCHIATRISTS, AND Pediatricians, state that if an infant doesn't get the proper attention, such as someone to kiss, talk to, or cuddle, the child will die at an early age or come up emotionally deformed. That is exactly what happened to me. From the beginning I felt rejected and deprived.

On March 30, 1971, the doctor cut the umbilical cord and slapped me on the ass. I've been catching hell ever since. Living with my grandmother allowed me to get some serenity and solitude, but I had arrived at a certain point where a good girl was needed in order to make my life complete. God made man and woman to complement each other. I felt as if something was missing.

From my perspective, it was only three types of women; whores, freaks, and good girls. Whores and freaks are basically the same, just for the purpose of good and quick sex. I've had enough of them to be a director of a horror movie.

After my second time catching crabs, I was convinced that it was time to slow down some because I didn't want to be the Rock Hudson of the black community. It's real easy to speak about slowing down but a whole lot harder to do.

Good girls are the ones you take home to meet moms. With a limited amount of resources, that was going to be a hard one for me. My intuition had already forced me to believe that I would be very persuasive with females since the time I was in the fifth grade and girls used to argue over who was going to buy me ice cream for lunch.

One evening Marcus, C.B., Michael, and I were sitting around my grandmother's house getting high. We decided to catch the city line bus downtown to go to Michael's auntie's house, then from there to the Mardi Gras parade. We got on the bus from Wilson Avenue and we went straight to the back of the bus and started drinking our wine.

On the next stop five girls got on the bus, one of them we all knew well. We immediately started putting in our bids. My choice was the high-yellow girl, cute, with long pretty hair, short, and bow-legged. She was so pretty the other chumps were afraid to approach her. Short girls are so sexy to me. They add the necessary balance to a man's life and I will crawl through the snow butt-naked like an Alaskan Husky to get one of them.

The fellows and I remained on the bus until we got midway downtown, then we departed the bus and headed for Michael's aunt's house. She had planned him a surprise birthday party. We were in her den doing it up. Michael's oldest sister, whom we had never seen before, was there along with some of his female cousins. We were there entertaining them.

Michael intervened, "Come on, y'all, don't do my family like that." He knew what we were up to. Therefore, he was a little overprotective of his family members. We all ended up getting so drunk we had completely forgot about attempting to do something with them. We were even too drunk to go downtown to the parade. When we finally left we were sloppy drunk, staggering, and cursing like sailors. We were walking in the direction of McDonald's and saw so many pretty different girls.

Likewise, in Snug Harbor I immediately became the envy of all the males and heart throb to all the young women. The only thing I was doing was resting, dressing, and finessing.

My good friend Pinkie lived in Snug Harbor. She was big with a real pretty face. Whenever I saw her I'd make her know how pretty she was. I was at the washer shooting pool when Pinkie walked in. She had her little sister with her; Pinkie introduced me to her sister Michelle. Michelle tooted up her nose and real sassy-like said, "Ah, girl, he isn't all that."

Michelle was a real around-the-way girl, dark-complexioned, with some delightful sad eyes, and a round ass.

We walked around to their house; her life was almost as complex as mine. She barely went to school and got high to the point of intoxication. This is some of the things that made me like her more than anything else because I could be myself without putting up a front and having to conceal my deep lustful desires and thoughts. Her eyes would always express how she felt about me.

If I didn't come by their house she'd always show up at my grandmother's house and ask me to come be with her. I really liked talking to her but she wanted more so I played along because it was absolutely nothing I could lose.

We was sitting around getting high when all of a sudden she tried to kiss me. I moved my head out of the way in order to tease her and see exactly how serious she was. When she attempted again, I gave her what she wanted; she just smiled and squeezed me like she was holding on to me for life support. This sensational flinch went through her body. Something told me that she had lost control of herself. I propositioned for us to go over to the school; she was afraid to go there. That was the first place to come to mind because my grandmother was at home. She let me know whenever time allowed she'd still be ready, so I hung around.

Time came farther than we expected. The day my grandmother got her food stamps, Michelle immediately came to mind. My grandmother was asking, "What do you want me to bring you back?" and I asked her, "How long do you think you are going to be gone?" Jean came to take my grandmother to the store.

I ran to get Michelle like Jesse Owens. We were walking to my grandmother's house. It seemed like every nosey bitch in the projects had come outside to sit on the porch. This is how they act on the first of the month. We delayed our plan until dust dark. When we got inside the house, I turned the television on B.E.T.; fortunately for me they was playing slow music. Al B. Sure's new video had just come on. She wanted to watch it.

When LL Cool J's "I Need Love" video came on he helped me out. I needed the exact same thing. As I kissed her and rapped along with LL, she undressed and laid across the bed. I was getting into it good; she was just lying there watching TV.

Unfortunately, Jean pulled up and blew the horn. I was trying to get one more grind in when I heard the horn blow again. I cursed everybody out, the nosey neighbors, Michelle for being so good, and Jean for disturbing me. I had to rush Michelle out the back door half-naked. If they would've caught her, it's no telling how long I'd have to hear their mouths. When I opened the front door, Jean was tapping on the window; she was a few seconds too late.

Jean came to the door, "Champ, who is that in there with you?" "What took you so long?" "Why you don't have no clothes on?" Jean looked in the house and kept on complaining, "When I catch you, Champ, I'm going off!" I didn't pay her any attention; I tried to hug her to get her to shut up. She just pushed me away and said "Your mannish ass, get those bags out my car."

My grandmother would complain a little bit in front of Jean, but as soon as Jean left she'd say "Champ, you don't have to be scared of Jean's black ass, she is not your mammy!"

Michelle and I remained real cool and always will be. Her mother liked me a lot. She was just lacking the necessary quality I needed.

However, the back street became a very popular thing in the hood for me. I'd sneak plenty of young girls in the back door, and a lot of older women chose me as their back door lover while their spouse was gone away. This is the best aspect of the ghetto. The men go off to work or hustle and the women lie around all day having sex and watching the soaps. Once this lady had me over to her house and her husband came home early, I had to jump out the window because the upstairs apartment in Snug Harbor didn't have a balcony.

Approximately a week after my sixteenth birthday, I got a job at Chris Rogers Steak House on Cottage Hill Road. My assigned job was a dishwasher and cleaning off tables from time to time. This wasn't my idea of work but I needed money to have a good time with. They paid me minimum wage for slaving in their kitchen. It was a lot of tests involved in working with white folks.

My sixth night on the job, everyone was gone besides me and the white assistant manager. A real Harley-riding, leather-jacket-wearing white man; he even wore cowboy boots with his slacks and tie. He called me off into the dining area and asked me to go get a pair of name tags from his desk drawer.

When I went into the office, his desk drawer sat right over the safe in the floor. The safe was wide open, full of money from the day's take-in, checks, and other receipts. Something told me to take it and run but I noticed the camera on the wall. Deep down inside I realized that that's what he wanted me to do. I grabbed the nametags, looked in the safe again and thought about it. I just took the name tags and gave them to my boss.

His facial expression read, "Nigger, why didn't you get the money and run, you know y'all like to steal and can't be trusted." The smirk on his face made me want to whip him.

The more I thought about it, the more I wanted to whip him. It had been a few months since I'd slapped a white person. I ignored the fact because I needed to do something positive for myself. I went back to my task.

My stepfather came to pick me up from work around 12 midnight; the manager asked me to stay over so he could teach me how to operate the new dishwasher and another machine, so I stayed.

On the way home, talking about my manager, I informed my stepfather of what happened and that I didn't believe I'd be able to work under white folks' supervision.

He told me, "Stick with it, that's just how they are." This reinforced my determination and I was trying to avoid the streets. Some nights I'd be so damn tired, I couldn't do anything the next day but sleep until it was time to go to work again. On my day off, I was completely out of the habit of going out because my partner lived on one side of Prichard and I was living on the other end. So I stayed in the house and rested.

I was on the back porch smoking a joint when Shaunta stepped outside and asked "Champ, what are you doing?" I said "Getting high, want some?" She replied "I don't need that stuff, I possess a natural high." I looked at her like she was crazy. This was my first time noticing how pretty she was.

Shaunta had big, beautiful lustrous eyes, which would make you think you'd arrived in paradise, long pretty hair, dark complexion, and was sexy, sexy, and sexy. She had a serious crush on me but I'd never really talked to her because I stayed busy.

We sat on the back porch talking until it was almost dark. Those little love bugs started flying around us. I felt cherished and very much connected. Shaunta asked, "Would you please walk me to the store?" I agreed because I wanted to spend more time with her. My grandmother and her grandmother were really good friends, by them living right next door to each other. They'd be on the front porch gossiping; when they saw us together they'd just smile like they knew something we didn't know.

As Shaunta and I were walking to the store, some winos were standing in the pathway and complimented us: "Y'all really do look good together, y'all would make a good couple." She smiled because she knew I'd be like a dream come true for her. She had such a beautiful smile, her presence alone helped beautify the ghetto. I said to the winos, "When I get some money, I am going to give you a dollar for that." They held me to my word on it. Every time they saw us together they'd pull the same trick, but I made sure that she never walked through that pathway alone again.

She invited me to come inside. We spent time getting acquainted while listening to music. She was the oldest child and had two younger brothers. She lived on Dauphin St. but spent a lot of free time over at her grandmother's house. Her mother and father had respectable jobs and were very supportive of their children. She was going on her tenth grade year at Murphy High School and was a year younger than me. At fifteen, she already knew that she wanted to be a nurse.

We had absolutely nothing in common but good looks. Shaunta knew all of my character defects. She knew that I had quit school, loved to get high, and considered myself a Casanova. She also knew Michelle was my best friend.

She reminded me of Shaunta a lot. Both of them had read too many Ebony and other magazines geared towards relationships, which messed their heads up at a very young age. All young girls' greatest fantasy is to have a player in their life. Shaunta was convinced that an act of magic would change me. I ended up doing a lot of compromising; therefore, she gave me her undivided attention. She had the class of a Rolls Royce, very fashion conscious, and conducted herself as a grown woman.

We stayed in her grandmother's living room talking until late night, hoping to stretch the night a little longer because we hated to depart from each other. She had such a magnificent personality and a real pretty smile that often left me mesmerized. I would say things to flatter her. She was really a special challenge to me because she had preserved her virginity up to that point.

A lot of young women don't know that their body is the most precious thing they could give a man. Shaunta did and it wasn't going to be a chump that got it first. She became my wonderful experience. She taught me how to love, share, trust, and that spending quality time with a woman is the best thing on earth.

I rejected some of my other girls for her because she was my romantic companion. I'd go to work, come home depressed, take a shower, and spend time talking with her over the phone. She would read me our horoscopes and encourage me to keep trying. I'd be glad when my off days or weekends rolled around so I could spend time with her.

The day after I received my second paycheck from my restaurant job was the day Arthur was released from the youth center. Arthur's mother had let him use her new Ford Escort as an attempt to pacify him. He came and picked me up and he looked real good. We rode to the Black Jack in

Saraland to buy us some weed. I wanted to go out to the mall to make a small investment. I bought Shaunta a Coca-Cola T-shirt with "Champ" air brushed on the back of it. With Champ on the back of her T-shirt, it was like saying "protected by a three-fifty-seven magnum."

Arthur snapped and said, "Cake daddy, you fixing to spend twenty-seven dollars on a girl you have never been with yet?" I replied "Damn, Chump, I just spent twenty-five dollars on a quarter bag of reefer for you." When I talked like this he knew to just shut up.

We went to my mother's house; I gave her twenty dollars for taking me back and forth to work. Arthur told my mother I bought a shirt for Shaunta. She didn't believe it. She told Arthur, "You got to be crazy! Champ doesn't spend his money on no girls and if he did I need to find out who she is and shake her hand." She went on to ask me who I bought something for. I wouldn't tell her. Arthur and I left my mother's house. My mother with her nosey self jumped in her car and went to my grandmother's house trying to find out who I had been spending time with.

Arthur and I rode around getting high and kicking ideas around. I told him my plans were to chill out for a while and try something new. He thought I was just talking crazy. We went by some old friends' house. Arthur had developed some more get-rich-quick-and—in-a-hurry schemes.

We rode around all day telling different girls we had just been released from the youth center and we needed money to pay our probation officers. Since people hadn't seen us in months it worked. This became our hustle for a while. Every time Arthur came and picked me up he had a new victim. Sometimes he'd give me his mother's car and he'd stay around the corner and I'd go tell his girlfriend that he was in jail and that I needed a hundred dollars or so to get him out.

We just took the money and split it up and would do the same thing to a lot of my girls.

We rode through Roger Williams Projects. It was mid-springtime, young girls were walking around with short pants on and tight biker shorts on with the front of their pants sticking out like they had fox tails stuffed down there.

We jumped out the car on Brazier Drive and started putting our game down. A little girl about six years old pointed at the car and said "Hey mister, your car is on fire." We looked back and the car was smoked up. I rolled the window down and smoke shot out the windows like a chimney fire. Those small compact cars held smoke for a long time. We talked with the girls briefly; they didn't want to ride with us so we left.

I had Arthur drive through this Vietnamese community in Midtown Mobile. The rumor is that Vietnamese eat dogs and if you have a nice little small dog you can get three or four women to give you some sex in exchange for a dog. As we were riding through there real slow, checking the scenery, we saw two little boys playing with a dog and another little boy chasing a dog. We both said at the same time, "Oh shit, both of them trying to get something to eat." We were both tripping hard.

Arthur was too anxious to hang out on the corner, so I had him drop me off over Shaunta's grandmother's house. I introduced him to Shaunta and I gave her the shirt I had bought her. She had one of them ecstatic looks in her eyes. She kissed me and said thank you.

Arthur and I walked back to the car, divided the weed up and he said, "Champ, she got some big eyes and is skinny." His comment kind of upset me so I said "Weak-ass nigga, let me worry about that, you just take care of yourself." We shook hands and he left.

When I went inside, Shaunta was still smiling, but it didn't last long. She started questioning me, "Where you been?" "Why are your eyes half-closed?" She appeared to be real humble but was bossy and aggressive. When she saw me outside without a shirt on she would say, "Champ, you look good but if you plan on being with me you need to put a shirt on." She was sensitive as hell. If I called her a black bitch she'd cry and want to fight.

I always was a selfish person, so I started seeking refuge in Shaunta. Besides my grandmother she seemed like she was the only person that cared for me. She put me in touch with my inner self. We did a lot together. Some of the things that we did, we were both too premature to be doing. I really felt comfortable with her. Shaunta constantly came to mind; therefore I took Shaunta's feelings into consideration.

We went to the movies. This was my first time in a long time going anywhere not being high. After the movies we'd go to Godfather's to eat pizza. I had to pinch myself to make sure I wasn't dreaming. I had to be intoxicated off of good looks. She was good to me and treated me just the way my ego demanded.

Whenever she fed me, I'd lick her fingers just to see that pretty smile. Our feelings for each other were inexpressible. At one point of our relationship we would've jumped off the Empire State Building head first, holding on to each other's hand, screaming "I love you!" She turned me to a nonviolent person in her presence.

Her mother saw that I was getting close to her daughter. When she came home from work I'd be at their house. She'd roll her eyes at me; I just played the original shy guy role in front of her. Shaunta would always tell me everything negative that was said about me. I would always tell her, "I don't care about my momma, what make you think I care about yours?"

When I would tell Shaunta how I really felt, she would get sad and start crying. "Champ, you don't care about me, you just trying to take my virginity."

She would always try to put stipulations on the importance of family bonds. She'd call my mother and talk to her over the phone behind my back, and they would trick me. I violated the first rule of being a player. Every holiday, she'd make plans for us to be over my mother's house; like a fool I'd go for it. Ingrid liked her very much. My mother couldn't believe the way she had me. They always claimed I acted civilized whenever I was with her.

No one really believed it. Shaunta and I went to a rap concert at the Greater Gulf State Fair Grounds. My fat partner Temo jive-ass came up and offered me a joint. I declined it. Temo said, "Player, you don't get high no more?" Shaunta spoke up, "He ain't no player no more, he changed. Tell him, Champ." Temo stepped back and looked us up and down, put his hand over his mouth, and started jumping around acting real crazy. Temo left from where we were standing, smiling.

He went and rounded up almost everybody we knew and came back, pointed at Shaunta and said, "Y'all look at lover-boy Champ and his girl out here holding hands and making imaginary hearts in the air." The entire crowd just started laughing, but as they were laughing I just smiled because we all knew they wanted a good girl as well but didn't have the fortitude to get one.

I got mine by accident and we had a lot of fun together. I knew things would never be right for me without her. She was the most powerful stimulus I could have. So when my partners would be joking about "your girl got you trained, she even buying clothes, got you gaining weight, getting fat so nobody else will want you," I just ignore all that shit because if I had to be hooked on anything I had to be hooked on her.

Shaunta was way smarter than I had expected. We had been playing around for way too long and I still hadn't gotten what I wanted. Every time I convinced her to trust me, she had already found out about another one of my girls. But persistently pressuring her helped me get my player's card in gold.

We were alone at her grandmother's house early one morning. I kissed her, laid her out across the couch and introduced her to some extensive foreplay. Her body language suggested that she was ready. When Shaunta got a job, as a receptionist at the YMCA, that left me lonely.

A lot of females viewed Shaunta and I as a match made in heaven. On the outside it looked that way. Often they'd tell me how much they respected me for getting a girl, settling down, and how they liked the way I treated her. Most of them were being nosey trying to figure me out. Some even attempted to force their daughters on me.

One in particular was Joyce. She was in her late thirties, heavyset, and a motherly figure in Snug Harbor. I believe she been living around there ever since they first laid the foundation. Joyce caught me coming out of this young girl's house one day while her mother was at work. She looked directly in my eyes. A few days later it happened again with this lady who lived on the other side. This time she pointed her finger at me and smiled.

I'd start cursing to myself because I had a lot of respect for her. She eventually started calling me over to her house and telling me how the women in Snug Harbor felt about me. She was the only woman I allowed to call me "Pretty Boy" and didn't get mad. Occasionally she made remarks like "if you weren't so young I would make you my man." I'd be looking at her big ass thinking basically the same thing. People often thought we had something going on but we were just cool. She would tell me what other women were saying about me and I'd try to please some of them.

I went on and became a legendary dick man in Snug Harbor. Normally I keep two or three females on every street. They couldn't resist a slow walker and smooth talker. My presence alone made them rub their thighs.

Occasionally I'd be over to my auntie Jean's house looking at the only picture of my father, wondering if my life would've been different if he was still alive. Every time she caught me off in a deep thought, she'd tell me that I looked just like him and that he really loved women.

We'd talk for hours. She'd also end our conversation by saying, "Champ, you want something out of life but you're going by it all wrong. Why don't you use my address and go to Vigor and start all over?" I had been spending a lot of time looking for a job but nothing came up, so this sounded good because I was really missing all those young pretty babes.

A few days later, I went over to Blount to get my transcript. Marcus, Michael, and Manuel were standing outside of the office.

They had quit school the same time I did and was trying it again as well. Besides Marcus, I hadn't seen them in almost a year. We all kicked around briefly. I got my transcript and was about to leave when Marcus stopped me and told me that a girl that used to be crazy about me had a job at Jean West Clothing Store in Bel-Air Mall and that every time he went out there to steal, she asked about me. He convinced me to go out to the mall with them.

We caught the bus to the mall. I went inside of the store first to see the girl. She was ugly as ever. It appeared that she had been washing her face with sandpaper. We all used to tell her in school that she was so ugly that her momma should've crossed her legs as she was having her. Time has really done her some injustice. When she saw me come into the store, she smiled the ugliest smile I had ever seen in my life. We hugged.

Marcus followed behind me and when she saw him she looked him up and down. "Don't tell me you're with him." "Yeah and I also came to see you."

I watched as Marcus and the rest filled the bags up with clothes. They had three large shopping bags; it still wasn't worth what I had to face. I flagged for Marcus to leave the store. The girl and I talked for a little longer. She asked for my number. I gave her Arthur's mother's phone number and told her that's where I've been living. As I looked around the store, jail came to mind. I left the clothing store. I told the girl "Call me; we really need to get together."

We all went across to Springdale Mall across the street. We had just missed the bus by a few minutes. So we had an hour to wait for the next bus. We were all sitting around joking about how stupid and ugly the girl was.

As we were walking through the mall wasting time, we all went into Hibbetts Sporting Goods Store. It was only one clerk in the store and a few customers. We walked up and down the aisles, just looking. I immediately spotted some expensive pellet guns that would easily sell for fifty dollars apiece. I told Manuel to put four in the bag. He did. I grabbed four. We headed towards the exit.

A white lady who was a customer informed the cashier that we had put something in the bags. I heard it clearly so I walked real fast. I told them what the lady said and they lagged behind in the store. As I was walking out the door the cashier ran behind me. "Wait a minute, mister, you forgot something! You forgot something!"

When I heard her voice, I took off like a runaway slave from captivity; running down the sidewalk full speed. An old white man who was trying to be a Good Samaritan stood before me with his arms spread wide open. I jumped in the air and kicked him in the chest. He grabbed for my bag as he was falling to the ground. The bag tore in half. The only thing I was able to save was the tennis shoes; the rest of it was stolen anyway. I just kept on running.

He hollered, "Damn thieving nigger! A nigger stole something, get him!" His words made me pause for a brief second. I wanted to go back and stomp him to death, but a small crowd had formed. So I ran on until I got to Dauphin Street. The rest of them stupid asses stopped and the police got them.

I went off into the apartment complex where Shaunta lived. There wasn't anyone at the house. Arthur's older sister lived in the same apartment complex. Her husband gave me a ride back to Prichard; I got dropped off at my mother's house.

She had already known because Manuel lived right next door to her and he had told his mother that I was the only one who ran. Michael's mother made him tell on me as well. The only way their mothers could get them out of the youth center was if they snitched on me. But luckily the youth authority doesn't accept snitches' information unless it's a serious case.

My mother continued to ask, "Why was you stealing?" I showed the receipt for where I had paid for the tennis shoes and explained to her that I wasn't stealing, but I was with them and, regardless, if I would've stayed I was going to be guilty by association. She probably knew it was a lie, but had to accept it because my cousin had just received a life without parole sentence for stealing a carton of cigarettes under the habitual offender law.

Michael's mother had called my grandmother and told her what happened at the mall. I told my grandmother the exact same thing I told my mother. Everyone was making a big deal of it. They only got six months probation time with a curfew set at seven o'clock and a fine of six hundred fifty-seven dollars to cover the clothes we were attempting to steal.

When school started, I was more than ready to do something. My cousin Tiffany and I shared a locker together. She was a freshman at Vigor at this time.

All the people I had attended K.J. Clark with were glad to see me, but disappointed in the fact that I had to repeat the ninth grade. That was the talk of the school for the first week. Every last one of them asked the same question. "What are you doing with ninth grade books?" When I explained to them I had quit school last year they all responded, "That's why I didn't want to attend Blount." "It's nothing but a recreational center!"

No one actually believed or knew how miserable my life had become and it was constantly changing fast. However, I went to every class for two weeks, passed tests, studied, and even did my homework or had my cousin Tiffany do it for me.

Things looked as if it they were going to work to my advantage until I was leaving the school's auditorium one day and bumped into this dark-complexioned young female with bowlegs. She was kind of crazy about me when we went to Clark but she was younger so I didn't pay her much attention, but now she had developed nicely. Her ass was poking out of her jeans like she had two basketballs in her pants.

We walked and talked considering our next classes were next door to one another. After that class, we walked home from school together and spent the rest of the night on the phone rapping until it was time to go to school. Then I asked her to skip school with me. She agreed and said she would bring a friend along.

I called Arthur. "Baby boy, I got you an early birthday present, don't go nowhere."

"Nigger, I'll be waiting on you." At school, neither one of us went to homeroom class. We left the school campus and went directly to Arthur's mother's house. I burst through the front side door of the house screaming, "Happy Birthday!" Arthur seen those dark girls and smiled like it was his birthday for real.

The bowlegged girl and I went off into the room and had sex until we were both exhausted. For a young girl, she was a snapper. The girls went back to school. Arthur and I sat around thinking about how we were going to come up with some money. Nothing came to mind. We were sitting around smoking a joint, both of us off into deep thoughts. I broke the silence.

"Baby boy, the next time I'm going to bring you a white girl. What you want, a blonde or a redhead?" Arthur hit the joint, coughed, and laughed. His mother came home so we had to immediately get in compliance. As soon as she hit the door, she's giving out orders. "I smell that funny smoke! Y'all need to be looking for a job! If y'all been cooking, you better wash the dishes." Every time she came home she blew our high.

Arthur got his mother's car and took me down to the driver's license place. I had already obtained my learner's permit so I needed my driver's license. All while I'm driving along the highway with this state trooper pig, I'm nervous as hell. I can't even concentrate. Pigs are my natural enemy. Therefore, I failed the driver's exam. I was never able to get my license. I feel more comfortable running from the police than riding along the highway with them.

That one incident was enough for the principal to find out who I was. The following morning the principal called me to his office and told me that there wasn't any room at his school for people like me. When I tried to talk him out of kicking me out, it was useless. My words weren't nothing to a white person. He couldn't say that I skipped class because I never did go to homeroom or any class. His overall decision was based on the fact I had influenced the girls to skip class and one of the teachers saw us walking together.

Besides that, I had used a false address in the beginning to enter school. Everyone was doing it but they were so-called good students.

So I left school, went to my grandmother's house and asked myself, "Damn, why me?"

I started back looking for a job. I probably filled out ten or twenty applications a week. I even got a job interview, but where the job was located was going to make it complicated for me to work. As the days progressed, I'd become more and more frustrated until I saw Shaunta and she settled me temporarily.

One time, I was with this chump who pulled out a knot of money. "Yeah, Nigger, I'm the player now." We kicked back and forward for a while. I told him, "Fat Timmy, I still get more women on a bicycle than you get in a car." Temo just went all the way off. Before he stopped running his mouth, Shaunta and one of her girlfriends were walking in our direction. Temo spotted her first and hollered, "Here come your only girl chump! Get on away from the player."

With every step she made in our direction, it seemed as if she was getting prettier and prettier. I walked up to her, bear-hugged and kissed her. Temo's fat ass started back running his mouth, "Told y'all that nigger was a chump!" Shaunta asked, "Why is Fat Timmy always giving you a hard time?" She didn't understand that she made me violate some major rule and that's just Temo's style, to be the life of the party and never run across any strangers.

Shaunta and her girlfriend walked away and Temo and I went at it again. Something told me to throw some dirt on him for talking so much. Shilander walked up, she looked so good it was a shame. Everybody on the sideline got quiet. I hugged her but couldn't hold her long because she would cause major problems. Temo was looking stupid holding his chest like he was about to have a heart attack. This was his first time seeing her. When she walked away, I broke the silence. "I bet your fat ass fifty dollars I can pull more women than you."

My auntie Jean had almost spoiled me. Whereever I saw her all I had to do was kiss her and she'd go off into her purse and give me some money. I expected this from other females. My accumulation of girlfriends was greater than the local charter of the girl scouts, but that shit didn't work. Most of the time I stayed so broke that I couldn't even pay attention.

Later in life, while serving time in Alabama prisons, I came to the conclusion that females are the true players. Fact is, there are thirty male prisoners in Alabama for every one female prisoner.

CHAPTER 7
CRACK COCAINE

THE MOST POPULAR and well-respected hero and role models in the
Ghetto are the drug dealers, pimps, and hustlers. I idealized the players who had plenty of women and a pocket full of money. In the poverty-stricken community of Prichard, we couldn't relate to superheroes like Superman and Batman. We said the hell with Mickey Mouse. We worshipped the ground that characters like Scarface and the Sopranos walked on. We loved movies that glorified the street life. These movies gave brothers like me false hope of getting rich by selling dope and that money and women could erase all of your worries.

In 1988 crack cocaine, also known as crack, rock, nigger killer, had monopolized the street as the drug of choice. Selling crack became a million-dollar operation. You didn't need a high school diploma or a college degree to succeed in this lucrative industry. The only requirement to qualify for this position was a desire to make money and the thrill of risking your life or freedom.

The game of selling crack was cold. You had to be street smart and have a desire to gamble. Everyone knew that there were unwritten codes to this game. You had to play by the rules. The penalties were miserable: going to jail, getting killed, or getting hooked on drugs. There was only one way out once you entered.

It was my destiny to become a player. I tried very hard to resist the temptation to become a full-time hustler, but after constantly getting my grandmother's money and spending money on getting high and attracting women, I decided that this was the life I wanted to live. Being dissatisfied and disillusioned about my financial status led me to selling drugs. My goals were to make fifty thousand dollars, buy a car, and then quit selling drugs. Implementing this plan was more complicated than I expected.

My homie Arthur and I were small hustlers for the longest. We cashed stolen checks, used stolen credit cards, shoplifted at the mall, and hustled people out of money on a daily basis. I can remember one incident so well that it seems like it happened just yesterday.

Arthur, Kenny and I rode to Delchamps in Eight Mile in Arthur's mother's car. It had just begun to rain and this white lady was exiting the store. Kenny drove our getaway car to the back of the store, while Arthur and I snatched this lady's purse. The lady only had seven dollars in her purse, so we attempted another purse snatching.

Arthur and I watched the next lady exit the store with two full shopping carts. Our first thought was that this bitch didn't have any money; she spent all of her money on the groceries that occupied her carts. We proceeded to snatch her purse, jumped in the car with Kenny, and sped out of the parking lot. We thought we had scored $400.

After snatching the purse we went to Bessemer Projects to purchase reefer and crack from my Uncle Big Bro who was a known drug dealer. When we arrived in Bessemer, the streets were empty due to the inclement weather. We proceeded to Alexander Court in hopes of buying drugs, but we couldn't find any of our usual drug dealers. We laid low in Alexander Court and continued to search the purse before we dumped it.

The owner of this purse must have been in something illegal herself; she had money balled up in all different compartments. There were two old beat-up looking watches, a Rolex, and other jewelry in compartments of this purse. After emptying the contents of the purse, we returned to Bessemer and purchased dope. I went to the mall and went on a shopping spree with my cut from the purse snatching.

A few days later I hooked up with Arthur. Arthur was lying in bed, looking like someone had beat the hell out of him; eyes were bloodshot red and he was in much need of a bath and a clean shave. I knew something wasn't right. I said, "Arthur, what happened to the Camaro we supposed to pick up hoes in?" Arthur replied, "Champ, those niggers on the corner beat the living shit out of me."

I knew the truth: Arthur smoked up all his money; no one was crazy enough to take his money. I still had my half of weed from a few days ago so I decided to lift my partner's spirit by getting high. After we finished that bag, Arthur insisted that I buy some more weed, and I did. I soaked his sorrows in drugs.

Arthur smoked his first joint laced with crack. He was now on a mission, and it wasn't to get right with God. Arthur was busy running up and down the streets hustling cars. He was so high some days that he would screw women that had been robbed of their good looks by drugs. I became so intrigued with all the attention Arthur was getting that I decided to join in the drug game.

At first, my mind was on the money, but when I realized what crack hoes would do for a score I was all game. Women auditioned their body for a hit of crack. Occasionally, I would allow them to get their knees dirty to score drugs. Women would even offer their daughters to score. I wanted the women; they were more experienced, and knew just how I liked it.

While riding around Bessemer Projects one evening in hopes of buying beer, Willie, Arthur, and I saw two of the students from Blount dressed in a tie and slacks; one of them was my brother. I approached them and asked, "Where are y'all sissy asses going with ties?" The students responded, "Man, we just graduated from school tonight." I said, "Damn, my older brother graduated tonight and I didn't get to attend."

My older brother was the only nigger in my family that graduated high school. I had no idea of what was going on in my family; I hadn't talked to my mother in about three to four months. My mind was on chasing girls and getting my money.

After leaving the service station, my partners and I rode around all night getting high. We rode through Saraland, a cracker city, and happened up on four monster trucks that were waving rebel flags. We knew that these white crackers were looking for niggers to hang so we went back to our normal spot in Bessemer Projects.

The streets were deserted so we looked for our big-booty hoes that were sitting in front of a house to kick it with. When we reached the house this chick had all of her faming friends over looking for a high. We let the ladies perform their dues for a score.

During this time, I lived three lives: my grandmother's grandson, a drug dealer, and a womanizer. My grandmother never suspected I was doing anything wrong. Occasionally, my grandmother would question me about the new clothes and the money, but I would tell her that women took care of me.

Shaunta, one of my main ladies, helped me keep my sanity. She knew exactly what I was doing because her family members were my regular customers. Shaunta was my strength; hearing her voice made me feel good. She accompanied me when I visited my mother, which made the visits a little easier.

My brother Ricky was headed to the Navy the next day. He and I talked that night and realized how much we had in common. Temo, one of my buddies and a known drug dealer, arrived at my mother's home to take Ricky out on the town. Temo hooked me up with a lucrative deal of selling drugs on a full-time basis. Before we shook on the deal, Temo informed me that Arthur was doing badly.

I left my mother's home that day declaring my independence from my social security check that she received on my behalf every month and pledging that I would never be a broke nigger on the streets again.

From that day forward, when the eagle flies (mailman delivers social security checks) I would fly right behind him and knock off a few social security checks. I would cash the checks at a local grocery store and break off the owner a piece for cashing the checks.

I took the other checks to larger stores and purchased eggs, milk and chicken for my fictitious grandfather. I used the money to purchase crack and have crackheads sell it for me. Crack was selling like hot cakes. After getting my business off the ground, I decided to look for Arthur.

I began at his mother's house. Arthur's mom stood in tears in her kitchen, explaining how someone broke into her home and stole her appliances. She hadn't seen Arthur in months. We both knew who had stolen her appliances. I looked in our normal spots—the alley of Alexander Court and King and Mary's Club—but Arthur was nowhere to be found.

Arthur went way off on the deep end. Drug dealers were looking for him because he stole four ounces of crack and a couple of thousand of dollars. The last thing I heard was that Arthur was in a drug rehab.

I began my drug peddling in Snug Harbor. Snug Harbor was where the big dogs hung out. I developed regular clients in this area. People would spend their entire payroll checks on getting high. I would even grant credit until payday to keep people hooked. Business was booming.

Women in the projects would spend their welfare checks, food stamps, and child support checks on drugs. Crackheads would sell their blood to buy a crack rock.

One particular crackhead, B. P., had it bad. B. P. hustled crack just to get high. One night, B. P. ran for me all night. He even gave me his dentures for collateral. I told him to sell this $400 worth of crack and bring me $300 back the next morning. I looked down the street and shook my head in disgust.

The next morning, Greg and I were standing in front of the projects when B. P. came up, all red-eyed and worn out. B. P. smoked my $400 worth of crack and didn't have shit to show for it. That day I realized B.P. was running a game on me. He took my drug money and paid Greg and took Greg's drug money and paid me. Restitution had to be paid.

I beat the hell out of B. P. with a $5 wooden bat that I bought from some little boy. People stood on their front porch and peeked out of their window, watching as I whooped this grown man's ass. I earned my name, Champ, that day. Everybody in the neighborhood knew not to mess with Champ.

Crack cocaine was the most demoralizing drug of the century. The love for this drug contributed to the demise and destruction of the black race. This drug degraded our community, multiplied whorehouses, increased homosexuality, and robbed men and women of any hopes of a future.

Many women sold their self-respect for the use of drugs and many of their babies were born crack-addicted with AIDS.

I saw many nameless, faceless crackheads go weeks without eating, bathing, and changing clothes. They wouldn't sleep either; the only thing that was important in their lives was getting high.

The inventor of this drug had to be a mad scientist in order to develop a recipe of cooking cocaine, procaine, and Novocain. Hustlers would stand around and compete to see how low a dope fiend would go to get a hit of crack.

One night, while standing around a fire, a crackhead agreed to remove a burning tire rim from the fire for thirty dollars worth of crack. He bet that he could pick up the tire rim with his bare hands. The rim was fiery red from burning so long. None of us believed that he would actually do it, so we gave him the crack. He looked at us like we were a bunch of fools; we poured some more gasoline on the fire to make a big blaze. This fiend stuck his hands in the blaze and pulled the rim out of the fire. He threw the rim down quickly and it caught the rest of the grass on fire. His hand was burned to the flesh; the smell of burnt flesh was awful.

He was smiling like he had just received the Nobel Peace Prize. He went off into an old house and smoked the crack. He returned to the campfire. We gave him $20 worth of crack to kick the walls down in the house so we would have firewood. The firewood kept the fire going so we could continue to get paid. We almost demolished the house. As we stood around the fire, this drug fiend worked his heart out running to the liquor store, running to McDonald's and making it back to the campfire before the french fries were cold.

I witnessed some freaky shit while selling crack. As long as I stayed high, I was able to pay my grandmother's bills, send my uncle money in prison, shop as much as I desired, and keep my whores on my arm. Regardless of the evil transgressions that I did in the streets, I never hustled on Sundays.

Every Sunday I visited my mother's home while the rest of my family was at church. Shaunta accompanied me for our special love rendezvous. She and I talked and made plans to get married and leave this depressing area. She tried to convince me to quit my transgressions while I was ahead. She tried, but my mission wasn't complete. She wouldn't stop talking about me quitting the business so I distracted her by running my hands through her hair and messing it up.

Night time in Snug Harbor was a little city within itself. Everything took place on Craftmore Drive at night. There was a dope house, a whore house, and a club that occupied Craftmore Drive. The oak tree was my spot. Regular housewives, lesbians, and dope fiends frequented my spot. The oak tree afforded me the opportunity to sell drugs in three different directions of traffic. After selling to several cars, I peeped this girl and we continued our arrangement in an upstairs apartment.

After our arrangement was complete, Michelle and I went to People's Lounge Club to witness the bikini contest that was going on. The bouncer wouldn't let me in because I appeared too young. I joined the group of drug dealers who were selling crack; it seemed as though there were more people standing outside completing drug transactions than inside the club.

While standing outside the club, another red bone propositioned me for sex in exchange for drugs. She was one of the regular whores who sold their pussy for drugs. I accompanied her to her house and she proved to have a wonderful head on her shoulders. Smoking crack made most females horny as hell; once they got started it was hard for them to stop.

Some females say that crack makes them want to stay naked; these females became my favorite customers. I gave females crack just to see their reaction. They hit that pipe and they immediately undress themselves, get on their knees like a dog, and do the do. I'd pimp these females out to my friends for crack.

I had one fat friend, Hump, that I would supply with whores. When a whore was disobedient, I beat the hell out of her with a 2 x 4. The thickness of the board against her fat ass sounded like a pistol.

For the longest, people at Snug Harbor thought I shot the bitch. After I beat her ass with the board, she agreed to sex Hump. The crack along with the whipping made her real freaky; she was extra horny. As she sucked my dick, Hump smiled like he was a kid in Toys "R" Us.

Hump was a virgin and this was going to be his first time. He was so scared that his dick wouldn't get hard. The girl gave him head until he was hard. I had to coach this fool through the entire process. Hump was behind her hunching like a fat puppy. We changed positions about several more times until I couldn't take it anymore.

As I was about to leave, they both begged me to stay. I stayed until I became limp. I retired to my grandmother's house for a nap only to be faced with nagging. My grandmother was up waiting on me and complaining about me staying out all night.

After getting out of the tub I retired to my bed. Hump knocked on my window. Hump desired more female engagement. I got him hooked and he became another one of my flunkies. All Hump wanted was whores and money for

McDonald's. Hump's dedication allowed me to stay off the streets and spend time with a girl I had my eye on.

On the first day of the month, Mother's Day we call it, I sold drugs all day long. I went to Happy Hills Project, a multi-million dollar drug spot, to buy a cookie (an ounce of crack). Happy Hills was home to more caddies than you'll find in a used car lot. Traffic was jammed with Mercedes Benz and Jaguars all dipped in gold rims.

After buying the crack from the Hills, I returned to Snug Harbor and prepared the drugs for distribution. While Hump and other dedicated fools ran my drugs, I hooked up with a female. Females have something between their legs that make money faster than the government can print bills. Every man who works or hustles is trying to satisfy a woman.

My cousin wasn't exempt from using what was between her legs to get what she wanted. Her house was a pimp's dream house, whores were everywhere. I tried to avoid doing business with her but this whore wouldn't give up. One of the whores at my cousin's house called me a sorry sissy and it was on. This was a big-ass lady so I was scared as hell.

After she embarrassed me in front of my groupies, I had no other choice. I accompanied her to her house where she rubbed me down in oil and then licked it all over my body. She seemed so big and strong I thought that she was going to carry me to the bedroom. I stood at full attention like a flagpole. She walked me to the bedroom, informing me that she had been waiting on this moment.

The next morning I returned to my grandmother's house only to be patted down while I was asleep. When I woke up, she began nagging me about the money she found in my pocket ($1,000). My grandmother began telling me stories about junkies dying from AIDS, a lady on her death bed, and her husband infected with HIV. The last thing I wanted to hear about was AIDS. My grandmother watched too much news. I sat there cursing in my head, hoping she would be quiet. I pretended as though the phone rang so I could escape that nagging.

All that day the conversation I had with my grandmother kept coming back to me. I lay in the bed staring at the ceiling, thinking about all the sexual escapades and my chances of contracting AIDS. After smoking a joint, the thought of contracting AIDS was gone.

When I left the house that day my first stop was a drugstore to purchase condoms. I was embarrassed as hell so that I waited until the line was gone and then I approached the cashier. She made such a mockery of me that that was the last time I bought condoms.

Selling crack was paying off good, regardless of the risk involved. More and more people were getting hooked on drugs which meant more customers for me. Money was coming in faster than I could spend it. My clothes became more and more expensive to live up to the image I had created for myself.

I spent a lot of my money on getting high to escape the reality of the situation I had created. I began to neglect the things that mattered to me most because of the time I dedicated to building my empire. Things between Shaunta and I were up and down. She accused me of being with females with sexually transmitted disease.

Then she complained to me about not spending enough time with her. She also complained about driving me around in one of her family member's cars. Shaunta began affecting my money flow. One Friday she rolled up on me while I was selling drugs in Snug Harbor. We continued our conversation in her grandmother's house.

My mind was on getting paid. Shaunta had threatened to leave me millions of time and I wasn't worried this time. I didn't have time for this so I threw her $200 to get her off my back. She threw the money back and told me that if I didn't make it back at 8:30, don't come back.

Needless to say, I didn't come back at 8:30. I stood outside the project hustling drugs, money, and rubbing on the fine-ass women coming through. Shaunta witnessed everything that night and decided that our relationship was OVER.

At first when I broke up with Shaunta I thought she would come back running. That Sunday she didn't come over for our usual rendezvous. The next morning I went to her grandmother's house, but she was gone. Although I had other girls to accommodate me, I missed Shaunta. After a couple of weeks, Shaunta's grandmother informed me that Shaunta was sick. Shaunta and I spent the whole day together making up. She convinced me to go back to school.

I enrolled into a JTPA program on Government Street. While attending this program, I met people who were at different places in their lives. En route to class, I would sell a few hundred dollars worth of crack and then jump on the city bus line. I was the youngest person in the class, followed by a 24-year-old lady. My other classmates were forty and older. The older people envied me, wishing they could be 17 and have a chance to get their lives together.

The twenty-four-year-old chick befriended me and began telling me about how she had her first child at thirteen, quit school, and became pregnant two more times.

As I listened to her, I began to feel sorry for her and thought about how I would love to take her to the Red Roof Inn down the street. I didn't attempt to get with her because men had abused her too much already.

120

In class, my work centered on how I could use this information to help me prosper in my lucrative drug business. I also spent my time contemplating how to show Shaunta that I loved her. I spent my time making Shaunta a card. The strange thing about this whole ordeal was that I got the best grades in class.

On the street, I still had Hump selling for me while I was in school. While hanging on the corner one night, another nigger rolled up and told me he was headed to the Navy.

Shaunta came to pick me up from school and take me over to her mom's house to keep me off the streets. Her mother encouraged me to do the right thing. This wasn't the life I wanted to live; it was too slow. I was stuck in the game; addicted to living fast and staying high.

Finally, Arthur got out of the rehab center and returned back to the streets. We embraced as if we hadn't seen each other in years. We went on a shopping trip to the mall. He wanted to start back selling drugs but I was in a different chapter in my life. My objective was to get my GED as quickly as possible and become rich.

After attending classes, I felt I was ready to take the GED exam, but the policy was that a person must attend classes for six months before taking the test or be eighteen years old. This policy discouraged me, so I returned to my daily business of selling drugs.

I regret thinking of taking this opportunity to move up in the game. I really wanted to stay in the JTPA program and make something out of myself. Being a nigger and wanting to be a player made me learn the hard way. This was my prerogative.

CHAPTER 8
TRIGGER HAPPY

"For the love of money is the root of all evil: which while some desiring after, they have wronged from the faith and pierced themselves through with many sorrows."
1Timothy 6:10

OUT HERE ON the streets your life is in jeopardy. Everyday a person hustles, you must be aware of your surroundings: the many robbers, the informers who are willing to set you up with the police. At all times, you must almost assume that everyone is armed and out to rob or even kill you. This life is very capricious and cruel. The game was filled with a bunch of trigger-happy niggers who suffer from a delusion of grandeur. Niggers had been deprived so much that once they get a little money they go crazy. More and more people were coming off into Snug Harbor to hustle and buy crack.

The traffic was constantly going up and down the streets. Snug Harbor was better than watching cable TV.

Elderly women had purchased special pillows to brace themselves up in the bedroom windows to watch the action. They would see prostitutes walking the street all times of day and night and car doors always slamming and rushing off down the streets. The ambulance was continuously rushing off bloody bodies.

This ugly life makes you a victim or a victimizer. For me I had seriously developed a keen dislike for those people that I was expecting to make me rich. Daily I would express my dislike to them in a very strong way. I would kick them to sleep and spit on them for coming up short with my paper.

One particular evening, hustling was going good in the hood, money was rolling my way good, already I had pocketed nearly two thousand dollars. Dark was nearing my time to leave the streets. As I got close to my grandmother's house, I heard some cars speeding down the street, shots being fired, and screams of "get down" by the task force. Then I would take off running full speed.

Within minutes I had made it inside the house. I saw four policemen run around the side of the building. They were roughing someone up that was lying on the ground in our backyard. All alone, I was peeping out of the window trying to figure out who this was. All of a sudden I heard loud kicking on the door and the doorbell began to ring. As my grandmother ran to answer the front door, I ran to flush the crack cocaine down the toilet.

Before I realized it, four or five of the policemen were all in my face pointing guns, and asking where the drugs were. This was the task force searching my grandmother's house in its entirety. They searched the stove, closet, drawers, and shoes. They handcuffed me and searched my pockets. They even put their hands in my boxers. My grandmother asked me if I had any drugs. I promised to her that I didn't. My grandmother and I asked the police officers for a warrant, which they were unable to produce. They stated that they did not need a warrant because someone had just bought some crack from me.

I just sat there quietly, hoping that they didn't find a gun. By this time my mother and my aunt Jean had arrived. They watched the officers closely. After a few hours they did not find anything illegal, so they finally uncuffed me.

I rushed to my room and noticed that my bed had been flipped upside down. Money was thrown everywhere. As the police were leaving, they said to me that they would get me later if I kept on. As I began to count my money, I noticed that fifteen hundred dollars was missing. Later that night, I discovered that my three-fifty-seven magnum was gone as well.

Over the next few days I laid low, putting together a master plan.

I went to Eddie's Pawn Shop and bought a bike. I would ride the bike around Snug Harbor selling crack. This worked to my advantage. While other hustlers were standing still, I was constantly moving. When I recognized someone that I knew that was looking for drugs, I would ride my bike in their direction to make a sale and keep on going. All day I would be up and down the streets, telling everyone that I was exercising because I was getting ready to go into the army.

This didn't last long. Other hustlers caught on to what I was doing and everyone began to ride bikes. The police got informed as well.

One day I was sitting on the stairs counting my money and the police came up and asked who was riding the bike. No one answered; therefore, they continued to ask but were unable to get a response. One of the police picked up the bike and slammed it against the pavement. Tears immediately formed in my eyes.

The police ordered all of us to come off the stairs. I ran up the stairs through a lady's house and out of the back door. The police did not even chase behind me. Later that evening, the police went to my grandmother's house and told her that they were going to arrest me.

Snug Harbor had gotten so violent that the owners hired a security firm to patrol the streets. The security guard would walk the streets for a few days and then start trying to hang in the park or even try to see which females were easy to have sex with. The security guards that tried to be tough, we would wait until night and shoot at their cars. The security guards would then quit.

After that the owners hired Prichard policemen to patrol on their off days or after work. Most of the policemen would explain to us that they were only trying to feed their families. They would say to us, if we stayed out of the middle of the street or didn't shoot anyone we wouldn't have any problems. Therefore, we hung in the alleys. The policemen's warning slowed down a lot of the unnecessary shooting because we wanted to make money. There were a few that continued to shoot.

There was one person in particular by the name of Outlaw. Outlaw had just been released from state school. He had a strong hustling game. Outlaw always had a loaded forty-four revolver and was always ready to shoot. It was very easy for him to make a couple of thousand a day.

Most of the time he would be high off of laced joints, walking around with a pistol in his hand, looking bug-eyed and wild. Every time an unfamiliar car would pass by, he would begin to shoot. The cars would speed off with windows shot out. When Outlaw got high he became extremely paranoid. Outlaw and I would hang out late at night getting high off of laced joints and chasing money.

One late night we were all hanging out on the back street. Several shots were fired. This had become something common. No one paid it any attention. Then down the street came the red lights from the fire truck, followed by the ambulance and police. This made a huge crowd appear.

As I gathered around the crowd, I saw a man lying under the tree, dead, with a gunshot to the head. There was another man with his eye shot out. I knew both of those winos well. Death and people getting shot so much wasn't anything new to people living in the hood. We all focused on hustling.

Around 1989, a band of robbers was released from prison after serving long prison terms. They were all close acquaintances with my uncles.

Each day they would ride through Snug Harbor looking for someone to rob. They had put the word out that they was going to rob everyone with money besides me and Temo. The robbers were close friend with both of our uncles. I viewed it different. There's no honor among thieves. Although it felt good to hear them say that, they watched those trigger-happy niggers closely with a vicious eye.

At night I would be sitting in the living room snorting cocaine, wishing a nigger would kick on our front door. I had promised myself that if someone ever kicked on my door they would fall in dead.

I had begun to carry a pistol just as if it was a belt; I wore it every day. Places where guns were not allowed I stayed away from. It was so crazy on the streets that I would be selling drugs to people with the crack in my left hand and a pistol in my right. I would point to the crack with my pistol while asking people if they wanted it. A lot of times my message was probably misunderstood.

Through Outlaw is how I began to hang with Phelon. We had seen each other around Prichard but never hung with each other until crack cocaine became popular. Phelon had a lot of heart and was a real hustler. I had to learn the hard way that that doesn't mean a nigger won't snitch. Both Phelon and Outlaw were overgrown juvenile delinquents. The three of us began to hustle and hang together, although Outlaw was falling off.

At times Outlaw would be coming short with his money and we would have to help him out. This is when I realized that he was hitting the pipe. After he sold me his forty-four revolver, his appearance was going down. His jawbones began to sink in and it was showing in his eyes. He kept claiming that he wasn't getting high, but everyone knew that he was.

Outlaw started staying off of the streets a few days at a time. He was supposed to have stolen a couple hundred dollars of crack from Phelon. He began to hide out for a few days. I would go to his mother's house and she would tell me that she hadn't seen him. His mother was also smoking crack with him.

On the first of the month, Outlaw came to the back street, looking tired, and had lost about twenty-five pounds. We began to get into an argument because he kept saying that he needed to rob someone and I wouldn't give him the pistol. I was concentrating on getting money and did not need him shooting.

Around this time Phelon appeared. Phelon and Outlaw then got into a physical altercation and Outlaw beat him down quickly. Phelon ran and got a pistol from someone. Outlaw tried to get one from me, but I refused to give it to him. Phelon tried to hit Outlaw with the pistol. Outlaw jumped back to avoid Phelon's swing. Outlaw danced around and hit Phelon with a strong right. Phelon then staggered back and shot Outlaw in the leg. They both fought over the gun.

The police then arrived and we all ran our separate ways. Later that evening Outlaw returned with a couple of guns saying that he wanted revenge. Phelon was nowhere in sight. Over the next few weeks, Phelon and Outlaw shot at each other every time they met. Both of them were cool with me. Therefore, I stayed out of it and stayed my distance from both of them. They had Snug Harbor hot as hell but the police caught up with both of them and convinced them to settle their shootouts.

The police were still messing with me. I stayed in the house most of the time. People wanted to know how I was getting paid while the police were parked across the street in front of our house. I was using the back door. By this time people were going to jail, getting caught, or getting robbed. It was so much going on that I was drowning myself in liquor. One night we were all standing around a bonfire and I bought a case of gin from a crackhead. I wasn't hustling, so we sat around and got drunk.

So we stood around the fire getting drunk when this freak approached us and wanted to get high with us. I told her no but she insisted on getting high. She ignored my demand and grabbed the bottle. At that instant I picked up a burning piece of wood and pressed it to her face.

She screamed, "Nigger, you burned me." Immediately, I slapped her in the face with the stick. She took off running, screaming that she would be back.

Within minutes she came back with her brother and stepfather. As they walked across the street, someone screamed, "Champ, run. He has a shotgun." My pride would not let me run from this nigger because everyone standing around the fire was packing a piece, too. I had a small twenty-two pistol that I pack in my pocket at all times.

As they made their way through the path, I could see that they only had a wood stick. Temo pulled out a forty-four and shot in the air. He said that he wished a nigger would get wrong.

I charged and took the stick and hit him across the head with it. Phelon and Greg kicked them down and about ten of us stomped them good. By this time he was lying on the ground in a fetal position. His stepson ran. His stepdaughter tried to pull him away from us. Someone in the crowd slapped her and we continued to stomp him. Somehow, he broke away and begin running towards his house. Temo and I began shooting at him. By the time he reached the front door, he fell. The windows were shot out of the car parked in front of the house.

During all of this commotion the blue lights came towards us. We all split our separate ways. I ran to my cousin's apartment and watched the commotion from the window. I watched as the ambulance brought a man out on a stretcher covered with a white sheet. I could see the bloodstain come from his head. Spectators stood around watching.

Someone pointed to my grandmother's house and my heart began to drop. As they approached my grandmother's house, she fainted. I knew prison was for me. Everything was rushing fast through my mind.

My cousin asked if I would turn myself in but surrendering was not an option. I could only think about where I could run—Mississippi or Florida.

I washed the blood from my tennis shoes and ran down the back stairway. I unloaded my pistol and threw it in the fire. That night I lost my favorite pistol. I had that pistol since I was fifteen years old.

After two days of hiding in a motel in Pensacola, I got the word that the guy wasn't dead, he was in a coma. I needed to see my grandmother so I had a friend to drop me off on the back streets of Snug Harbor. Everyone was looking at me and pointing in my direction but my mind was on seeing my grandmother. I felt lost. It was a feeling that I couldn't understand because this was the first time I could remember being outside without a gun.

I made it to my grandmother's front porch. She was so happy to see me that she hugged me and then asked me if I had any intentions to turn myself in. I said, "For what? I haven't done anything wrong." She pleaded and begged me to leave the streets and go to Cleveland, Ohio, where I had family. My mind was on going to the Job Corps, getting a trade, and getting a good drug connection and becoming a major cocaine dealer.

I lay around my grandmother's house until nightfall. At nightfall I hooked up with Outlaw and Phelon. We rode around getting high. Everyone was still busy hustling but Outlaw and I played around boxing. He kept telling me how good it was to see me. I grabbed Outlaw and told him that I had a proposition for him. I told him that if he shoots the lady's house that pointed to my grandmother's house that I would pay him and give him his forty-four back.

He accepted, but I told him that he would have to wait until I go to the movies with my girlfriend so I would have an alibi. Later that night, I went to the movies and to dinner and Outlaw took care of the business as we discussed.

After everything was taken care of I laid low for a couple of days. The two apartments across the street where Outlaw shot up were now empty and no charges were ever pressed against me. The police were angry because they wanted to pin that on me. The authorities knew I was on the verge of turning eighteen and wanted me behind bars.

Phelon and I began to hang tight. We rode around in his beat-up Pontiac getting high. He was wilder and more thuggish than I was. He handled more drugs than I did. By this time, I was staying in different motels so no one knew what I was doing and what I was up to.

One evening Phelon and I left Happy Hill, buying crack to flip it. As we left Happy Hill and headed to Snug Harbor, the police had the streets blocked off. Phelon was driving. He turned the radio off and pulled over. I laid back on the passenger side. As I looked in the rearview mirror, I saw the policeman remove his gun from the holster.

My mind told me to do something, so I reached over and placed the car in drive. I told Phelon to stomp the gas. He didn't move fast enough so I stomped the gas. Before we sped off, the police shot the back window out. I am ducked in the seat. The policeman ran to his car and chased us.

We went down several one-way streets until we were out of Prichard's city limits. The police fired several more shots, but we were out of their firing range. The police were at us hard but at this time I didn't know why. When I was in jail, I was told that a lot of old-time drug dealers were snitching to stay free and keep their nice cars and homes. Nowadays a lot of this is going on. They call this a part of the game.

I often felt myself losing control snorting cocaine, smoking laced joints, and drinking, that I often forgot what happened the day before.

One time I had ten thousand dollars hidden at my grandmother's house and it took me three weeks to find it. Another time my girlfriend came to pick me up with a black eye and I couldn't remember that I had given it to her.

A few times I woke up with blood on my shoes with no idea how it got there. I knew something bad had happened, but I couldn't remember what.

When I finished my transaction of business on the street, I went to my grandmother's house, talked to her, gave her money, and ran water in the bathroom while I snorted cocaine. My conscience was playing tricks on me. I knew there had to be a better way. I leaned my head against the wall and let the coke take full control of me. It seemed as though death was chasing behind me.

April 1, 1989, was a day in my life I would never forget. The streets of Snug Harbor were like a block party; everybody that had been my regular customers were waiting on me. My plans were to hustle for three days and then leave town.

On the second day, I had monopolized the hood. I was dressed in Bugle Boy shorts with big front pockets, a pair of black Jordan's without a tee shirt. I had so much money in my front pocket that it looked like I had a bowling ball stashed in them.

I was trying to make it to my grandmother's house when four policemen approached me. I began yelling for people to come outside. A huge crowd gathered around the four policemen. I didn't want the police to take my money. I had plenty of money, but no drugs. The police took all the money from my pocket, stripped me of my money and my clothes. They took pictures of the money.

I was doing nothing illegal and felt violated. I asked them do they perform those types of searches in West Mobile. The police walked around the building trying to find something. They asked where I got all of the money. I replied, "This money belongs to all the old people. I was going to pay their bills."

The police responded, "Champ, we aren't worried about you. In a matter of six months, you will be dead or in jail." This was the day the task force videotaped me selling drugs to undercover officers and gave an informant four hundred dollars to buy crack from me.

A couple of months later, Phelon and I were riding in his car. He had just paid me five hundred dollars he owed me. I had just sold my last ounce of crack.

As we made a block around the People's Lounge, a white pickup truck flagged us down and wanted to know if we were straight. Phelon told them to follow us.

The truck pulled up on my side of the car; the occupants said that they had fifty dollars so I sold them some crack. They passed me some money all balled up. When I opened up the money there were two dollars wrapped in newspaper. The truck pulled off. Phelon always had a thirty-eight on the seat. I picked up the thirty-eight and shot five times.

The person on the back of the truck took three shots and died. I reloaded the gun and fired six more times, attempting to shoot the other three occupants in the truck. I missed the other occupants but shot up the truck.

Realizing what I just did, I regretted that I didn't have any more bullets to empty into Phelon's head. I knew that Phelon was the only one to finger me for this shooting.

Immediately we rode through Prichard listening to the sounds of sirens drawing close. I still had the pistol clutched between my fingers. Phelon and I agreed to split up and never talk about this incident.

I jumped over a fence and threw the pistol down the drain on Montgomery Street. I took off to Bessemer Project to work on an alibi. After this incident, Phelon and I didn't see each other.

A few people informed me that Phelon was running his mouth about the shooting. People offered their service of killing Phelon for a price to keep his mouth shut. Through the grapevine I heard that Phelon was arrested for possession of a pistol and drug possession. I gave Phelon's mother the bond money so he could meet his fate he was destined for.

Two weeks after the murder, I was arrested at my grandmother's house for first-degree murder. This was just eleven days after my eighteenth birthday.

Approximately three weeks after being released from bond, I purchased a Buick Park Avenue for cash. My status as a dope man had increased tremendously. I felt I had nothing to lose; therefore, I hustled harder than I had ever hustled before. I changed whores like I was changing clothes, two to three times a day. I had more women than Mary Kay had clients, but they were all gold diggers.

Shaunta was still my main girl. She couldn't control her jealous rage and would make comments about me being a pimp. She asked, "What a pimp like you going to do in jail?" I responded, "I plan on having a lot of fun until my sentencing begins." My mind was set on having fun, with or without Shaunta.

On the streets of Prichard I was so hot I began expanding my business to Trinity Gardens and Roger Williams. This expansion paid off. Roger Williams was such a hot spot that I could sell five ounces of crack in a matter of minutes.

Roger Williams was home to many murders. During the first week of hustling in Roger Williams, I witnessed a man shot to death while riding his motorcycle. This spot was a breeding place for murders, therefore I moved from one location to another, not staying too long in any one place.

One night as I descended from Roger Williams searching for this fool that tried to trick me on some drugs, I apprehended him at J. R.'s Club. As I approached him, I revealed my .357 and pierced his right leg twice. No one in this area of town was familiar with me, so nothing else was heard of this incidence.

On November 11, 1990, I was on trial for first-degree murder. People from my mother's church served as character witnesses. Sister Gales knew me from infancy. The district attorney portrayed me as a villain, drug dealer and murderer. My attorney defended my honor although Phelon testified that I was the person who pulled the trigger. He turned state evidence and fingered me for the killing.

After three days of jury deliberation and the lack of evidence, the verdict was read. "Hung jury." I beat the rap during the first trial.

Two days later I was back on the street selling drugs. The only thing that could stop my dope game was a pine box six feet under. My life revolved around hustling. I hustled hard, with style and grace. I often felt lonely, but couldn't show it. Everyone thought I was on top of the world, but I was miserable.

CHAPTER 9

INCARCERATION

JANUARY 1990, I went to the guillotine for first-degree murder. The only character witness that was on my side this time was my auntie Jean. My lawyer didn't subpoena Sister Gales. The entire trial was a malicious process.

During the opening argument the district attorney quit. Witnesses changed their testimonies from the first trial; at the first trial no one knew me. Now all of a sudden everyone was able to identify me as a bad drug dealer. Those actors should be in Hollywood getting paid for their talent, as those crackheads were on the witness stand crying and carrying on.

I looked at my lawyer and said, "Man, do something." My lawyer objected but the judge overruled it. Phelon testified against me that I was the one who did the killing. During the recess my mother and I had lunch for the last time.

On the way to the restaurant, my mother told me, "Champ, if they find you guilty after those people lied on you, God must want you in jail." I should have jumped out of the car right then on busy Airport Boulevard and committed suicide.

After we ate, something felt real strange as we headed back to the courthouse. I felt sleepy. When we got back to the courthouse, Pee-Wee and a bunch of girls I had been messing around with were standing in the hallway trying to be nosey. They asked me how I was doing. I didn't have anything to say to them; my life was on the line.

As soon as I entered the courtroom, it was a few task force officers sitting in a corner, but I didn't pay them any attention.

I was on trial for murder, and they were there to get me. Court started back, my auntie testified on my behalf. Then I was next; I tried to maintain my innocence. I didn't know anything about any killing or any drugs. Then they called a task force officer to the witness stand.

"What in the hell is going on?" I asked my lawyer. He claimed he didn't know, but he was in cohorts with them to get me off the streets. The officer testified that he had been watching my every move for the last six to nine months and had arrested several people that worked for me in two different projects. The officer had once worn a disguise and purchased drugs from me. I was considered as a major player.

By this time I broke out in a deep sweat.

To top this, they showed a video of me selling drugs. The tape was almost a year old. This was part of a secret indictment. I didn't know anything about the tape and had never been arrested before. The purpose of the case was the warrant for my arrest.

The jury went into deliberation and I was arrested on the spot in the courtroom. The judge set bond at $7,500, $750 to make bail. The bond for the murder case was only $5,000. My mother went straight to the bondman's office to post my bond.

The sheriff took me to the docket room to process me in. They placed me in a little cell with about 30 people who had also been arrested during that day. It wasn't enough room to even sit down. The cigarette smoke was irritating the hell out of my eyes; the wino's breath smelled like a 15-year-old whiskey bottle. For me this was a small portion of what was going to take place in my life.

After four or five hours of standing in a cell, the bondman came and got me and took me across the street to his office to fingerprint me and take a mug shot. It wasn't clear but something kept telling me that my life was over.

I was so exhausted, the only thing I wanted was to get out of this white man's office and get something to eat.

When I tried to go through Prichard to pick up my last little money people owed me, the streets were almost empty. One person who owed me $800 was on the corner. That was my last pick up; everyone else probably was out celebrating my arrest.

After talking with Shaunta half of the night about the court process it seemed as if she was telling me goodbye.

My mind was on skipping town. This woman I had out of town had offered me a plane ticket a few days earlier. I was seriously thinking about considering her offer. I didn't sleep much that night.

The next morning, I arrived at the Mobile County Court House around 8:33 a.m. Everyone was running around looking for me. My lawyer thought I was still in jail. My family was under the impression that I was at the airport. That would've been wise of me.

A few minutes after 9:00 a.m., the jury came out of deliberation and delivered a verdict of guilty for first-degree murder. Then the judge ordered the sheriff to arrest me. As the pigs handcuffed me, I told my mother to come take my jewelry off and not to cry.

They put me in the same holding unit, which seemed like a nightmare to me. More people were there, drunk as hell, just like the ones that were in there the day before. For the first time in my life I wanted to be a wino or a petty hustler.

The pigs brought some slop to the holding cell. I refused to even touch it because it looked that bad. He should've

139

taken my share and given it to his funky wife. I took my jacket off and rolled it up like a pillow and dozed off.

It's easy to lose track of time in jail. It seemed like time I closed my eyes the pigs called my name. They took me to the docket room and processed me in, this time for good. They took my clothes and balled them up and put them in a brown paper bag. The pigs started making wisecracks. "It will be a long, long, time before you wear something nice again." I should've spit in the potbelly pigs' face. They issued me some dirty county whites and took my T-shirt because it had color in it.

As soon as I reached the second floor stairway, I heard voices hollering and screaming, "Don't cry now, baby, you're in the big house." One squeaky voice that sounded real familiar said, "Champ! Stop crying." I looked through the hole in the cell door and it was Reginald Jones, one of my favorite customers.

Before I got in the cell good, he started telling me that everybody in the jailhouse had been talking about me. Then he asked, "Why did you beat up my old lady?" It was a case of mistaken identity. They had me accused of almost everything that was happening negatively in Prichard. Inmates love to lie.

The pig came and opened the steel door, let me into the cell block, and slammed the metal door behind me. Boom! It was a sound that will scare the shit out of you.

I was placed in a special drunk tank that the county had converted into a cell due to overcrowding. It was small and designed for four inmates, but was now holding ten. It wasn't enough room to walk around in; there was one shower, one toilet, and no TV. The air was filled with funk due to cigarette smoke and unwashed bodies.

Most inmates were afraid to take a shower because of fear of being raped. I'll admit I was scared but my fear only compelled me to want to fight harder.

Due to Reginald and I knowing each other on the streets, he immediately started schooling me on the jailhouse rules.

"Hell, Champ! You don't have anything to worry about. Everybody in this jail already knows who you are; all your homeboys from Prichard are upstairs."

Reginald had already done time before so he was jailhouse slick. He gave me everything I needed as far as personal hygiene items, T-shirts, and socks. I paid him back over a hundred times. He stayed up to some type of con game; we shared two sisters while on the street.

Every store day he'd start talking about women or his little sister, trying to sell me her. I always wanted his younger sister but never had enough time to get with her. When I would buy him a pack of cigarettes he'd call her for me. Well, I thought it was her I was talking with but every store day the woman on the other end voice changed.

I'd tell him about it, and he would say, "Man, its winter time out there. She got a cold." I'd get mad and tell him, "Nigger, you need to come up with my $300 you ran off with in Bessemer Projects." We slept so close to one another that every time we rolled over in our sleep we'd slap each other in the face.

Both of Reginald's parents were entrepreneurs. They owned several convenience stores in Prichard. I used to always stop by to purchase things to eat from time to time. He was raised with a silver spoon in his mouth always; he had everything he wanted.

Reginald rejected the good life so he could sell drugs and become the ghetto superstar. The dope game was good to him for a while until he started using drugs and was eventually sent to prison for messing with a minor. His first prison stay was only for a year. After that year, he got out and was never able to establish his dope game plan the way he had planned and started back smoking crack again.

Now he's in jail for stealing clothes out of the mall and for parole violation. Because of his first prison sentence he didn't learn to conquer his drug habit. Once you get that monkey on your back, he rides you for a long time and either sends you to hell or jail.

On the streets, Reginald always kicked some positive information to me. "Champ, man, don't let them whores or chumps trick you to start smoking; get you a good lawyer and you won't have to worry about nothing."

Now we were both sitting in the county jail like a damn fool, talking about getting out and going straight. It would be years before we'd both be able to really prove our worth. The conclusion that we came to is that crime doesn't pay.

How are we going to resist that quick money when it is so easy to get and have so much fun with? The only cover salary that would compare to that in the dope game is being a doctor. With our conviction and lack of education that would be highly impossible for us.

It was an old-time player in the cell named Chick; he used to be big-time back in the day on Davis Avenue. Chick was sent off to prison in the late 60s. It was a revolving door for him ever since.

After he overheard Reginald and I conversating, he always would come and kick the bo bo (talk) with us. Chick would tell us how other brothers who were big players had been sent to prison, gotten out, and was doing real good. Some were preachers who I'd never believe were once criminals; others owned their own businesses with a good, respectful, career-oriented wife. He'd always say, "Young blood, I did pretty good working and hustling on the side until I fell in love with cocaine and then the big-butt gal in the projects."

The entire cell block would share bits and pieces of their life stories; some tried to glorify themselves. All of them had done time at some point in their lives. Most of them were career criminals—three years in prison, six months on parole. They considered the times they spent in prison as the most enjoyable time in their lives. Being the youngest in the cell block, I'd just listen in disgust.

I regretted the fact that my life was becoming just like theirs. Our goal was all the same: get rich fast. The entire jailhouse was full of a bunch of junkies and artificial pimps who had traded their freedom on many occasions for a used Caddie or a woman living on welfare, and now they are bragging about getting over on the system. They couldn't post a $50 or $100 bond or even call anyone to bail them out. I had enough money in my pocket to make six of their bonds with no problem. If we could have traded places, I would have easily left them $500 to spend. But I was stuck.

The quick, unexpected, life changes are enough to run a man crazy. One day I'm rolling, having sex with some of the finest women in town, dressing nice, and eating good. Just enjoying the best of everything. "Damn"—it's over. I'm locked up in the county jail with a bunch of former customers, the people I looked down on, the same people who paid my rent; now we are equal and wearing the same dirty jailhouse whites.

I didn't know what to do. I had just spent the last three years getting high, now it's difficult for me to sleep without some form of intoxicant. My nose had a serious drain because the tissue was now raw from sniffing that pure cocaine. I didn't eat for the first few days because the food looked terrible; it had to be unfit for human consumption. Who in their right mind would eat boiled wieners, lima beans, and corn bread?

I just lay on the hard jail bunk eating cookies and candy bars, looking at the ceiling like I was in another world, wishing this would've never happened to me. I thought I was going to die.

All the screaming, hollering, and the filth from the unwashed bodies drove me crazy. I'd been bathing and changing clothes twice a day.

What in the hell is going on.

My whole life flashed before my eyes. I wanted to be at Central Baptist Church; I'd even settle for being at Blount High School. I should've listened to all the people who were trying to help me before I got to the point of no return. I just had to talk to someone with a soft voice to explain my situation.

The phone was rotating every hour. The first person I called was my mother. We didn't know what to say to each other because neither one of us was expecting this to happen.

She told me to pray. "I know you have never prayed before in your life, but God will deliver you." This was the last thing I wanted to hear. My mind was on the lawyer and a helicopter.

She went on to say "Your grandmother took it real hard when she found out you were guilty. She's over to Jean's house and you need to call her right away." Those words hurt me worse than anything else. I could deal with losing my freedom, but not taking my grandmother through this.

Then my mother came with another devastating blow. "Shaunta said why you haven't called her. She was about to go crazy worrying about you." I definitely didn't need to hurt her either.

When I called my grandmother, all she did was cry. "Those damn folks got all my sons in jail and two of my grandsons." I assured her that I was going to be alright, although I wasn't. I couldn't allow her to worry about me. She told me that she was going to die without me. I promised her that I'd be out soon, and that a new lawyer was working on my case.

Shaunta and I had been on so many emotional roller coasters before I got locked up that I was embarrassed and afraid to call her. I'd taken her through so much. I felt like she was going to use my incarceration against me to get back at me. Therefore, I didn't call for another week.

When I did call, things were totally different. "Champ! I love you and miss you." She sounded so sexy I wanted to cry. But I couldn't, too many people were watching. We talked for two and a half hours. She informed me of everything that was being said about me on the streets. She found out about other girlfriends that I was hiding from her. She was trying to tell people I was out of town until they wrote an article on my case in the newspaper.

I asked her what role was she about to play before I make up my mind or what woman I was going to have on my visiting list. She told me I'll be with you until the end regardless of what happened or how much time you have to do. Shaunta had always been honest and straightforward with me over three years. Relatively late, I realized this was a lie. I rode with it because she was all I had that would be worth anything.

Shaunta did try. During my first visit in jail with her, we had to talk through thick glass and holler through a hole at the bottom of it. The visiting area was so small and noisy I couldn't hear anything she said.

I was grateful that she came. I wanted to hold her so bad. I was weak. I'd been holding back the tears for the last one and a half years. After seeing her big, beautiful, lustrous eyes, I couldn't hold them any longer. I broke down and cried like a bitch. Tears formed in her eyes as well, but she had been going through this ever since I had been locked up in jail.

This was my first lesson in prison. A woman is much more emotional than a man. If she would've been in jail, it was no way in hell that I would've had the strength to support her the way she supported me. I've always appreciated her because no one else ever took the opportunity into consideration to attempt to understand me before. Shaunta had always been all ears.

Visitation only lasted for 30 minutes and time went fast. Before she departed the visiting area she asked me to call her every day and promised she'd visit me twice a week. I said, "I love you" as she got up to walk away. I just sat and admired her beauty. The first thing ran across my mind was kick the glass out, then you can get a kiss.

As I was departing the visitation room, my partner Arthur McFadden had been watching me cry like a bitch. He said, "Champ, you down there putting your game down like we used to do it back in the days, ain't you boy?" I said, "Yes." But he didn't realize I was crying for real.

Arthur was upstairs on the third floor; we kicked it for a minute from there. We had to send notes to one another through the trustee. Arthur was shocked at how much weight I had gained since we last saw one another.

The saying "out of sight, out of mind" went into effect quickly for me. My friends and artificial fan club had disappeared. I couldn't turn a corner before I got locked up, without someone attempting to jump in my car. On the streets they treated me like a king. Now I'm in jail and they treat me like I am nothing. My only true friends were Shaunta and Pee-Wee.

My family members had turned their backs on me again. My two uncles that I had working for me owed me more than three thousand dollars. Neither one of them gave my mother a dime. I no longer believed that blood is thicker than water. My family had proven to me that they are not worth a tablespoon of chicken shit.

Time was moving extremely slow. It seemed as if I had done years in jail. When I made phone calls or watched the news, someone that I knew had been killed or arrested.

Darryl Jessie had gotten killed in front of a grocery store parking lot. The reason for his murder was because he was driving his white girlfriend's car.

I just sat in the cellblock thinking what in the hell is happening. My mind went back to the time the police shot the windows out of the car shooting at me. All the times my partner had been shot and I'd escaped. Things seemed really strange. I'd never viewed life from this perspective before. It was too late, the white man had me and wasn't planning on letting up any time soon.

I am not a Charles Manson or Ted Bundy type of guy. I just wanted to make a bundle of money and have nice things.

There are some fools that I'm being surrounded by and they are getting sicker as time progresses. In order to feed their drug addiction, they smoke banana peelings with crushed Tylenols and Sudafeds. This has a terrible smell; but they claim it gets them high. They'll climb up on the bars like monkeys, looking up and down Government Street. From time to time, I'd participate in this foolishness.

A streetwalker would be released from jail, walk by, pull up her dress, and give the inmates a freak show. Most of the time we'd stand up in the window during visitation time, waiting on visitors to arrive.

The recreational yard was surrounded by a 16-foot brick wall, with a guard with a riot pump shotgun. If I could've got my hand on it, I could've solved my problems.

Arthur and Mike-Mike kept bringing up how much weight I'd gained and suggested that we start working out together. I told them that the only exercise I was going to do was wrestle with the guard to get the riot pump from him. As we laughed and exchanged ways to get the gun, we thought about how we would blow the guard's head off with it first.

A fight broke out around the basketball game. A big ole joker was swinging a broom; he was about 6'4, 245 pounds. Niggers were falling like flies, but he kept on swinging. The guard shot in the air; it didn't stop him, he kept on swinging. So the guard turned on a high, powerful, water hose and hit him with it. The water hose staggered him for a second but didn't knock him down.

The county sheriff had to come and stop him. He fought them off for a second but they eventually overpowered him. We all just stood back and watched in amazement. About 10 more sheriffs came to run us off the yard and then whipped the monster they created.

Arthur, Mike-Mike, and I gave each other five and went back to our cell. Early that morning, Arthur and Mike-Mike were transferred off to prison. They sent me a note telling me to take care and try to get stationed at Draper, a camp for first offenders where they would most likely be sent to.

An artificial revolutionist was in the cellblock preaching about the fighting that took place on the recreation yard. Perry claimed the fighting was over a bet that had been placed on the game; the bet was only 10 individual cigarettes. Perry was one of the fakest niggers I've seen in my life. He'd tie his head up like a Muslim, but always read the New Testament. Perry would sit down for hours at a time talking about how white folks are trying to kill off all black men to prevent us from being a strong nation.

My ears weren't available for all this preaching shit so Perry and I would argue all day. Sometimes it got close to a fist fight between us. The majority of the other inmates listened whenever Perry talked. Sometimes they would fast for long periods of time. I was glad, that meant that I could eat their tray during meal time. Every day one of them would say, "Champ, get yourself together." I knew that most of them were only involved because of fear and they needed protection. I didn't play on the street, so therefore I wasn't going to play in jail.

Perry was doing a good job at keeping some of the trouble down, but he knew better than to interfere whenever it was time to get some get back on the white boys. He just went in his cell and got on his knees and prayed for them.

Once Perry did catch my attention, when Mayor Barry of Washington D.C., was caught smoking crack in a hotel room. This was my first time ever hearing of a black man being mayor of a large city. I didn't sympathize with him for being so careless. Reality was becoming a lesson in development for me because that's one of the many incidents that occurred that helped me realize that the war was on.

Absolutely no one can outsmart the F.B.I. We perfected and spent billions of dollars on anticrime equipment, which is useless because if they was serious about stopping the drug trade, they'd just stop bringing it over here for minorities to sell for them.

After three weeks of incarceration I had more partners in jail than on the streets. People would always say, "That's how the game goes." When I watched the news, all I saw was young black men getting killed. I said to myself "Damn." Perry would read my facial expression and say, "Champ, another young black man just got killed; it could've been you." I'd curse him out for wishing bad luck on me.

The way I was viewing things, I'd rather be on the streets, taking my chance running from the police, getting shot at and avoiding all the snitches, than sitting in a funky jail.

On February 8, 1990, I was escorted into the courtroom for sentencing. A female officer and another male guard attended. They had some pretty 9mm on their side. Beautiful thoughts crossed my mind. The female officer thought I was looking at her behind, but my mind was on the gun.

They took me to a courtroom on the far end of the building. No one in my family was present. A few of the victim's family were there.

My lawyer ran up to me and said something. His breath smelled like he had eaten a pint of shit for breakfast. I asked him to step back and repeat himself. He went on to say, "The faster we get it over with, the faster we can start the appeal process."

The judge called my name, reread the charges and the jury's verdict, and then asked how I felt about the situation. My lawyer spoke something about appealing and some more bullshit.

The judge looked at me through his glasses and asked "Do you have anything to say before I pass the sentence on you?"

I couldn't work up enough nerve to open up my mouth, nothing would come out. What could I possibly say, before my slave master tightened the rope tighter around my neck, that would be a benefit to my defense? I couldn't tell him I love him. So I said, "No."

The judge went ahead and said, "I sentence you to life in the state penitentiary." I couldn't believe this; it had to be a nightmare. My lawyer said something but I couldn't understand. My hearing was gone completely and my mind was in another world.

"You cracker!" was running through my head at a rate of 3,000 times a second. I was dizzy and thirsty at the same time. I tried to swallow my spit, but my mouth had become dry like only sand was in my mouth. I had enough strength in my arms to raise my hands to try to choke the lawyer. All of sudden, the handcuffs felt like they weighed 1,500 pounds.

The guards grabbed me by the arms and pulled me away. As I was exiting the courtroom, I looked back at the judge with his childish smile on his face. Right over his head sat the scale of justice; that bitch is blindfolded, meaning justice is blind. When it comes down to black people, those scales must be filled with money or gold if you want justice in a courtroom.

Most people think the KKK no longer exists; ha, ha, ha; they just traded the white robe for a black robe. Instead of hanging with a rope, they've replaced it with a more sophisticated tool, a gavel.

In a very wise way, they are murdering millions of black men through this process. Every other black man in (AmeriKKKa) will go before a judge in his lifetime, whether it may be a criminal act, child support, or for traffic tickets. The verdict will be guilty unless you have some money to pass around.

When the pigs placed me back in the cellblock, all the inmates were standing waiting to see what happened to me in court. I ran straight for the phone to dial my mother's number and told her that these white people are trying to kill me. That's been my philosophy ever since. "How are they trying to kill you, Champ?" "Mother, these crackers gave me life."

She burst out crying. "I thought the lawyer was going to get you an appeal bond." "That had supposedly been the plan, but the lawyer knew it was a life sentence. It's no way the judge will give me a bond."

She started telling me to pray. I listened but couldn't understand because the people I'm dealing with don't believe in praying; they strictly believe in getting paid.

I got off the phone with her, and this female guard who I had been shooting game at reached for my hand and gave me a note. Her hand was so soft I wanted to lick her fingers. Her intentions were to console me, but I knew my life was over. She had written me some beautiful words of encouragement.

We started exchanging letters from there. I didn't know I could still write, my handwriting was terrible, but she liked it.

She would make her rounds to the cellblock every day to see how I was doing. When she realized I didn't eat jailhouse food she'd bring food for me to eat. This beautiful sister must be rewarded one day because I didn't know how to respond to her needs from a position of weakness.

I paced the cellblock thoroughly after the officers left, wondering how in the hell I was going to do a life sentence. Eighteen years old with a life sentence and I'd never really lived, but some ugly cracker wanted me to do life in prison.

Everyone else in jail seemed happy playing games and making boats out of popsicle sticks. I'd imagine they would, since they had nowhere to go. If a person don't care enough about you to post a one-hundred-dollar bail, you ain't got nobody and that's reality.

I paced the cell until my feet got tired, then I tried to go to sleep but the words "life sentence" kept coming to mind. When I stuck my fingers in my ears, I still heard the judge's voice "Life Sentence." The gavel hit the oak.

When I called Shaunta to notify her of what happened in court, she cried like a baby. Hearing her cry I broke down in tears. She said, "Baby, that doesn't mean you'll have to do life, you'll be able to get out in seven to ten years. I'll still be waiting for you." She always found a way to brighten up my day. Whenever I was weak, she'd make me strong. But I had to be straight-up with her for once in a lifetime. I told her that I wasn't expecting her to stick with me. "You have too much going for yourself, you are about to graduate and go to college, so have fun."

Shaunta insisted on riding with me because she thought I was trying to get rid of her for someone else. She didn't know she was all I had left. The rest of my girls were just with me to have a good time, but she actually loved me. When I actually realized how much she cared about me, it was too late. In actuality I didn't know how much I loved her until I was in jail. My frustration wouldn't allow me to talk long, so I told her I loved her and I'd call her back tomorrow and hung up the phone.

Time I got off the phone and was walking toward the cell, someone who was sitting at the table said, "Redbone, you been over there crying, ain't you?" I walked over to the table and asked, "Who called me a redbone?"

Johnnie was an old-time junkie who didn't like young dudes because he was making them rich on the street. A few times I heard him state how all lightcomplexioned men in prison be whores. So I knew he was trying to challenge me indirectly.

I turned and walked to the cell. I sat on the bunk and then the thought occurred all redbones are bitches on the streets. Only whores are referred to as redbone. I jumped up and got a long sock and put four bars of soap into the sock, tightened it up on the end, wrapped it around my hand, went off into the dayroom and hit him across the head from behind.

A good fight is what I needed. This made me feel a whole lot better. I continued to hit him some more. I had to whip him good because in jail your reputation will follow you to prison. He didn't have a chance to fight back and this is how it was supposed to be. I became panic-stricken and beat him unconscious. Someone grabbed me from behind. I broke loose and beat them with the sock about 15 times.

The guard ran off into the cell and hit me upside the head with a flashlight to stop me. My head was busted badly, but it wasn't anything compared to what I'd done to the other two inmates. The nurse had to come get one of them because the bleeding was really bad.

The sight of blood excited me. I rubbed my head and licked the blood off my fingers because I knew if I had to do time this is how it had to be for me. The soap in the sock worked wonderful for the occasion; when I was finished the soap was crumbled up like fine washing powder.

The rules of the jailhouse dictate the loser of a fight was put into another cellblock where the same thing will most likely occur. The winner always gets the opportunity to become the bull. I became the bull and took full advantage of it.

When Nelson Mandela was released from prison after doing twenty-seven years, Perry's house nigger was going to every cell asking everyone to come watch the news. When he came to the cell I was sleeping in, he had an Uncle Tom smile on his face. He asked, "Brother Champ, are you going to watch the news?" I went all the way off on him.

I was angry. "I just got life for killing one nigger. If you don't get the hell out of my face I'll kill you, nigger. Mandela ain't did nothing for me."

I was good and stupid with zero understanding. I didn't know who Mandela was or what he represented. All I've been familiar with was hustlers and jackleg preachers. Later in prison, prisoners would call me Mandela or Malcolm X because I stayed solid and never compromised my moral standards. That was the last run-in with Perry.

Three old-timers came from prison to go to court on some charges they had pending. They revealed Perry's identity. We all found out that Perry was an ex-Prichard police officer who had been using his position to rob drug dealers and set people up.

When he got exposed, he was moved to protective custody. A goldfish don't stand a chance among living sharks. No one heard from him again. Then everyone who had been listening to him lost faith, stopped faking, and went buck wild. We had to mop up blood off the floor daily.

Now on the recreation yard all the old-timers were congratulating me. Everyone was under the impression that I ran Perry to protective custody and I accepted full credit for it. Anything that would help, I needed. These cheers were simply "Champ, you're handling time like a pro. You show 'nuff isn't going to have no problems surviving in the big Camp."

We'd all huddle up and plan what we were going to do once we entered the cellblock, and talk about what our boys were doing up the road in the big house.

We'd walk from the recreation yard back to the cellblock chanting, "We are going to whip us some white boys today and it's going to be real soon." The white boys would automatically get in compliance after they heard us chanting this. They would clean the cell, wash our dirty underwear, and wouldn't even think about eating their food during meal time.

My mother and Sister Gales decided to come visit me for the first time after two months. Shaunta showed up as well. Shaunta suspected Sister Gales as being one of my girlfriends because Sister Gales looked so young. I had to explain to her who Sister Gales was. She immediately apologized and told me I had so many women that she didn't know who was who.

My mother didn't say much. She just told me that she was pregnant again. Sister Gales and Shaunta mostly did all the talking.

Sister Gales came to preach the gospel. I sat there and listened because there was nowhere to run to. Under normal circumstances I would not have listened to this at all and they know it. Women do men real bad while men are in jail.

Shaunta just stayed there and listened with a big smile on her face. When this visit was over I was more than glad. They had me about to say "Hallelujah." But I felt that something was terribly wrong. I asked Shaunta to go over my grandmother's to see her for me. She gave me a real strange look and said, "Call me by the time you think I'm at home."

As soon as I got upstairs to the cellblock I called. She had just walked through the door. I said, "What's up?" She tried to equivocate but I didn't go for it. So she told me straight up

"Your grandmother's health has been deteriorating since you've been in jail."

"How bad?" I asked. "No one wanted to tell you about it because they knew how you're going to act. She had a stroke and is paralyzed on one side of her body." I immediately hung the phone up and said, "Those sorry bitches."

I called everybody who would accept my phone call and cursed them out. "The only reason was they didn't want you to know." Some black people are still stupid like that. They feel that your family's health shouldn't mean anything to you. I fell asleep and hoped that I would die in my sleep. Too much was going on for me to deal with.

March 11, 1990, they took me to court for an arraignment on a drug charge, distribution of crack cocaine. I pleaded guilty to the charge for a seven-year sentence to run concurrently with the life sentence. I was already doing time for murder. It couldn't hurt me any. So I was ready to leave jail and head off to penitentiary. The jail was too crowded, so it should be soon. I just had to wait for my time to come.

Temporarily, I was moved from cellblock 303 to a cellblock on the dark side of the jailhouse. The cell was designed just for killers. Everyone in this cell had already been sentenced and was waiting to be shipped off to prison. Majority of the cell block had a life sentence, life without parole, or death penalty. Some of the death row inmates were coming back to court in order to get their case reversed on appeal.

I was shocked to be surrounded by these types of people. They seemed so humble. My curiosity got the best of me. I had to talk to them to see what they were thinking about and see how it felt to be sentenced to die in the electric chair.

My sentence was life and I felt like dying already.

Vernon Madison was the bull in this cells; he had the chair for allegedly killing a white off-duty police officer. The officer was his white girlfriend's ex-boyfriend. Vernon had suspected his girlfriend of having an affair with someone. One night the officer came to the lady's house in plain clothes. Vernon was drunk and out of his mind. He didn't know the cracker was a police officer; he just walked up to the car and blew the man's head off.

Whenever Vernon wasn't writing letters or talking on the phone, we'd sit at the dayroom table and talk for a while. He was in his early forties and was talking like he was about to go home in the morning. I would always ask him how he was doing it and what was keeping him alive and from jumping across the brick wall. Actually, I couldn't believe he had done what he was accused of, he seemed too humble.

It was eight of them in the cellblock, all of them with the chair. Some of them were incarcerated for anything from killing their wives for insurance policies to serial murders. I couldn't understand why they didn't just hook up and attempt to escape. Eight men with the chair should be able to fight harder for their freedom than all the officers in the Mobile County Sheriff Department. I'd talk to every last one of them and ask them the same question; their answers were to the same effect.

"We are waiting on God to grant our appeal." They were depending on God and dope to carry them through. I couldn't accept this. These people disgusted me so bad. I hated even meeting them. All they wanted to do was pray, shoot dope, and watch TV, but when they were in society they murdered a fourth of Mobile County.

Then it was Gary Hart in the cell. He was 16 years old with a capital murder case pending. Gary robbed a seafood restaurant to prove his loyalty as a part of an initiation process to be in a gang.

When he entered the restaurant, things didn't go according to plans. The restaurant manager refused to give him the money. Gary was half-retarded with one small arm. His gun accidentally went off and the restaurant manager was killed. Due to the manager being young and white, the white folks in the courtroom were talking about giving him the chair. The bad thing about Gary's case is that the person was trying to prove his loyalty and turned state evidence against him in exchange for a life sentence.

The last I heard, Gary received the death penalty at the tender age of 16. All while Gary and I were in there together all he did was cry; often I'd sympathize with him because he never really had an opportunity to live and never will.

My nineteenth birthday was spent in the Mobile County Jail. My family sent me a few cards and some money. This was an attempt to pacify me because they hadn't heard from me since I found out about my grandmother's condition. That same night, my stepfather came to visit me talking about

"Happy Birthday!" What in the hell do I have to be happy for? I'm serving a life sentence and I just turned nineteen in jail. "Man, did you buy me a getaway car? I don't want to hear nothing you got to say unless you are talking about paying my lawyer to help him fight my appeal." The remainder of that visiting time was spent in a heated argument.

CHAPTER 10
PLANTATION

AROUND THREE O'CLOCK in the morning, a guard came to the cellblock and informed me to pack my bags. I was on the chain to Kilby Prison near Montgomery, Alabama. They came at you like a thief in the night in the most organized fashion. I grabbed my bags and stood in front of the cellblock. I was more than glad to be getting away from these lunatics.

The guards escorted me to the basement along with other inmates. They gave me all of my personal property. It felt really good to have my clothes on again. I felt like I was making love to a woman.

My jeans were stiff because the starch had been sitting in them for so long. Every step I took the jeans would crack. They were loose around the waist because they had starved me bad. I had lost close to ten pounds in less than four months.

When I put on my leather jacket and boots, all the other inmates were looking at me like I was a movie star. Everyone else was dressed like a bum. This forced me to realize I was surrounded by the wrong type of people.

I asked them, "What were you doing on the streets smoking crack?" We were all handcuffed together, put in shackles, belly chains, and placed in the back of a van with metal walls. There was not one window in the back of the van. You were unable to see where you were going. The misery I felt on this trip had to be similar to what my ancestors felt when they were shipped from Africa.

As we were moving along the interstate, I couldn't see anything. The metal was cold. We were rolling around the back of the van like marbles. There was nothing to brace up against. Every corner that we turned you felt it.

After two and a half hours of this, we stopped. We were inside the gates of the Kilby Correctional Center. In the yard sat a big white tower shaped like a penis with an erection. This meant that the white man was about to mess with you good once you were inside.

Kilby is the processing center for all the prisoners in the state of Alabama. Once you hit here you have really made it to the big house. They take you through a total process of demoralization; spraying you with spray, checking for lice or crabs, cutting your pubic hair and the hair under your armpits. Everyone who came through this unit had to get a regulation haircut and shave regardless if you needed one or not. I wasn't even growing facial hair and they still made me shave.

If you didn't comply with all rules, the big illiterate hillbillies would beat you across the head with an oak stick and flashlight. The officers were very anxious to do so.

My first ten minutes there I witnessed them beat a man almost unconscious with their big stick. It was so many of them. Their sticks were hitting together on top of the man's head. All the inmate had done was step across a yellow line that had been painted on the hallway without their permission. Keep in mind that the only qualification needed to be a correctional officer in Alabama was to be big and stupid, too stupid to deal with the discipline of the army. Most of them were illiterate army rejects. They can't fit in anywhere in any form of employment, be an ex-athlete, or an undercover homosexual.

All inmates were issued an AIS number (Alabama in slavery); the number replaces your name. Everywhere you went it had to be used. It was used for mail and to eat. The number was stenciled on all of your clothes. My number was 157061. After you go through this harassment, you are then placed in quarantine. While in quarantine you are given many psychological and physical tests. This worried me the most because before my incarceration I had unprotected sex with over a hundred different women. I didn't care while on the streets.

My first night at Kilby, an officer came through quarantine with a yellow outfit on with a plastic shield over his face. The officer was getting inmates who had tested positive for AIDS to escort them to the AIDS ward. Every time I saw one of the officers enter the cell with their suits on, my heart would beat extra fast. My mind was made up.

Therefore, I got me a blade. If the officer ever stopped by my bed, I wasn't going by myself. I was going to cut myself first, then the officer, and the rest of the inmates. I was going to be doing a lot of cutting, biting, spitting and scratching as many people as possible.

It was approximately ninety inmates in the cellblock. I wanted half of them to go with me. I was safe but my conscience just kept on messing with me.

The second day of this madness we all marched to the social services office to see a classification specialist, to do some more educational tests and to be interviewed so they could decide what prison you should be sent to.

This was miserable for me because my reading level was below sixth grade. I was having trouble pronouncing simple words; my mind had completely shut down on me. Cultural shock got the best of me. I was frightened to the utmost. I attended school for eight years and didn't learn anything. The only reading that I had done in the last three years was read dope scales, sale papers, and sometimes I read to see who got arrested.

The first Mother's Day card I sent my mother was so pitiful. I couldn't figure out how to spell "dear." I didn't know which spelling to use (deer or dear) therefore I just wrote "I Love You" on the inside of the card and sent it off. Being embarrassed wouldn't allow me to ask anyone there how to spell the word "dear."

Immediately, I started learning how to read and write. I read the newspaper three times a day, mostly the comic section. Dennis the Menace and Curtis were my favorite. Those are still my favorites today.

We were not allowed to go on the yard or the general reading library until all test results came back. Therefore, every time we departed the cell we had to leave in a group.

Once we were all released from quarantine and sent to the general population, it was more like a circus or a family reunion. Inmates were around each other like they were happy.

I never realized what an inmate had to be happy for; trapped behind a chain-link fence with trigger-happy guards anxious to gun you down if you ever looked across the fence for a long period of time. A bunch of happy niggers confined within a cage with other inmates standing along the fence hollering all types of derogatory sexual comments to the newcomers, "Hey, pretty young lady."

The white boys would drop their heads in shame. A few blacks tried to play it tough. I was walking tall and making serious eye contact, trying to remember all potential predatory faces in case one of them approached me later on. It wouldn't be a surprise ambush.

It was about five dormitories lined up together. I was assigned to M-block. Inmates were standing in the entrance doorway. They would try anything to get over on a newcomer. They would come up to you acting as if they were willing to help you carry your bags but they would run off with them. They would take all your personal property such as your hygiene toiletries and pictures.

Inside of M-block depressed me to the extreme. As far as the eye could see, I could see approximately one hundred ninety bunks occupied by black males in white prison uniforms. Every time I sat on my bunk to attempt to relax, my mind would go blank; sweat would form all over my body as I thought, "What in the hell is going on?"

Somewhere along the course of my life I had been cheated of something real valuable and not just of freedom. I thought about my grandmother's life and my family. As I thought about being nineteen years old in a prison somewhere I've never heard of, serving a life sentence. Damn, something surely went wrong in my life. As reality set in, the angrier I became. In prison your mind really plays tricks on you.

The administrative rules changed based on the administrator's attitude and their constant dealings with the petty-ass inmates, all with split personalities.

I spent hours in the law library trying to fill out papers to get a copy of my transcript. From there I'd walk down to the general reading library; it was a little bit larger and had more people in it. Prisoners were more concerned about reading bullshit fiction than working on getting their freedom. Being trapped in prison is psychological warfare. The strong rule and the weak and the wise rule them all. Before it was over, I was determined to be the winner.

In prison there is a famous saying, "You can be everything that you want to be in prison." Prisons are filled with people from all social classes and professional backgrounds. I've encountered former doctors, lawyers, school teachers, many businessmen, and con men.

Another thing you will find in the Alabama prison system, are a bunch of prisoners who are not from the state. I have met and exchanged conversations with people from all over the United States. Some of the places I didn't know even existed. They also let you know that if you come to Alabama on vacation, you most likely will leave on probation. It's full of all types of people who are regretting ever coming to the State of Alabama.

While sitting in the library reading the newspaper, one of the Muslims I had run past came to speak with me. "Excuse me, brother, no offense at all, but the attitude you demonstrated earlier can get you seriously hurt."

I listened to him closely, trying to figure out whether he was planning an attack or was he super-humble. We talked briefly and established an understanding. I let him know that I was not interested in religion while in prison. He shook my hand and walked away.

Every day, newcomers would arrive at the back gate receiving unit. The newcomers would receive the exact same harassment from the guards we received when I first arrived. The inmates that arrived with me were supporting this foolishness by screaming derogatory remarks. In a matter of days, a man changed from being afraid to death into being a hard-core criminal.

A van pulled up at the back gate. The guards started unloading the van. Someone stepped out of the van with a short mini-skirt on with long braided hair, and then another one. Some of the inmates took off running to the back gate area. I said to myself, "Damn, they're bringing women in here." I walked towards that direction.

As we were getting close to the van, those big stupid guards pulled out their old sticks and ran us back to our dorm. The word spread throughout the prison yard that those two were a transvestite and a trans-sexual who had taken hormone shots to inflate their breasts. They both had to be placed in protective custody so no one could get to them. If they would have been allowed to stay with the general population they could have caused a major prison riot. I felt really bad about this that I allowed myself to run behind some fools to see some sissies.

After ten days of different types of evaluations, I was put on a train and transferred to Draper Prison, a prison for first offenders located near Montgomery. The ride was brief. They took a lot of back roads. The small part of the city that I did see was beautiful. The officer pulled the van along the side of the road.

As far as the eyes could see only farm land could be seen. I saw a few spots of white out there. I assumed it was cotton but as the van got closer, I realized that it was inmates in the fields picking vegetables; nothing but a modified plantation and inmates are viewed as precious stock.

The healthier you are the more work they expect out of you. There were very few white inmates assigned to the farm. Slavery hadn't changed much since the Emancipation Proclamation. The inmates who worked in the fields received one dollar a month for pay. There was nothing in the canteen that you could get for a dollar but a pack of cookies and one candy bar.

When I entered the back gate, the farm squads were just checking in. The inmates were hollering, "Welcome to hell." Their skin was burnt so badly from the sun, it appeared that they had just returned from Satan's den.

Some more slaves (inmates) that were hanging around the basketball court started hollering degrading sexual comments. The same thing happened to the people in front of the line. Their bags were taken away. We ignored the situation and went straight to the chow hall and ate our portion of slop.

While in the chow hall, four or five different inmates were peeping in the door asking, "Which one of y'all Champ?" I didn't say a thing because I was for sure I didn't know those people.

On my way to the laundry room to pick up bed assignments, there were about two hundred inmates ganged up waiting on me. The word had already been put out that I was on my way. People I hadn't ever seen before were asking, "Who is Champ?" I just eased though the crowd trying to put my back close to the wall. Everywhere I went they were looking for me, and asking for "Champ."

My partners Arthur and Mike-Mike were there. Mike-Mike I knew was a real trader. Therefore, I asked Arthur, "Where do these people know me from?" Arthur said, "Champ, it's a nigga who supposedly want to kill you for pistol whipping his sister in Orange Grove Projects. Then the dude you killed, his brother is the head gang leader here. But we can deal with them."

Mike just stood there with a real puzzled look on his face. I asked Arthur, "How many people from Prichard here with some heart?" He informed me that it was only a few, but they were riding against me for something. I supposedly did not look for them. I told him to go get some homies and meet me in the cell.

When I entered the hallway, it was complete silence. The inmates were leaning up against the wall, staring at me with their arms folded and some with their hands in their pockets. I was watching them out of the corner of my eyes. As I walked down the hallway some of them followed behind. I then went in the cellblock where I was assigned, dropped my property off and went looking for Arthur. The correctional officers jacked me up and took me to the shift commander's office.

In the commander's office I was told, "They're planning on killing you in your sleep tonight. What have you done?" I wouldn't say anything because the streets had taught me to never trust the police.

They went on to say, "You causing too much trouble for this to be your first day here. We're going to place you in administrative segregation for protective custody."

The inmate from the projects just wanted to jump me for nothing. I've never pistol whipped a woman in Orange Grove Projects. My dealings there were limited to a few minutes. I never spent more than thirty minutes there. Temo was the one who pistol whipped the girl.

Administrative segregation is a man-made hell; "the hole" it's most commonly known as or "lock up." It is an isolated unit of the prison. The cell is six feet in length by eight inches wide. It includes a prison bunk, an iron toilet, and sink. The walls are painted dark gray. There is not even enough room to stretch your legs.

You are in "the hole" all alone with absolutely no one to talk to but the walls. The peacefulness is good for a day or two, but after four or five days the walls start to seem as if they are talking to you. Sometimes you'll think the walls are closing in on you. The iron toilet made a hollow sound like an ocean. I just sat there and listened to it all.

I was sent back to Kilby to be reclassed. The remainder of my time at Kilby, I stayed close to my cell talking on the phone for hours. Talking on the phone was one of the best things to do. The rules changed based on the officer's attitude.

Regardless of how they felt, they were always anxious to inflict oak-stick therapy on anyone.

CHAPTER 11
THE BOTTOM

THE BOTTOM - In prison they use words and phrases normal people just can't understand; but in the bottom it's the language of the land. You will see fighting, stabbing and killing over another man mostly every day. In the bottom there are the laws of the land. Sometimes they walk hand in hand! Author unknown

MAY of 1990 was my very first day in "the bottom"— Atmore prison. I immediately realized it was a big plantation. The activities and attitude the administration had toward the inmates will have witnessed to that fact. The top administrative figures suck; the warden, assistant warden, captain, and chaplain are white. They had no productive programs. On the farm they truly believed in working you to death just like they did the first time they had us in slavery.

According to the United States Constitution, slavery is legal upon the conviction of a crime. Since blacks are more likely to commit crimes than any other racial group, it is logical to assume that the laws were written to entrap black people.

In prison you have everything that's in the projects except women, cars, and guns. Prisons are just like the projects. The only difference is that you are trapped behind a twenty–five-foot fence. Projects and prisons are systematically designed to destroy your mind.

In the projects you have nine people living in a two-bedroom apartment; whereas in prison there are one hundred and seventy inmates living in a cellblock with six showers, nine toilets, and one TV per cell with only four channels. Then you have a cellblock full of arguments and confusion. It has been many stabbings over that one-eyed monster (the television). Some want to watch sports, some want to watch the news, and others want to watch the soap operas or instigate arguments that end in bloody affairs.

Everyone that I hadn't seen in a long time was in prison. People who knew my father, some knew my uncles, and people I had met while I was growing up in different ghettos. I thought these people were either dead or living in another state.

I decided to walk around for a few minutes to get an overall view of the plantation. The savage environment most definitely earned its name for being "the bottom" because things seemed to happen.

There were homosexuals walking hand in hand like they're husband and wife. I peeped in the TV viewing area and there were two guys sitting in the TV room kissing and watching the news. They supposedly had been sending me to a prison, not an insane asylum. They looked up at me like I was doing something wrong. As I walked through the hallway, inmates were staring at me like I was a giant—six feet tall and two hundred seventeen pounds without a smile.

I went looking for Snap. Snap and a few other slaves were sitting around the prison like they were at home. They were exchanging lies. I went up to him and shook his hand. At first he didn't even know who I was. Snap was one of the niggers who ran with my father. He took a second look and said, "Got damn, Champ, you must been eating fertilizer." We talked for a while, but I didn't want to disturb him from doing his thing.

When I hit the prison yard everyone was interested in the type of tennis shoes I was wearing. These people had been locked up so long, they had never seen a pair of Air Jordan's.

The ones who were out on the streets just couldn't afford a pair.

My tennis shoes even caused animosity between some of the officers and me; those back-road, no-class hillbillies didn't even own a pair of Air Jordan's.

Once I was going through the cellblock and this pretty female guard and I were talking. When one of her male co–workers came up and asked, "Who in the hell do he think he is?" I just went all the way off on this chump. "Broke-ass nigger, my tennis shoes and gold chain cost more than your raggedy-ass car." He looked at me like he was doing a brief estimate and walked away. Talking to officers wasn't my style. She was just curious about my age, because I was probably the youngest inmate there.

While standing outside watching the basketball game, I realized that it wasn't nothing but a bunch of old slaves in this prison, not one young-looking person was in sight. Over half of them looked as if they had been working on oil rigs or changing a transmission in someone's car. Since there are no cars in prison, it's safe to guess it came from the hot sun while working on the plantation.

The half-time show in prison basketball games is a real trip. The half-time show is a prison wedding. Two punks jumping the broom and kissing; I actually mean standing dick to dick kissing like it was legal.

I saw enough madness my first day at "the bottom" to depress me for the rest of my life. After the half-time show, I went and stood up against the wall wondering how in the hell am I going to occupy my time. I just sat down thinking.

Before long this old-timer came up to me. Everyone called him Brother-in-Law. He said, "Just stay to yourself; homeboys are the most dangerous species; just watch and learn."

That advice stayed in my subconscious mind throughout the duration my incarceration. Brother-in-Law and I became cool. He was fifty-one years old; he had been in and out of prison since nineteen sixty-two. He was a wise and cunning old man, an education within himself. I learned a lot just watching him wheel and deal.

Everything you need in prison, he could help you get it. My shampoo was running low. I would ask Brother–in-Law to find me some shampoo. I gave him a pack of cigarettes for it. This con man gave me a bottle of shampoo he had been using himself. He just filled the bottle up with water and sold it to me. I was green and didn't know any better.

When I confronted him about it, he said, "I told you, homeboys are the most dangerous species. Watch me get down and you will learn something." This had me fighting mad. If I had had me a good stick, I would have taught his old ass something. This forced me to observe my environment more closely. There are some mean tricks and games being played on you in prison.

My first night there I didn't sleep at all. I had to watch my back because I was the youngest prisoner in the entire camp. I saw some strange things that night. People who looked like men turned out to be gay as hell. He's say, "Freaks come out at night."

Everything in prison is done in line formation. You have to stand in line in order to receive your mail, inmates have to stand in line for their assigned work detail, and for mostly all prison activities you have to stand in line. This is done to make sure the state has complete control over your life.

The feeding process is the strangest thing I've ever seen in my life. Inmates stand at the bars like cattle, as the officers open the gate hollering, "Chow call!" or blow a whistle. The inmates then would stampede to the chow hall.

Segregation does exist. White inmates on one side and the black inmates on the other side. Never was it real friendship involved within the two races behind the wall. Anytime you see a white inmate sitting with black inmates, the white inmate is normally a homosexual. When a black inmate sits with a bunch of white inmates, he is also considered as being a homosexual.

They have one side and we have the other side. It's that way in every prison I've been to.

The wall where the black inmates sit to eat there are many pictures painted of white fictitious heroes such as Jesus, George Washington, and Bear Bryant. This is consciously done to project a high image of white people and to subject the black inmate with an inferiority complex. The floor on our side of the chow hall looked like a hog pen. The white's side was spotless clean.

Around my third day there, I went to the inmate orientation. They said my first parole date wasn't until November 1998. My conscience spoke to me saying, "November 1998 is a long time, Champ; they will have stopped making cars by then." November of 1998 was not guaranteed because parole is a privilege and not a right.

The warden highly stipulated that each workable inmate work in the fields. For a newcomer I had to work in the fields. Those fields are so big it takes hours to walk across. The hot sun is terrible. The heat is so hot on the fields it seems as if the sun is setting just inches away from your head.

As we were walking, I started hallucinating that it was two heat monkeys tap dancing around two kegs of beer. I saw McDonald's and Church's Chicken signs. The heat had me so thirsty I needed a beer bad.

Some inmates would fake heat stokes. The guards be sitting on top of horses screaming, "Come on now, and get up from there." When the inmate didn't move, he would shoot his gun in the ground beside the inmate's head. Instantly the inmate would jump to his feet. The officer would write the inmate a disciplinary for causing a security hazard. Then the inmate would be ordered to go back to work. The inmate would have to spend forty-five days in lock up for this behavior.

The main work area during the spring was the cucumber fields. We picked so many cucumbers that I declared that I would never eat another cucumber in my life. Another scheme to avoid work is to start a fight in the fields. After my first day working in the fields all day, I just stood in the mirror looking at myself. This was the dirtiest I'd ever been in my life.

I immediately realized that I couldn't go through this type of slavery. My ancestors had worked enough for me, I shouldn't have to go through this. Everyone in prison was trying to avoid work.

One big slave (inmate) went on the weight yard and intentionally dropped a forty-five pound weight on his foot. He would do this twice a year. Others would get a piece of sandpaper and sand the skin off the heel of their feet so that they couldn't wear a pair of shoes. They would brag their ass off about it, too, standing on one leg.

You are written up if you refuse to work, and put in the hole. The hole was the last place I wanted to be. Therefore, I bought four packs of cigarettes and paid this house nigger inmate that worked hand-in-hand with the police to pull my work card and give me a non-work profile until I was able to get into trade school. Cigarettes in prison are just like cash money in the mall. When my card was pulled, I still regretted seeing the other inmates go out in the fields.

The day many of my classmates graduated from high school, I supposedly would have graduated if I had stayed in school; but I was now in prison looking like a damn fool, working on a shotgun squad. This was another one of the many painful experiences I'd have to endure.

CHAPTER 12
SEXUAL MISCHIEF

THE DESTRUCTIVE HELL-fire of the cities of Sodom and Gomorrah should have been a sign for a conscious mind. In the Alabama prison system those signs are highly ignored. Prisons are notorious places for corrupt sexual behaviors. Therefore, anyone who supports this type of activity, the hell-fire should be their reward. God created Adam and Eve not Adam and Steve.

These people are so confused that they have made things that are abnormal appear to be normal. This sinister sexual deviance is a very big problem and is as common as the noonday meal. Public masturbation is one of the strangest acts in existence. They call it gunslinging or dick jacking.

Lusting at a woman leads to something far worse than you can understand. This only reduced a man to playing pocket pool or participating in homosexual activity because you'd eventually get tired of staring at a woman. When you become sexually aroused, your mind will tell you to relieve the pressure one way or the other.

When I realized these facts, I wouldn't even look in a Playboy Magazine. When my female friends sent me pictures in lingerie or anything sexy, I got rid of the pictures. In prison, a photo of a woman in underwear will sell for five or ten dollars easily.

With female officers working in places like this, it made things even harder for a real man. If anyone wanted to bring the chump out of a man, bring a woman around.

When the female officers came through the cellblock to count, chumps would go crazy and start hollering, "Shake your money maker." Some inmates would be wishing for a recount so the female pig (officer) would walk back through the cell. Many female pigs (female officers) actually like this and support this madness because women do love attention.

I would just sit there staring at the ceiling. I refused to compromise my integrity, dignity, and the things that make me a man.

Any man who allowed his wife, or woman he claimed to love, to work in a male prison got to be a fool. When a female officer comes through the prison gates, her intention is to have an affair and be unfaithful. You can smell the cheap perfume from miles away and that enticing, penis-sucking red lipstick will automatically get her plenty of attention around one-thousand horny men.

These conversation freaks would do anything to get a woman's attention, from dances all day long and hanging from the cell bars like monkeys. Some even shine the officer's shoes for free in order to look between her legs while he's shinning her shoes. When a woman officer is assigned to work the cellblock, chumps would be standing in line to talk while lotioning down their body in front of her, offering her a pillow for her to sit on so they can sniff her scent later on.

Earl was from a small country town in Alabama and had been incarcerated since he was like twelve or thirteen years old in different detention homes. When he turned sixteen, he was transferred to prison and lost his virginity in prison. Earl had never in his life been with a woman. Earl was a compulsive gunslinger. Whenever he saw a female, he would masturbate off of her regardless of where he was.

Sometimes there were times when the female guard was in the guard tower 30 feet above the ground, and Earl would be out there in the cold weather masturbating, staring up in the tower. The only thing he could really see is the top of her hair. If she rubbed her fingers through her hair, he thought it a sign of approval for him to go ahead and get down. It only took for him to see a silhouette and he would masturbate off of it. A male officer with a Jeri curl was enough for him because he was only impressed with seeing hair of any length.

Earl was so obsessed with gunslinging that the administration put a memo in his institutional file to have all his front pockets on his prison uniform sewed up. This didn't stop him. He would just tighten a shoe string together and put one end on his penis and the other end tied to his big toe. Whenever he saw a woman he just stood around tapping his foot, smiling, and jacking off.

I didn't believe this at first until one of my homeboys explained it to me. "Champ, it's better than smoking crack." So I listened to this fool like I was a fool myself.

Sometimes I'd watch the female officer react to see if she really went along with it, and some of them did. Then I'd go ask the officer why she let inmates disrespect her like that. She would say "I'd never imagine a man would find me so attractive that he would watch me and play with himself." She probably didn't believe a man would find her attractive at all since she had more stomach than ass.

One Saturday I was headed to the visitation yard; it was about ten inmates standing on the infirmary walkway. As I passed through, I overheard their conversation. "She letting everybody get straight." The conversation I'd heard a lot on the streets. I hadn't quite learned any better in prison. I walked down there, because if a woman was giving away sex, I didn't want to miss out on it.

As I got closer, the inmates were standing peeping through the pill call window of the infirmary, masturbating off the nurse who was passing out medication. I still can't understand how they do it. These women were fully dressed and standing a great distance away.

A female officer came up pregnant. The gunslingers were so messed up in the head that they were running around the prison arguing that they had gotten her pregnant, because she had given them permission to masturbate off her, more than she allowed the other one to do so. This was the big talk of the prison for months. They were serious about it.

One gunslinger told the others not to masturbate off his baby momma because he was sure it was his child and he didn't want anybody disrespecting her. We'd all sit around and laugh at these fools. They would keep going at it. He got mad and got a two-by-four and chased the other one with it for masturbating off of her. These chumps had probably never even touched this woman, but he thinks he got her pregnant. These people are really sick.

Who created this madness? The disciplinary code for this violation is #38.

They've only programmed themselves to be potential rapists. If a man is so sick that he can imagine himself having sex with a woman while she is fully dressed, and he only sees her hair, then it shouldn't be a problem for them lying down on top of a six-year-old boy or girl after they've seen them with a pair of short pants on.

When Pee Wee Herman got caught masturbating in a movie theater, that gave the gunslingers grounds to justify their deviant behavior. They think everybody's into it. It mostly affects young black inmates. White boys prefer to be homosexuals. Homosexuality is common among white inmates.

As much as I'm in disagreement with the white man, he deserves credit for not allowing his woman to work in a male prison. There is only a handful of white female guards. They're considered as beat-down trailer park trash.

It's enough black sisters here to celebrate Kwanza and they were being disrespected and disrespectful. Inmates go to the extreme to disrespect a black female officer. When white female officers would appear, black inmates became speechless.

Around the time of the gay March on Washington, D.C, the faggot shit went out of control. The male officers started coming to work with their pants tighter and tighter. In my judgment, over 70% of the male officers were gay and came to work in a male prison because it's an easy place to find a man.

Whenever the showers were on, the officers always had a hard time counting and it was only 1000 inmates there. In the shower area they counted too many heads—phallus worshipping does exist.

The prison warden used homosexuality to his advantage, and as a form of pacification of a terrible situation. Whenever the warden wanted to find who was smuggling drugs into the prison, he locked up the homosexuals until he got some answers. This way, before sundown, he had the names of all known prison drug dealers. Once he got the information he wanted, he would let the homosexuals back out into the population. When more drugs came into the prison, he would lock the punks up again.

A lot of the officers ended up having sexual relationships with a homosexual. At night the homosexuals would go up to the visitation yard and come back with a bag of free-world items such as silk panties, lipstick, and chocolate candy.

To prove the allegation, one year in Atmore, some of the inmates came down with a bad case of gonorrhea. The county health department was sent in to clear up the problem.

Everyone who was a known participant in homosexuality was called up to the infirmary to give a list of names of who they had been having sex with. Two guards' names came up on the list. The sissy that reported them was transferred to a maximum-security prison.

In a sneaky way, every man who's incarcerated will be a victim of some form of homosexual activity. Your own homeboys will try to turn you out. They will approach the newcomers. Homeboys would tap them on the shoulder, trying to size them up and getting free feels. Then go back and tell everyone else that he's open game.

Everybody plays the rub game to a certain extent, that was one of my reasons for not playing any type of game or tolerate anyone getting within arm's reach with a smile on their face. It's absolutely nothing in prison to smile about.

The undercover punks are the ones that are the most dangerous. They'll approach you and just talk with you, hoping you'll be attracted to them as a mentor, and then flip the strip. Once trust is built, they'll let you know they're gay. At this point you'll be attached to them as a friend, not wanting to let them down. A lot of good brothers got turned out this way, saying "he's just another man." I don't view it this way because if a man will have sex with another man, he'll do anything, NO EXCEPTIONS!

Whenever a punk or someone I wasn't familiar with would try to talk to me, I'd immediately stop them. I didn't come to prison to be friendly. Their impression of me was that I had a little money. A lot of parasites are looking for someone to take care of them. Something wouldn't allow me to be in their presence for long. If one of them was in the shower, I'd wait until later. Old slaves would say to me, "You're homophobic." Homo sapien described me better.

Someone wrote me a love letter stating that they'd been watching my dick in the shower and they'd like to suck it. The letter was unsigned. My conclusion was that everyone in prison wrote it. I stood by the bed area for nearly thirty minutes thinking, and hoping this was a joke. Someone was playing. This was one of the many games that are being played on a young man in prison.

That evening I was taking a shower and this off-brand nigger started talking; the shower area was the last place in the world I wanted to hold a conversation.

So I told him, "Bitch, I don't know you; furthermore, I don't talk in the shower or while eating." He ignored me and kept on talking. So I lathered down my face rag real good and slapped him across the eyes with it. The soap burned his eyes. Immediately I grabbed a broom and beat his ass with it.

From that day forward, I always took some type of weapon to the shower with me. Everyone claimed I was wrong for whipping the old slave. If they had tried to talk with me in the shower I'd have done them the exact same way.

Old man Brother-in-Law pulled me aside and told me that the old slave wasn't up to any game and I was just over-reacting. He went ahead and philosophized the situation. "Champ, man, you might be just schizophrenic paranoid. Don't give these white folks a reason to hold you for the rest of your life. Everybody knows you got life and don't play."

My reasons for reactions were perfectly clear. I'd seen too many young men fall victims to homosexuality. I felt good proving that I'd harm again in order to survive. They say, "Only the strong survive." Surviving was my mission, by any means.

They would call it packing peanut butter when the sissies walked by with their prison-made mini-skirts on. The chumps would holler, "Baby, I want you to shit on me."

185

In the streets these so-called players would beat the hell out of a woman. Now they're in prison taking care of another man, saying, "That's my wife."

One time my homeboy Kemp tried to convince me that it was nothing wrong with messing with sissies. The way he explained was, "If your teacher don't come to school, you have a substitute; in prison you don't have a woman, therefore a sissy will do!"

When a new punk came off into the prison, those chumps would compete for the punk. These chumps would line up, profiling, trying to put their bids in; borrow other people's jewelry trying to impress with, dress up in new prison whites, and walk around with a bag full of cigarettes and cookies.

Rick, a young dark-complexioned punk, came off into the prison and caused major confusion. This punk actually looked just like a sixteen-year-old bitch. All the old booty bandits were ready to kill over him.

Rick went off into the shower on his first night there and about three hundred inmates followed him. Chumps were coming from three other parts of the prison to see him. He was afraid.

Within the next few days, the gangs from Birmingham, Montgomery, and Mobile competed hard over him. It was so much fighting and knives being drawn on each other, the warden had to come down the hall and settle the dispute.

Rick was telling everybody he was born gay. I know some people were born stupid, but this was my first time hearing a person talking about being born gay.

Rick eventually chose a dude out of Birmingham. He was one of the biggest drug dealers on the streets and in prison. The dudes out of Mobile were heartbroken. Every day they'd intentionally jump on the person Rick chose for some silly reason or another. Rick turned out to be a real drag queen,

186

the Queen of Atmore. All the officers were in love with him. He grew his hair long, arched his eyebrows, and ate fried chicken from Church's almost every night.

One night, after the lights were off, he strutted through the cellblock with a white silk gown on with a two-piece red bathing suit under it. An officer had given it to him. The entire cellblock went crazy clapping, hollering, and screaming. I went and jumped on the bunk and asked God to help me get out of prison.

This one chump wanted Rick so bad he was going around eating Snickers bars out of Rick's ass. At first it was hard for me to believe until he came down the canteen line asking who had candy bars for sale, and he went on and confessed that he was a certified candy licker on the streets. This stopped me from eating Snickers bars. Whenever someone be walking through prison trying to find Snickers bars, my mind got to wondering what they're going to do with them.

Darius was a homosexual, light-complexioned, about 5'11, and should've been a running back for Auburn. He was the only punk that had plenty of sense to me. He had to squint his eyes to see because someone had broken his glasses. He was looking at me one day and I said to him, "What's your damn problem?" "I don't want you, I'm almost blind."

Darius had been transferred to Atmore because he was a real troublemaker. His last prison lover had gotten real jealous and stabbed him six or seven times.

When we talked, he would always inform me of how the sissy game goes. His advice stayed with me for years. "Champ, don't ever mess around. Everybody who mess around either takes care of their sissy, kiss them in the mouth, or exchange sexual favors with them." A lot of that proved to be true. Darius was penitentiary smart; he knew by him being new that all the booty bandits were after him.

One Saturday, Darius made up his face, put on some shorts, and walked throughout the entire cell auditioning himself off for half-time show of that day's football game. He sold numbers for a pack of cigarettes. Before that day was over, Darius had over five hundred dollars worth of cigarettes.

My homeboy and I were standing outside when Darius walked by with a pillowcase full of cigarettes. He bragged, "Champ, I told you these men ain't nothing but tricks."

The competitors realized how much penitentiary money Darius would make for them if he chose one of them. The competition was strong. They immediately went to war with one another. Darius stood in the middle of it all, manipulating the entire process.

He'd have a chump out of Birmingham buy him some shoes, and a trick out of Mobile to get a gold chain, and another sucker out of Montgomery to get him a watch. Once he had so many cigarettes, candy bars, and cookies he had to rent out other prisoners' locker boxes until someone caught on and blackened his eye. The warden placed him into protective custody to prevent a murder. All while he was in lock-up he was being taken care of.

The players out of the northern part of the state had that old-fashioned pimp mentality. While incarcerated they worked on preserving their game by pimping sissies. They tried to regulate all the known homosexuals.

My homeboy Kemp had just got married to an older lady who had big money. Kemp was a real con man. His philosophy about women was he didn't care if they were blind, crippled, or crazy, from eight to eighty years old, as long as they sent him a money order.

Kemp got married on the visitation yard on a Saturday. Darius was released from protective custody on a Monday. They got married that same night in the seven dorm.

Kemp was one of my partners. He was a few years older than me. The word was spreading that Kemp had hooked up with Darius. I had to go see for myself. Sure enough, they were lying in the bed together. Kemp was smiling like he had just won the lottery. When he saw me coming, he got up and went and made a phone call. I went to his bed. Darius said with a smile, "Champ, whatever you do, don't drink behind him no more." I replied, "Why?"

Darius opened up Kemp's locker box and held up a Snickers bar and smiled. "This why! Remember what I told you, don't you!" I had always known Kemp was a chump but this was too much. Darius informed me of something I wished I wouldn't have heard. I didn't want to believe him because that's one of the quickest ways to slander a man's name in prison.

We talked until Kemp came back from making his phone call. I let him know what Darius had told me. When he didn't kill him on the spot, I figured it was true. Kemp and Darius argued and then fought. Darius whipped Kemp's ass. This shit was funny. I just busted out in laughter. I wanted to break it up but it would've looked bad on my behalf.

As I was walking off, Darius said, "Champ, don't come back around us causing problems." Something told me to curse them both out, but the words I really wanted to say, they both probably wouldn't appreciate them.

Kemp fell in love with Darius more than he loved his wife. His wife would send him five hundred dollars a week and Darius spent it the way he wanted to. They walked the yard all day long, hand in hand, went to chow together, and showered together. Darius would always brag about it behind Kemp's back, to me and other people out of Mobile. "Y'all don't be jealous because y'all homeboy is a trick for me."

The dudes out of Birmingham wanted Darius badly, but couldn't afford him the way Kemp did. Darius had this dude out of Birmingham that was his man as well. He couldn't take it any more. He got mad and went out to seven dorm and took Kemp's tennis shoes, knowing that Kemp's homeboys out of Mobile wasn't going to allow this to happen.

Likewise, he knew his homeboys had his back. Everybody knew Kemp was weaker than sugar water. The homeboys out of Mobile cliqued up and made Kemp go get his shoes back. It was about a hundred dudes out of Mobile. Kemp was my partner, but I wouldn't swing not one blow for a sissy. I went along to see the rumbling.

The dude out of Birmingham was standing in the hallway about thirty to fifty feet deep, waiting. It started with the look in the eyes, the flaring lips, and fists balled up. Kemp stepped forward; a dude out of Birmingham met him with a knockout blow. The dudes out of Mobile followed up.

This initiated a major riot; before it was all over, two people got stabbed badly. One of them was an innocent bystander who got paralyzed because he was out of Birmingham and at the wrong place at the wrong time. My back was up against the wall, all while the blades were being swung. The hallway was crowded. The sound of the blades was like the sound of a helicopter landing.

Over half of the stabbings and killings in the Alabama prison system are over some form of homosexuality. Homosexuals are the masters of mischief. A female guard, it was her first day on the job, was caught in the middle of it. She almost got stabbed herself. They were respectful enough to push her out of the way.

She ran down the hallway hollering, screaming, and crying, "Why are they doing this?! Why?!" A male officer grabbed her because she was in a state of total shock. She was one of the few sisters I met who was able to be wise enough to resign from this demoralizing process.

After the battle over Darius, the dudes out of Birmingham ended up with him. Kemp walked around the prison sad, with lips and eyes swollen like he'd been in a fight with Mike Tyson. His pride got the best of him and he caught protective custody. Many other inmates had to be transferred and hospitalized.

Rick and Darius eventually got into a fight over who was going to be the queen of Atmore prison. A lot of young men coming off the streets had succumbed to this negative sexual behavior. Some had turned down work-release replacement so they could stay in a main institution to be with their homosexual lovers. They would even go to the extreme of getting disciplinarians intentionally so they could miss first parole. Even when the administration forced them to leave, you'd see them standing in the middle of the hallway, crying and kissing.

Johnny was another notorious booty bandit in his late forties who had been in and out of prison since the age of eighteen. He would get all the razor blades he could find so he could cut the young white boys' drawers off while they were asleep and rape them.

It was a small group of them. They called themselves the militant booty bandits. They all hated white folks with a passion. Their defense was that they raped young white boys in order to get back for the many years of oppression and they worked together in an organized fashion. They would drop sleeping pills in the white boys' coffee. When the pill knocked them out, they'd pick the white boys up and carry them to the back of the cellblock and rape them. If any house Negroes wanted to be white, after spending a day in Atmore prison I bet it would force them to change their mind.

Late one Friday evening, a chain load of white boys came to Atmore; all of them had caused problems at another prison. They had tattoos that read "white pride," with a swastika on their elbows. Their punishment was to be sent to Atmore and assigned to the roughest cellblock, the thunder dorm (seven dorm.) The average young weak black man can't survive in that cell.

The old-timers, along with the militant booty bandits, raped the white boys all night long. There were niggers standing in line like they were waiting on welfare and food stamps.

The next morning the shotgun was going off in the gun towers. These white boys would've been willing to face death than to allow this to happen again.

In society, I was having sex at the minimum twice a day, trying to get enough to last in case of incarceration. It wasn't ever enough. Being away from a woman is the most awful aspect of life. Regardless of how hard you concentrate to block out the desire, the thought remains.

Physically, I learned to arrest and to subdue my desires. I would lift weights in order to subdue the urge even in that. I would lift just enough of that weight that I would imagine what I wanted my ideal queen to weigh. When I gripped the weight bar tight, I'd imagine that I was holding her precious hand.

I had read (the first book I read in its entirety) "Waiting to Exhale," by Terri McMillan. In that book, I fell in love with all the characters. I'd ask myself where are all the black men. Jail and prison are full of us. Immediately I began to redefine my character so one day I'd be able to satisfy a dissatisfied sister.

This motivated me greatly. I even wrote letters of apology to some of the sisters I'd disrespected, abused, and used in the name of the game by calling them filthy and derogatory names. A lot of them never received my letters because I didn't know their address or their real names. Regardless of my lack of information, I wrote thousands of letters to them in my heart, saying I apologize.

My thoughts evolved around women more than they ever did in my entire life. Often I'd just sit back and daydream about women.

I'd go to sleep and dream about them and we'd do all types of fun things together. I'd pick her up from work. We'd ride around town in our convertible. She'd express to me how the white people stress her out on her job. I'd console her and let her know to give that white man his job back. At my request, she'd do so. Then we'd vacation in Jamaica, walk the beaches talking, smiling, hugging and kissing, while on the sailboat we'd make love.

In my dreams, at the close, a woman always appeared wearing a light-green silk gown. We'd kiss and I'd wake up in prison crying, boxer drawers wet, and angry as hell.

CHAPTER 13
CONSCIOUSNESS

"Education is our passport to the future, for tomorrow belongs to those who purpose for it today."
Quoted by Malcolm X.

CHECK YOURSELF BEFORE you wreck yourself. As I do a moral inventory of myself and others, I'm surrounded around on this mental plantation. The question that must be asked is, "Why is the recidivism rate so high in Alabama's prison system?" Over 85% of the people released from prison return within five years. A large percentage return before two years on the streets.

The department of corrections is a joke. It's more like the department of corruptions. Where are the penologists, criminologists, sociologists and social workers? Prisoners only got an opportunity to see an institutional psychologist once a year and that visit was brief.

The pigs will gladly support you in your illegal activity. They know that it perpetuates the hustler mentality and increases drug addiction, and keeps the recidivism sky high. The officers come to work smiling because they're viewing inmates as economic security. When you ask the pigs to bring you a book or a magazine to read, they'll respond, "Oh nigger, you don't need that!"

Due to the release of movies such as "New Jack City" and "Menace II Society," criminals were able to see their ugly pictures. These movies motivated a desire in me to change for the better. For once I realized how people in Prichard must have viewed me, because my associates and I were really striving to live close to it all, striving to be our worst. Seeing myself in the scheme of things and feeling the consequences helped shake that hustler mentality.

So far I've only been incarcerated for a little over two years, and the domino theory has already taken effect on all of my old associates. Temo got killed mafia style: shot, stabbed, burned, and his dick cut off. He was found in a house dead, another unsolved murder.

The authorities never did investigate the killing seriously because the law hated Temo. He was a big shark swimming in a little old pond. Whoever killed him had to be close because he was too smooth to be caught with a gun. The only letter I ever got from Ricky was to notify me of Temo's death. "Someone killed our favorite homeboy Fat Timmy the other night."

After I got this piece of information about Temo's death, I reminisced about how we used to rent hotel rooms and throw parties; this left me crying like a baby.

Greg got sentenced to five years in prison for possession of crack cocaine.

Hump killed a lady for hitting his car with a bottle, accidentally. He killed the wrong woman.

Pee-Wee was indicted for money laundering and conspiracy to distribute crack cocaine. Pee-Wee was facing life in the federal prison, but he did just like Nino Brown in the movie and received seven years in the federal prison.

So many others fell victims to crack cocaine they became non-productive crackheads, got killed or were sent to prison. The subliminal message behind this all was profound. My imprisonment was a blessing in disguise.

Right after the movies were released, the violence increased in black communities. Everyone watched the movies to imitate the characters. As the violence increased in society, so did the county jails and prisons.

Almost every week now, it's about fifty to sixty young black men who come through the prison gate from age sixteen to nineteen; they're fearless, angry, cold-blooded; a total product of the environment. Most of them are not even old enough to vote, but they can buy beer or have a car in their name.

I feel their pain because mine is basically the same. The laws are corrupt when you can be sentenced as an adult when you are still a minor. Over 65% of the brothers who commit crimes are in gang-related crimes or the crime is for some form of money getting. The father figure wasn't seen in a positive perspective, so they had to become misdirected warriors.

In my judgment, newcomers should never be in the same prison with old convicts. The old-timers will only corrupt their character, old fools producing young fools. It happens every day in prison.

One old-timer in particular, Jimbo, was nigger-rich in the late 70s and the early part of the 80s and he wass stuck in those times. He hated young players who had money on the street. I just sat back and observed these people, never saying much, just listened to all the many lies that were being told.

We would be on the farm squad, slaving hard for the uncivilized tobacco-chewing hillbillies, Jimbo and a young player would go at it, "Young nigger, I had so much money on the streets, I was a dollar away from being a millionaire." Everybody stopped working to listen at his lying. The officers on the horse was about to fall off the horse laughing about

Jimbo. The officer forgot about making us work when Jimbo started laying it on us; he's hard to stop, he can go for hours.

The officers said, "Jimbo, tell us about your truck." Jimbo said, "Y'all young niggers talking about a Mustang 5.0. I had eleven cars and two trucks. My truck was so fast, I outran a telephone call and C.B. I was in a high-speed chase coming out of New Orleans, the police got on the C.B. and walkie-talkie trying to set up a road block at the Mississippi line. I was already sixty-five miles into Mississippi. I was running hard. Every time I shifted gears, I knocked up a quarter mile of asphalt off the highway."

The young dudes would laugh their ass off, get mad and tell Jimbo, "Old man, if we had you on the streets we'd put the AK-47 on your ass for lying so much." Jimbo would snap again, "Damn drive-by baby. An AK-47 isn't shit to me. I had a gun cost $50,000; it was so powerful, I shot at a man in New Orleans and killed a man in Denver Colorado."

Jimbo was real smart but it's very seldom that you got him to talk about something positive. He just loved to lie and entertain; no one in prison could out-lie this man. I've heard a lot of crazy stories from him; some should be on Def Comedy Jam. He topped the list as the biggest liar in all of Alabama's nineteen prisons.

How are you going to live a productive life in society when you are trapped in a controlled environment and all you want to do all day long is exchange lies, watch soap operas, X-Man, Power Rangers, get high, run around prison playing grab-ass, and participate in every type of retentive degrading activity under the sun?

Most definitely these were people who were going to go through a stage of moral decay. Their lives revolved around foolishness. They hated books, couldn't think, and wouldn't listen. I was an angry lion awakened from a deep, deep sleep and my conclusion was "Who needs a mouse in a lion's den?"

As a self-imposed vision of my own education, I deemed it necessary to educate myself. An educated prisoner is a future empty bed. By seeking to learn more, we rob the oppressor of its most powerful weapon against us "our ignorance."

Besides studying the law and working on my case, hoping through an act of Congress someone somewhere would acknowledge the many reversible errors and grant me immunity, I had more time for study. So I started reading history books. Mainly black history. Not to be a slave to history, only to study it to help me have a better understanding and clearer insight of my future and to obtain a more positive insight of where I wanted to go in life.

My studies were profound and full of understanding. In my discoveries, I realized that I am not a criminal; I'm just a victim of some criminals. Everything white folks have accomplished was taken by forceful and malicious means. They murder thousands through the passage.

When I read how blacks were shipped from Africa in chains, this was enough to motivate me to take my gold chain from around my neck. I placed it in an envelope and sent it to Miranda. It would take me several more years to fully understand that my incarceration was on another level. In order to be free, you must become aware of how you were enslaved (physically, mentally, spiritually and morally).

Booker T. Washington's book, "Up from Slavery," explains how he was able to overcome all different types of obstacles in the late 1890s. Washington was able to get an education, experience racism, and poverty, then advance to establishing Tuskegee Institute with very little resources.

Why can't black people do it in the 1990s? We are surely depriving ourselves by striving to control the ghettos and nigger business through illegal activity. It looks as if as time progresses, the condition of black people regresses. The same dedication that those soldiers had in those days could be restored and converted to contribute to something productive. "Cast down your bucket where you are."

The administration has implemented a Transactional Analysis Program. This was the only self-help and rehabilitation program in Atmore. Inmates Kareem, Shabazz, and Zo facilitated the program. Both of these brothers were self-proclaimed silver-tongued players.

Zo was a real Prichard nigger, a high school dropout, hustler, robber, and drug user, but had studied intensely during his incarceration. He was on his third bid, serving a twenty-five-year sentence for robbery and had eleven-and–a-half years built on his sentence.

Zo never did conceal the fact that his only motivation for being involved in the program was to shake the shackles and a chain which has impeded his growth. He constantly reminded the class "Bro, I'm trying to get out of here by any means necessary! And to help yourself you need to get something positive into your institution file so you can get out."

Kareem was a devoted student of Islam. He had a bachelor's degree in psychology, but it wasn't any good because he had to incorporate the teachings of Islam with what he previously learned in order to be the man he always wanted to be. He was real eloquent. This brother became a victim of the white power structure. They used the devalued educational system to trap him.

Early in his life he thought he'd be accepted by white people because they had bestowed a degree on him. Then he wanted to achieve the American dream: a white man's job, a white man's car, and a white woman. That wicked white flesh doomed him to prison gates.

Kareem was the smarter of the two, but I could relate to Zo a little bit better, probably because we both were a product of Prichard and that forced our lives to be a living hell.

Occasionally, I'd stop by the cell where Zo slept and talk with him. Our conversations helped me face the reality of my situation a little better. Zo had very high expectations of himself, but he couldn't shake those iceberg-slim aspirations. All throughout the program, I was just trying to fake it to make it, but Zo insisted that I participate.

Zo gave me truckloads of literature to read on suppressing emotions, different states of the ego, inferiority and superiority complex.

This literature was a positive factor of him reforming my character, because earlier I'd really felt insecure around anyone who was taller than me. I'd be quick to crack them upside the head with something hard to prove to them just because they're bigger than me, don't necessary mean they're badder.

After reading this I started dealing with people as individuals and not stereotyping them. Zo would always say "Association forms assimilation, therefore you have no business hanging around people who ain't trying to help you develop yourself mentally. Hang around fools, you become a fool."

Zo eventually played his way to a work release center. Before he left he said, "Champ, don't let your hands contribute to your destruction and whatever you do get a GED."

I went ahead and completed the program and was granted the opportunity to say a brief lecture at the commencement exercise. Basically because everyone else in the class was afraid of speaking before a crowd, I was on a mission to prove that Champ was not afraid of absolutely anything.

My mother and stepfather attended; they were in total shock because they never imagined seeing me stand in front of a crowd of people speaking positive. As I was speaking tears came to their eyes. The audience gave me a standing ovation; this was only my first of many steps towards a serious transformation.

After the administration heard me make the speech at the Transactional Analysis Program graduation, they allowed me to re-enter trade school, provided that I wouldn't cause any type of disturbance. This time around I was placed in this big old fat white lady's class.

She was a little bit bigger than a beached whale; the other cracker resigned. By this being the only female instructor at the trade school, her class always stayed full to capacity for perverted reasons. These inmates wanted to lust after anything; believe me she was an unpleasant sight for human eyes.

She had a serious control issue complex. She was more in love with bossing men around than teaching every inmate that was assigned to her class. She tried to treat them like kindergarten students, straight romper room action, pledge allegiance to the flag. The only thing was missing was duck, duck, goose. Ten inmates terminated themselves the very first day out. The idea crossed my mind, but I was on a mission so this forced me to endure.

Her teaching was ineffective; inmates stayed intoxicated in her class for over a year and didn't get close to passing the G.E.D test. Something must have been wrong with the teacher because they all supposedly were certified in the education field. She had a Master's Degree.

One brother, Akbar, would be on the plantation a few times, mostly staying to himself and studying. Akbar was in his early 40s; he was enrolled in the adult basic education class for nearly seven years and hadn't obtained his GED. I was surprised because he looked like he had it together. I sat in the desk next to Akbar because I knew he'd give me the straight rundown on what was going on in this class.

"Bro Champ, in here you got to get it on your own. You can't depend on no one else. All she is going to do is sit on her fat ass and eat until she is ready to give a spelling test. She spends most of her time on the computer."

Something told me to dismiss this notion because it sounded almost like some of that militant shit I'd been hearing around on the plantation. As I quickly observed the classroom, the students were sitting around playing tic-tac-toe. Some were playing the word game Scrabble, while others were half sleep.

When I took a basic placement test, which consists of language, reading, and math, language and reading were my weakest subjects. My math was excellent because the street experience taught me to count money sideways. The instructor gave me my test scores and said, "If you ever get a G.E.D it will be a miracle." She probably crushed over half of the class's self-esteem like this by discouraging them, but Champ had to prove this cracker wrong.

Every morning I'd read every magazine in the classroom: *Time*, *Jet*, *People*, and even the gossip-filled *Enquirer*. When I ran across a word I didn't understand, I'd write it down, look it up in the dictionary, write the meaning down, and use the word in a sentence in order to put it in my subconscious mind for later use. In some type of educational magazine, I read where the average high school graduate only has a working vocabulary of twelve thousand words. So now if I add five new words to my vocabulary daily, after five years of studying I should be well ahead of all the people who graduated from high school. I let Akbar read the magazine; he agreed to it.

So we started studying together while at the trade school; we were at it hard. We even started to play Scrabble together for relaxation from the books and to help build a strong vocabulary. The instructor peeked out of her office at us. She probably didn't know she was about to be defeated. She even offered to play me in a game of Scrabble. I declined because I didn't want to give her the possible satisfaction of having bragging rights over me. If I could see her today, I'd tell her something so powerful it would turn her cerebrum into water.

After constantly studying, I felt ready to take the GED. practice test. They required you to pass a practice test first in order to take the real test. When I was given the test, my skills had improved tremendously, but my math had decreased. This is the reason the schooling system sends you through in order to keep you perfectly unbalanced.

So I started back studying math. When it was where it was suppose to be, I confronted the instructor about helping with algebra, and the pig said, "You don't need to be concentrating on that right now! Go ahead and do fractions and decimals." When I explained to her that I had been putting too much emphasis on those areas and I felt that I'd mastered them, she snapped at me, "This is my classroom; you do the lesson I give out, not the opposite!"

I can't allow white people to talk to me this way, so I asked to be terminated immediately! When she saw that I didn't give a damn about her or that white piece of paper, she refused to terminate me. This had me furious all my early years of my life. I've been a victim of missed education, now it was continuing while I was putting forth a sincere effort.

My homeboy Landlord gave me a clear insight of math, algebra, and geometry. Landlord helped me enough in order for me to pass the practice test. When the actual GED was given, I took the test and failed. I made 42.8 this time. I had trouble writing a 200-word essay. Out of the 30 inmates taking the GED, only seven out of eight passed. "I'm quitting," I said. Akbar took the test as well and he failed. He was tempted to give up as well. We realized that we didn't need a white man's piece of paper to prove how nice we were.

In all actuality, a GED is not worth the paper that it's printed on. Those classes don't teach anything about black people's affairs. Akbar encouraged me to hang in there.

Then I reflected on what Zo said about "Putting something positive in your files to deceive the administration." Since I was in prison, I needed to learn about someone other than reading *Jet* and *Ebony*. It was okay, but they only give you a false image of the bourgeois Negroes.

Akbar let me read "The Autobiography of Malcolm X." I'd heard a lot of prisoners talk about Malcolm X but never took time out to read about Malcolm. I kept the book for about a week-and-a-half and hadn't finished anything but 185 pages. Akbar said "Take your time because white folks want to keep us ignorant on purpose." I didn't complete the book because Akbar was transferred to a work release center. The little I did read fashioned a strong desire from within; I became thirsty for some real knowledge.

The old-timers would conceal all of the good books. When I approached the old slaves concerning good reading material, they would say, "You ain't ready for this yet!" They'd gladly give you some nudity but nothing good unless you were in with their clique. They weren't use to dealing with a young person such as myself who was a true maverick.

So realization set in. It came to mind that white folks incarcerated me physically. These slaves were attempting to do it mentally. My determination was strong; I asked my mother to send me "The Autobiography of Malcolm X" and a small pocket-size dictionary. I went to work.

The book had a very profound effect on my mind. I'm still impressed with it today. I read the book twice before I put it down. I probably read it fifty times since then. A person can't just read about Malcolm X; they must study him. Every young black man I ran across in prison I begged them to read that book.

My next letter to my mother stated "I've found my father and the man I've always wanted to be: "Malcolm X - Black Powers."

Malcolm X highly favored education—that became my mission. Every morning after breakfast instead of going back to sleep I would stay up and read. Early morning hours were the best time to get some peace and quiet from the pandemonium of the inmates; while everyone else was asleep, I was wide awake. I'd meditate to escape the madness of my surroundings.

I started setting more positive goals for myself, like eradicate profanity and slang from my vocabulary, mainly the nigger word. The nigger word is too degrading and belittling and prisons are full of niggers, all types of niggers, house niggers, weak niggers and rent-to-own niggers. In prison you can give a nigger a pack of cigarettes and that's your nigger. I no longer wanted to be addressed as a nigger.

Furthermore, white people manufactured niggers; a nigger is a person who has been trained to think and act a certain way—negative at all times. Since white folks made niggers, that means that the white man is the original nigger.

Another goal I set was not to hit anyone unless they became too disrespectful. Now, that's going to be a hard one.

After studying Malcolm X and listening to his tapes more often, it sent me searching for some spiritual salvation. I knew Christianity wasn't for me because they're too hypocritical and passive, especially in prison.

Everyone who claimed Christianity in prison were undercover homosexuals or in it for a form of protection. The homosexuals called the chapel their motel; that's where they went to turn tricks. When the officers announced "church call," the sissies grabbed the Bible. You could hear them saying, "We're going to make love and money in the chapel on the carpet, under any condition." Things got so bad out there that the maintenance repair men eventually put a safety lock on the chapel's bathroom door so it wouldn't close.

Once you see the jailhouse jack leg preachers smoking reefer with pages out of the Bible, it is very hard to believe anything they say. All Christians are not bad. Nat Turner was a very beautiful Christian brother.

Hypocrisy in Christianity pushed me towards Islam. Muslims don't mind fighting, neither did I. I was already in total disagreement with white folks so this should've been home for me. However, it's not safe to judge a book by its cover. Every conscientious person needs to pick up the book and read a few pages.

In Atmore Prison you have a very poor representation of Islam. Muslims were everything that they shouldn't be. They got high and practiced homosexuality. It was common to go around to their prayer room and find panties in there, and they didn't come from the officers. The religion supposedly is based on brotherhood, but it's not. A strong display of disloyalty was seen in their demonstration. Satan had poisoned their minds, robbed them of their thinking capacity, and sentenced them to solitary confinement of non-responsibility.

Shortly after I turned my back on Islam, a young brother about 19 years old arrived at Atmore by the name of Fateem. He was an "intellectual giant."

Fateem had strong integrity to bring people together. Within three weeks upon his arrival, he had monopolized and organized all religious organizations. One man drove millions of people into the sanctuary. It was approximately three or four hundred brothers. This was unbelievable; everyone was asking, "What is he teaching?" I observed from a distance because I didn't believe it myself, brothers addressing one another as "sir" and marching in military formation on the yard in double lines. Fateem walked and talked in dignity to everyone.

The old slaves who once were the leaders of the religious groups got mad and spoke real negative behind Fateem's back to the administration about how he was about to start a prison riot.

The officers came at Fateem around 9:30 one night, put him on a van and transferred him to a maximum-security prison for nothing. The administration wanted to keep their handpicked Negroes in leadership position; therefore, they could keep Islam at a small portion and control from within.

After Fateem transferred, everybody went back to being slaves because they didn't want to be misled. The younger brothers became gang members and whipped white boys damn near to death. As they were whipping the crackers they would be hollering "Allahu Akbar!" (God is greatest, in Arabic).

Their frustration was correct but the solution was wrong. As I reflected over it all, this is where the Negro who we used to run off the railroad tracks in Prichard must have gotten his teachings from.

My house nigger homeboy, Big Blood, was a real house nigger; anything he told the officers they believed it. He worked with them and they looked out for him. Big Blood kept boxes full of fried chicken and sardines. He was the first inmate I saw with a cellular phone and alarm clock. Regardless of his Tomish ways, whenever I got off into any trouble Big Blood always came to get me out of lock-up and made sure I didn't get a disciplinary.

Right after I obtained my GED, I had to move fast because the administration was about to reassign me back to the farm. My options of taking a trade were limited to brick mason, barbering, auto body repair, and computer tech.

There were many wake-up calls coming my way; more and more of my homies were getting sent to Atmore. A lot of them had heard through the prison that I was on some positive stuff and didn't associate with many people unless they were striving for what I was striving for and that's self improvement on all aspects of life.

The administration assigned me back to the farm to slave and pick cucumbers and tomatoes. I stayed agitated. I could barely concentrate; I didn't like the way these white folks were dogging us out. I was really trying to take it in stride because black folks had always been oppressed.

On March 30, my twenty-third birthday, my fifth year of imprisonment, I woke up angry about my condition. I refused to go out in the fields to work. All year they celebrated all type of pagan holidays. Therefore, I thought they should celebrate mine.

As a result of my attempt to rebel, I was placed in lock-up. While in lock-up I was put in for a transfer to a prison where there were supposedly more educational programs. Before I left I wrote a letter to my comrades stating, "If I would've been with Moses and the children of Israel when they departed the Red Sea, white folks, Pharaoh, and house Negroes never would've had any trouble out of me."

CHAPTER 14
MADHOUSE

HARD-CORE AND I, along with eight other inmates, were transferred to Bullock Correctional Center together. Hard-core stood 6'2, 188 pounds, muscle-bound and had a reputation of being a pro-black radical. He would whip white folks to sleep at will. He was about 25 years old. I was still 6'1, 211 pounds. The warden at Atmore had labeled me as a troublemaker which he called an intelligent hoodlum.

While we were sitting in the receiving unit at Bullock waiting to be processed in, the warden of Bullock came to give us an informal introduction, a speech full of lies. He was a little, short, George Jefferson-type Uncle Tom Negro to be precise. He was a perfect manifestation of an Uncle Tom. "I'm going to help you get out of prison."

This token Negro, the warden, was swift and well trained at deceiving his people. He really impressed me at first, but time always is the determining factor. By the prison system, inmates are so disproportionately black, that the white folks had picked them a few other Uncle Toms to mislead black inmates. They inclined we'd be more receptive by being punished by our own kind. In my honest opinion, the correctional officers are a bunch of over-paid baby sitters in blue suits.

Bullock Correctional Center was a prison like I would have never imagined. No farm and no known homosexuals, except a few male officers. The building was perfectly clean. The outside looked like a recreational center. There was only one guard tower outside the entire prison. Ninety-seven percent of the administrative staff was black. Majority of the black wardens had a Ku Klux Klan mentality, all the way down to the cooks in the kitchen. Majority of the correctional officers were black, even the nurses.

Here, Pharaoh's manifestation is being displayed strongly. Kill off the men and employ the women. Incarcerate the males and make them act real ugly and disrespectful towards the women officers, turning the women totally against men.

Well over 75% of the correctional officers at Bullock were black females. The only white folks there were the institutional psychiatrist and a few drug treatment counselors.

That was probably the worst effect of Bullock. Anywhere you go and see black officers, it's a problem. Black people are so used to being oppressed and deprived anytime, they get a little authority they abuse it. They immediately adopt that Uncle Tom and Aunt Jane mentality; they'll abuse that little authority to the fullest. Especially when you get a nigger out of the projects and give them a blue suit and an oak stick, they'll beat the hell out of any black person they see.

Another form of genocide is black-on-black crime. It was at its highest there. I've seen one Lieutenant A.K.A Mad Dog make inmates get down on their knees like a dog. If the inmates refused to bark like a dog, the officers would kick the inmates until they screamed for mercy. On another incident, they held a young white fag down and molested him with their night stick. Several officers were court ordered for this.

The only thing I learned to respect about Lt. Mad Dog was that if you didn't show him any sign of fear, he wouldn't harass you at all. When he saw a weak nigger, he would dog them out. Also, he treated officers just like he treated the inmates, with absolutely no respect.

Every dog must have his day. Lt. Mad Dog was forced to resign after a female officer filed a sexual harassment suit on him. These female officers have a penis envy complex; they was slapping inmates down like they were pimps simply for starring at them too long. Some got mad and extremely aggressive if you didn't give them the proper attention. They had me confused as hell. I didn't know whether they were professional linebackers or sumo wrestlers.

Now, I really love black people to death, but after doing time at Bullock my mind was made up; if there ever be a black president, I was going to Jamaica and be away from all the madness that would be produced. I would be to myself with plenty of sunshine, bananas, mangos and other citrus fruits. No Uncle Toms and Aunt Janes.

When I first hit the yard, April of 1994, everything looked wrong; this was my second day there. I was standing in the gym checking out the prison. Inmates were stretched out along the gym floor and bleachers, sleeping from being over-drugged, while others were walking around talking to themselves, playing the crazy man role, hoping to get an early release or a crazy check upon their release.

This one black stupid-ass Negro would get in the middle of the gym floor and sing old country music; he even had a country boy accent. After every song, the other slaves would applaud. He'd stand in the middle of the floor waving. Then he'd tap dance and the loud applauding would start back.

Then it was a white man walking around choking himself all day long. He claimed he was punishing himself for being bad. I was at Bullock for 2 ½ years. Every time I would see the cracker, he was choking himself. That day I got so angry at what I was seeing, my blood pressure shot sky high and dizzy spells hit me.

As I was exiting the gym door, Ali approached me. We shook hands; it had been almost eight years since we last seen one another. Ali went on and said, "Got damn, Champ, my big homeboy. Brother, it's been a long, long time. I've been asking everybody about you in the joint. People in Prichard think you've been killed by now or gone crazy." Immediately, I let him know that a lot of chumps want to hear about Champ being crazy or gotten killed but they must wait a little while longer.

Ali was one of my original homeboys from back in the days when we were all running buck wild, skipping school, hanging on the railroad tracks, and drinking cheap wine. Occasionally he'd hang around. He was mostly off into books and working. He was a few years older than the rest of us. This was the last person on earth I expected to see in prison.

As we walked the yard, he began to inform me of some of the tragic events that took place in his life that led to his incarceration.

One of those sorry Negroes and a big-butt crackhead influenced him to smoking the crack pipe. He'd quit school, trying to hustle in order to support his addiction. Overnight, he was out geeking and freaking with this crackhead whore. When he stopped feeding her crack, she called the police and pressed rape charges against him. By Ali being young, black, and poor, he couldn't afford a decent lawyer. He was automatically guilty in their eyesight. Therefore he was forced to plead guilty for sexual assault and was sentenced from four to nine years in prison.

Since his captivity, he had once became a student of Islam, but due to several conflicts of interest concerning ideology it turned him off and he became pro-black conscious. His study habits were excellent and I thought he had done a beautiful job at educating himself while incarcerated. He obtained a GED and took a few community college courses, but something was still missing.

By me still being in the infancy stage of development, this became my trusted comrade. We were about the only real two brothers from Prichard and my mind was made up. I wasn't going to even attempt to conversate with anyone unless they read a 48-page book a week at the minimum.

As we were walking, I asked, "What type of prison is this? I thought Atmore was a hellhole...but this really is a got damn insane asylum."

"Champ, Brother, I have to give you the unadulterated truth. It's a big ole mental health center; most of the craziest ones locked up in Alabama is here for some type of treatment, whether its drug abuse or sex offenders. They have here two dorms of nothing but rapists, all different kinds; pedophiles, pederast, and a few UAB rapist (University of Alabama in Birmingham). "

"What are we doing here?" Ali responded, "I wouldn't lie to you for nothing in the world. I was assigned to that dorm due to the nature of my case. Brother, you'll hear some wild stories in there. One brother stole a police car and was riding in B-ham pulling women over like he was the police and was raping them; he's one of my partners. He got a 108-year sentence for it."

Ali pointed at an old white man walking across the yard on a cane. "See that bastard right there? He's Chester the child molester. He had sex with his grandkids; they say he was walking around his hometown when they arrested him with a pocket full of artificial little boys' dicks made out of wood. He even had one on a silver chain around his neck."

Now this made me burst out and laugh. Every single day that I spent at Bullock was just like a tour through a mental health center. There is a strict mental health ward section of the prison where about 150 inmates are assigned there for psychological purposes. They probably started out playing but when the state gets finished shooting them up with all types of psychotropic drugs, they'll be a bunch of walking psychopaths.

You'll see them daily walking and talking to their invisible dogs and standing in the window of their isolated cell units with shaving cream on their faces, licking on the window, and waving at everyone who passed by. This wasn't funny to me because the administration was playing games with these people's lives.

As we walked, this gave me a migraine headache. I had to ask Ali was he crazy. Ali explained how he ended up at this prison.

He'd been expedited to Alabama from Ohio and did three years in a maximum-security prison in Northern Alabama. He signed up for the sex offender program, attempting to gain early release from the belly of the beast. The program was full of racism and foolishness, because the majority of the white inmates committed those types of crimes and the wealthy whites are the main ones. Ali was about to do a minimum of six months.

I didn't know why I was really here. I hadn't done anything to be locked up around these types of people.

Ali and I became tight. We sat around for hours at a time reading over black literature, talking about the streets of Prichard, family, and looking over pictures of old associates and family members. (Later, I would even become a conspirator in one of these adulterous affairs).

The majority of the females have secret love affairs with the inmates. How desperate can a woman get? Some had even resigned to come back to date inmates. Several became pregnant by inmates. Out of the approximately 950 inmates confined to Bullock, 60% or more of them were sex offenders.

The sexual treatment counselor was a female. In order to seduce and tempt their rapists, the most beautiful female pigs were assigned to work in and around the program dorm. Seduction was the order of the day.

I often felt the ancient hell-fire of Sodom & Gomorrah creeping towards the perimeter gates. You could easily tell when it was pay period. These pigs would go and buy every piece of fake hair in the city limits. The females would be standing in the hallway with their tight uniforms on, profiling their undesirable bodies, with more make-up painted on their face than the Indians.

Oooh! And the cheap perfume was affecting my sinus terribly. Sometimes I'd walk by them and attempt to fart to give them a taste of what they were issuing out. Every time they would feed me beans I would try this, but nothing ever came out at the proper time; even when I ate my dessert first, it was still useless.

A quick glance was all I ever took. I'd turn my eyes as I had trained myself to do early in my bid. I'd walk down the hallway in dignity, never paying much attention to anyone.

These officers had scrutinized my character in its totality. When they didn't see me eat meat in the kitchen, they asked me how I was so healthy; one even attempted to offer me an apple but I wasn't going to let her get me like that. "I'm not Adam."

After a few weeks of my arrival, four female officers stopped me to hold a conversation. They were blushing like little girls at their high school prom. Their impression of me was awful. They thought I was a spoiled child, only child, or a homosexual. I wanted to curse these sluts out so bad, but I was trying to respect black women.

As I strived to maintain a low profile, laid back, and quiet as possible, they insisted on being nosey and stupid. These were some real bitches with attitudes.

One asked, "What's your malfunction?" "You see us checking you out, why you don't ever stop and chat, why you don't smile?"

Why should Champ smile? I've been incarcerated for 4 ½ years. When I look in the mirror, I see my youthful features slowly disappearing, alopecia is making my head bald. I was trying hard to maintain my composure in prison.

A prisoner doesn't supposed to fraternize with the enemy. A female is no different in my eyes; once they put on a uniform they're my enemy. If by chance they ever found out how I actually felt about them, they'd assassinate me on the spot.

After a few more of the questions, I let them know I wasn't the talkative type and I didn't belong in prison. I was just a victim of unfortunate circumstances. Real stupidly they asked, "Is your mother a doctor and your father a lawyer?"

This was making me real uncomfortable. They were used to dealing with a bunch of boys masquerading as men. All the other inmates were infatuated with the cheap perfume when they came down the hallway. Inmates would flock around like flies and the officers would just smile. They should be offended because flies are attracted to shit.

Their opinion of me was based on their psychological insecurity and their inability to accurately distinguish the true qualifications of a real black man. The logical conclusion I came up with was telling them that, "I'm as close to Jesus as y'all going to get in y'all lifetime. So if you want to go to heaven, you better respect me."

This always made them scream, "Get away from us before lightning hit you. You're one arrogant-ass nigger to be in prison and conceited as hell. You are probably just like O.J, want a white woman."

"Good!"

This forced the female officers from harassing me. Occasionally they'd see me and holler "As salaam alikum, pork chop, ham and bacon." They had strongly accused me of being a Muslim. The types of books I read and my association with Ali helped them form that opinion and when I would tell them I'm Jesus, they would get scared.

I refused to compromise my position to please their sensibility. I had to do all that would benefit me and not worry about what people thought. My life is for me, not for a spectator to make me a victim of false propaganda.

When I kicked it with Ali about it, he said, "Brother, it's all good. You have nothing to lose but your chains." Of course he would say something to this effect because he had earned the nickname Black Superman by inmates for his sharp intellectual ability and class.

Every time he saw a female officer getting a verbal beat-down by a brother she was trying to harass, Ali would always run to the officer's rescue, put his glasses on, and start speaking like a Negro college professor. This was one of the few things we disagreed about—his potential of Uncle Tom.

About my third week there, the administration assigned me to work in the mess hall temporarily until I was able to sign up for the Substance Abuse Program (SAP) and the college courses. I'd already informed the administration off the top that I didn't like to work for free and that was my main reason for transferring from Atmore. They insisted that you have some type of minor details.

Working in the chow hall wasn't all that bad, but I'd rather have stayed in the cell and read a book or meditated. My task was serving food on the breakfast crew. The breakfast was so pitiful a lot of inmates don't bother to eat. It was absolutely no variety to the menu. Grits, eggs, jelly, 2 biscuits, and watered-down juice was served almost daily.

The mess steward was a fat bad-built country Negro with an extremely sluggish attitude toward inmates. His rules were that a half of a scoop of eggs was more than enough and that's equivalent to about three tablespoons full. Before he gave an inmate extra food, he'd throw it away.

One morning after breakfast some inmates tried to double the line to get extra eggs while the steward's back was turned. He caught them while they were lining up and quickly grabbed a bucket of mop water that was sitting in the corner and threw the mop water over the serving line so the inmates in line wouldn't get any extras. Now that was just low down and dirty. He stood back and laughed at it.

I couldn't tolerate that, so I approached him politely. "Why are you competing with white folks, trying to see how dirty you can be towards your own kind?" The Negro steward, with a slave master's mentality, looked at me and said real ignorantly, "Why y'all always talking that black shit? It's nothing wrong with white folks, I have a white fiancée!"

This Negro slave actually smiled like he was proud of himself. They say only the good die young. Sell-outs like this are the ones who should be attached to the back of a pickup truck and taken for a ride down a long dark highway. My tolerance level was low for these types of people. So I had to do something to avoid working in the chow hall.

One Saturday morning I was serving the biscuits. All the slaves knew you could only get two biscuits. Some slaves were coming down the serving line asking for extras. When they got to me, I politely said no. They responded, "We will see you down the hall." I couldn't wait to get down the hall;

immediately, I picked up some biscuits, threw them and hit one of the slaves in the face.

That was my last morning working in the chow hall. The steward kicked me out, claiming I had a bad attitude and needed to take anger management classes instead of working on an institutional job. He did me a big favor and made sure every time I came to eat, I was fed badly.

When I stepped to the inmates after the confrontation, they didn't want any problems. They were over-passive because of the strict rules of the sexual offender program they were assigned to; any rule violation automatically would get them kicked out. They both apologized to me and explained their situation. The slaves were angry and hungry. I felt sorry for these people, so I started to slap the shit out of them for wasting my time.

My attendance of the Substance Abuse Program (SAP) while at Bullock was the most frustrating time of over 10 years I've served in prison. The drug program was no different from those in society. The length was eight weeks, the same rules and concepts were applied—being a good boy, never showing any angry displeasure and conforming to stupidity.

The jackass instructor was a diehard patriot. He insisted that we began and ended all classes with a serenity prayer. Everywhere you lay your eyes in the class it was a poster that read, "God grant me the serenity to accept the things I can't change, the courage to change the things I can and the wisdom to know the difference."

I was trying hard to fake it to make it; otherwise I would never sign up for the class. I sat there three weeks listening at these junkies tell their stories, how God allowed them to be hooked on crack in order to show them a better life after incarceration and addiction, or how they became crackheads to fit in with the crowds.

Since this was a spiritual based program, most of the inmates attributed their suffering to God. Shame on them.

The instructor supported this himself. He even admitted that he'd been drunk in his lifetime, that he woke up in a gay bar with a dick in his hand, and he doesn't know what happened. That was a catch line to get everyone to open up and reveal their deep secrets that they'd been hiding in the closet. The inmates went for it; some admitted that they molested their sisters because their father did it to them.

Some admitted how they wanted to have sex with their mother, that's why they stole and sold her house, appliances, jewelry, car, and anything they could get their hands on for crack cocaine. There were crazy stories revealed throughout the program. They called it cleaning their slate.

I sat through it for three whole misery weeks. I tried to get terminated from the class eight times, but once you enter a program you must complete it out. You have no will and no choice in the circumstance surrounding the overall situation, so be wise and surrender, this is keeping compliance with the prison conspiracy to get money off of you. A denial looks bad on your progress review or parole board report. Dismissal from the program is an automatic treatment failure. My intention was to keep ahead, do my assignment on time, and remain silent.

This one session we had been completely spontaneous. I'd noticed that the instructor was a chain-smoking rebel—coffee breaks and smoke every thirty minutes. The instructor said, "Smoke time."

I stood up, "What about those who don't smoke?" This homosexual rebel looked at me like he didn't believe he heard me correctly. I went on and snapped, "You are a bigger addict than anyone in the class; you can't go an hour without a cigarette and a cup of coffee." The class went "Oh!"

He glanced around the room for some sign of support. His face turned red, his fist was balled up tight, and his belly was poked out like he'd been constipated for the last twenty-five years.

He spoke up stupidly, "Now, it's nothing wrong with smoking, I've been smoking a pack and a half all my life and it hasn't harmed me."

"First of all, it's highly impossible for you to have been smoking all your life and you're not finished living yet."

The class was quiet now, so I continued "Cigarettes contain carbon monoxide, the same poisonous gas that comes from the tail pipe of your car, and everyone know if you sit in your garage with the car engine running what will happen after you inhale that gas. Also, over three hundred thousand people die a year from lung cancer due to smoking. Smoking is detrimental to your health, it turns your lungs black and causes blindness. Nicotine is a serious addiction. I've known people who stopped smoking crack but can't put down the cigarettes. Why? They're addicts!"

He responded "I've never stole to purchase a pack, never have my wife sucked a dick for a pack of Marlboros, but they do it for crack rock."

It's impossible to intellectualize with fools like this; he's stuck on stupidity. I really enjoyed challenging the administration, humiliating them, proving they're unqualified, and preparing myself for my future task as well. So I went ahead and applied some basic tricknology "Now let's go back to Sigmund Freud, that is your God and Father of psychology."

He's smiling now. "Yea, yea you're right."

"Oh Sigmund Freud was a very brilliant man, but he died of cancer and refused to quit smoking cigars. If we go a little farther, let's look at the oral stage of development. Sigmund claims that if a mother breast feed their child, the child will be obsessive with oral sex. The child goes from the breast, the bottle, and sucking on his thumb, to sucking a penis." I paused intentionally to watch every one's reaction.

"Now, if you smoke a cigarette you'll suck a dick!"

The entire class fell out of their chairs laughing. "Ha! Ha! Ha!"

He looked at the class and then at me, rubbed his fingers across his fiery red face, lips, and nose. He went in his pockets. I thought he was going for his knife. I stood up; he sat down, looking confused and defeated. I felt a bit of sympathy for this fool but he'd been begging me for this.

After a few minutes of silence, he simply refused to quit. "You're just too militant and outspoken, people like you shouldn't be allowed to read books, and I bet you don't believe that Jesus is God?"

"Neither do you."

He stood up, walked back and forward in front of the classroom. He looked like he was communicating with someone in space. He stopped and said, "Jesus is God, and he died for our sins." The class looked in my direction. I had absolutely no business entertaining this unrighteous beast, but this was Armageddon. I couldn't allow him to continue to spread all the different form of lies, so I manipulated this dummy, "It's impossible for you to think Jesus is God when Jesus never, never prayed."

He went for it. "That's a lie, you are a liar. Jesus was always praying and worshiping."

"Well, if he's God, who is he praying to?"

"OOOhhh!" The class responded.

He submitted on the spot. He simply refused to remove me from the SAP program. The class was very well impressed by my presentation as well.

Every morning the class would punish me by asking me to read before the class right after the serenity prayer. I read and expounded on different things. One morning I read to the class out of an AA book where Dr. Bill Wilson, another racist, stated that AA meetings should be segregated. Therefore, I refused to attend AA meetings while incarcerated. The blacks in the class fell for it. My homeboy Ali would constantly have to come check on me because I really was on the verge of going off in the program.

Over half of the inmates who completed this drug program went straight back to using drugs. Most of them returned with three years in society. I encountered a bunch of them later in my prison stay serving life without parole sentences. We can't depend on anyone else's myth of rehabilitation. The only thing that is really needed is a strong desire to quit using drugs. The material is obsolete.

The administration sent for me again; somebody had been dropping snitch notes on me. The psychiatrist wanted me to do a survey for a group of interns from Tuskegee Institute. Their overall objective was to test the I.Q. of young black men in Alabama's prison system. Annually, these black spies would come to play with inmates' minds.

"Hell no, I protested." The Tuskegee experiment immediately came to mind. I quickly refused. Never will I allow anyone to crawl into my head and manipulate me. I may have been incarcerated but my mind was still free and my mind's desire will never ever be confined. If a psychiatrist, along with an able representative from C-Span, ever could analyze some of my thoughts and broadcast them on the air, the world would think twice before sentencing a young black man to do life in prison.

The majority of my time there was spent wisely because someone was dealing with us wisely. I attempted to reverse the game.

As I recalled earlier, Bullock Prison had more rehabilitation and educational programs than any prison in the state of Alabama. With the time that those brothers had to study, think, acknowledge their wrongs, and attempt to correct themselves it shouldn't be anyone on any college campus anywhere more aware of the positive worth than those brothers. Every program and class that I felt would uplift me as an individual I participated in. The more information I received, the more knowledgeable and morally stronger I became.

Faulkner University had a branch of four-year college programs there. The college courses were no different from the others; there it was even co-educational. A few female officers who worked in the daytime attended college there at night. It was great for them because an inmate would automatically do their work for a few hours of conversation.

The classes I enrolled in were Western Civilization, biology, and algebra courses. We were in algebra class one night on a test night. The female officer wore a pair of tight jeans. All the inmates in the class ran close to sit by her in order to give her the answers. She had so many people giving her answers, she made a 100 on the test while the inmates giving her the answers made 80s and 90s. I couldn't even get an answer.

So I quit that night. Later I regretted it because if I wasn't procrastinating and blaming others for my shortcomings so much I would've been able to obtain my associate in science degree. Procrastinating is a serious fault of mine; my spirit wouldn't allow me to deal with so much hypocrisy.

Annually, the Lau Bach Literacy Program went to the prison to give a two-day seminar to certify inmates to become certified adult basic educational tutors.

I went through the seminar and was really amazed to find out that there are over two million people that can't read or write. After absorbing the Lau Bach method of "each one teach one," it left me determined to do something about the problem of illiterate people. A very large percentage of the inmates in prison are illiterate and some are really satisfied at being that away. They're lagging behind.

The rules concerning the GED class stipulate that before you have a job as a GED tutor, you must volunteer for a minimum of 30 days. This was cool with me because I didn't have an institutional slave mind and being a GED tutor was something that I really wanted to do because I could really open up some doors for me in the future.

They assigned me four students, ages 24 to 43, my very first day of volunteering. They barely knew how to read their name let alone mention write. The other tutor was doing absolutely nothing to help them out. They all were in it for selfish reasons. They wanted to keep their whites clean or be able to drink coffee and eat doughnuts with the administration. Regardless of this, I still put forward a sincere effort to teach my peers.

One morning, I was in the computer lab of the GED area putting in some work. Everyone in the class kept replying, "I can't do this, it's hard." They were becoming real lazy, wanting to work on the computers instead of working the mind. The mind is much stronger than a computer. First, we must realize computers can't do nothing but what the mind allows. I wasn't going for the pitiful excuse.

If a person can imagine himself having sex with another man, imagining it's a woman, then he can imagine himself reading and writing.

Anytime you can memorize "Super Freak" by Rick James word for word or Michael Jackson's "Beat It," you should never, under any circumstances, have a problem writing or reading.

So I got a World Book Encyclopedia off the bookshelf, looked up Isaac Newton, and shared the story when Isaac Newton was a poor student, cared little for school work, at the bottom of his class, had no friends, and was so absent-minded that while out walking a horse the horse slipped away. He continued to walk with the empty bridle in his hand, unaware that the horse had slipped away. Soon Isaac was at the head of his class. He proved to his teachers that he wasn't an ordinary student. He read all the books he could get, especially those on mathematics and physics. They interested him the most. Isaac Newton eventually became one of the greatest scientists of all times.

Now this is proof that no one is unable to be educated. After my thirty days of volunteering, I was not selected as a full-time tutor. Someone or an inmate who currently held those positions who was in disagreement with my style of teaching spoke negatively to the administration tutor to block me from getting the position. To my disappointment they were some young black inmates who were trying to get close to the administration, and talking against me supposedly helped them gain brownie points.

However, I still volunteered whenever time allowed. I didn't like them or their judgment of me. The most knowledgeable prison scholars I've met educated themselves outside of the classroom. We don't need the white man's piece of paper to certify us as an educated house nigger. Most of us just realize that without it, we'll end up taking orders at fast food restaurants for the rest of our lives.

Ali was really a black conscious brother but he had some ass-kissing potentials. Never have I seen a black man kiss ass so well. He had all types of officers working to help him out.

Whenever I would get a disciplinary, one of the lieutenants would immediately push it under the rug for him. Several females in there were in love with him and the feelings were mutual. Ali had a plush prison job—third shift hall clean for only an hour a night. He was assigned to clean the prison's infirmary.

Ali had been trying to convince me to come and work with him for months. Every time he brought it to me I refused because I had done too much free labor work in prison. Therefore, I preferred to hang around the cell and be a bookworm and take advantage of the opportunity to rest.

Anyway, he convinced me to come out on the third shift. We worked in the infirmary mopping and waxing floors, basically janitor work. Ali did the inside of the infirmary so he would have exposure to the beautiful nurses and the female officers who always were assigned to the post. We would always do our task with the possibility of one day owning our own janitorial business. Another thing that would work to our advantage was that we had access to the gym and weights all times of the night. We could always work out.

My objective was to stay as far from the officers as possible. I'd work at night and sleep and study during the day. I probably went for a whole year without any type of sunshine, living life like a caveman.

It was one male officer I began to talk with by the name of Dee. He was brand new. Often Ali and I would catch him and attempt to inform him that it would be smart for him to give the white man his job back before he became a fully developed pig. He was young, black, and country. A year younger than me, often he'd stop me and ask me why I didn't smile. I'd explain to him my situation. I would let him read some of my books and ask him why should I smile. He agreed with me. We were cool but we never were able to completely remove the chains from his mind.

Late one night, Ali and I was in the gym working out, pumping weights, and jumping rope. I was attempting to drill Ali on my special style of martial arts, mixed with Prichard nigger street fighting. As we were taking a break, this crazy female officer came through the gym. I called her Reva.

My reason for saying she was crazy is because any woman officer who may have any interest in me had to be insane, because the police and I have always been enemies. She came through the gym and paused for a brief second watching us work out, and then called Ali to where she was standing. They exchanged a conversation briefly. She went inside of the receptionist area where the vending machine was located and the pigs' lounge. Ali came back with two Coca-Colas. He handed me one and said, "Champ, she told me to give you this and she want to see you later on."

"Ali, you're an American. If you are going to be my pimp, I should be worth more than a damn coke; besides, the only thing I drink is Dr. Pepper."

Ali snapped "American citizen! Champ, you're the only black slave who drank Dr. Pepper. You have been around the white people for too long."

We argued about taste and class. We went back to the infirmary to see what the crazy lady wanted. She was sitting in the infirmary, the light was off, and the radio was down low. She had this lustful look in her eyes which I had interpreted from many females before. She knew that the only way I'd find her attractive was to be in the dark. She dismissed Ali, said she needed to speak with me alone. This sounded like trouble.

She questioned me about my age, length of sentence, sexual preferences, and family background. Trying hard to avoid offending her, I answered all questions in respect to authority but often I had to catch myself from blowing. As I was going out of the infirmary doorway, she asked "Can't you see it in my eyes?" I responded, "Yea! You look sleepy." She laughed. In order for me to be successful I'd have to play much harder than she did.

In the cellblock I informed Ali that this woman tried to offer me the red apple; he already knew. Over the next several months he informed me on how to slaughter a pig. I'd caught the officers watching me carefully, both male and female, and I just continued to step in dignity. The officers even began to search my locker box regularly when they saw I only had books and hygiene items. They would ask, "What type of man are you?" I would respond, "A conscious one."

Time moved rather fast. Ali was on the verge of being released. We had grown tight and he had equipped himself with the necessary tools for success. He left me a few books and a Bible, the only one I've ever kept for a long period of time. The hardest aspect of doing time is departing from a close comrade.

Ali was released the middle part of December of 1994. We kicked it and made serious plans to stay in touch through letters and phone calls. Recently I heard from him; he's doing good, going to college and being a good boy. After Ali was released, many female officers bum-rushed me trying to get his phone number. Many of them we didn't even know had interest in him. At his request, I gave them the information they wanted.

Reva and I became real close. We began writing each other simple letters. I'd tested my old form of charming and flattering just to see if I still had it. From there we'd have verbal intimate conversations and meetings in the infirmary late at night, getting really intimate with one another.

The infirmary was the place where we jumped the broom. Eventually my feelings developed for her. She gave me the opportunity to enhance with the female persuasion which my soul had been longing for. Her feelings towards me were so uncontrollable. However, both of our motives were impure. She wanted to be able to brag "I got him!" and mine was for selfish reasons.

Life is just a game. All the built-up anger inside of me for the authority caused me to attempt to inflict on her. Then it got to the point where we no longer talked as man and woman, it became police officer to prisoner, her uniform against my prison whites. Then it came to the point where it was always, "You need to let that Champ image and pro-black stuff go." Never ever!

Trying to get her to understand what my life had been or would be like without Champ is like a chess match between a 77-year-old Alzheimer disease patient and a 5-year-old mentally retarded child; no understanding, just total confusion. Therefore, I isolated myself from her.

She couldn't accept it this way and attacked me furiously, making me the victim of false propaganda. She would spread rumors that I was a homosexual, and that's why she stopped talking to me. All the officers on the third shift believed it because they only saw me talking to Officer Dee. While coming from the gym one night, all the officers were looking at me with real strange facial expressions. I knew it was something. I wasn't aware of the slander against me yet!

This one officer stopped me. "Napier, we need to talk." She was one of my friends; she came close to me. Her face was only inches away from mine. I could taste her lipstick. I wanted to kiss her but she was an over-privileged dick sucker and I didn't want to be a secondhand dick sucker.

She went on to say, "I knew it was something strange about you, you looked just too good to be a man. Why didn't you tell me?"

Still not aware of what the lady had done, I asked her what she was talking about. "That you had a boyfriend," she responded. "What? Who is bad enough to be my man?" She smiled, "It's serious, everybody done heard about you." She explained to me in detail exactly how it transpired. Murder was on my mind but something inside of me was screaming, Noooooooooo!

Like I said, one of the quickest ways to slander a man's name in prison is by labeling him as a snitch or a bitch. Neither could ever be proven and the officers knew it. Often they will use it to their advantage to get many innocent people killed in prison. In a maximum-security prison, the one I would later do time at, an inmate got stabbed to death over a dispute that a female officer instigated.

An inmate named Steve was a baby rapist as well as a member of Reva's fan club. He added fuel onto the fire. Steve and Hard-Core was righteous homeboys. In spite of that, he told it to Hard-Core. As the rumor about my sexuality was in circulation, Hard-Core came to me with the idea of jumping Steve. "Bro, we need to whip that Negro slave good." Now I had been considering it, but I knew my rationale was beyond that. I'd never give a female an opportunity to say "Champ fought over me." They wasn't saying nothing worse than the judge in Mobile County when he said "Life."

Like always, the image thing kicked in and I confronted Steve so he could have a chance to speak negatively in my face, then I could inflict the proper punishment. Steve and some more young homosexuals were sitting around playing grab-ass, smiling and telling sissy jokes. As I approached him with anger in my eyes and murder on my mind, looking straight in his eyes, saying, "Steve! I've heard of the negative talk that you are spreading about me, but I'm not surprised because you are in prison for sucking a little boy's dick. If you will put anything in your mouth, I know you'll say anything out of it."

He cut me off, "Champ, you're alright by me. It was Reva who started it." After the confrontation, my conclusion was to catch them together and slap the shit out of both of them. When I'm angry, all types of irrational things come to mind. The only thing that kept me in check was the consequences involved, and hurting them wasn't it. The administration would've placed something so negative into my institutional file for fighting over an officer that it would be highly impossible for me to get out of prison alive. A lot of things were on my mind concerning these issues. I was trying hard to cope with it effectively as possible; as long as it wasn't nothing said to my face, I was determined to maintain my composure.

One night I was in the gym attempting to work off some of my stress and clearing my mind. Big Rick and I was working out and talking, taking a brief break to get some water. As I was walking across the gym floor to the water fountain, Brian was mopping the floor. I didn't pay much attention to him. He whispered something under his breath about me. I asked what he said.

Brian responded, "Bitch-ass nigger, don't you see me mopping?" Without thinking, I slapped him. He then hit me across the face with the mop. The lick dazzled me slightly, but it was on. I ran to close the gym door so no one could exit. Brian was right behind me. He hit me again across the back and this broke the mop in half. My focus was on closing the door. After the door was shut, I grabbed a broom and hit him across the head with it. The first lick cracked the broom; we stood toe to toe exchanging blows. I charged him, rammed his head against the brick wall, kneed him in the stomach, and followed it up with an elbow across the back. This broke him down. I grabbed a mop wringer and whipped him with it but was only able to get a couple of licks in before Big Rick grabbed me from behind.

That was a good fight! "Y'all stop; the officers are coming." Within minutes, the officers paired through the gym and asked why was everything so quiet. No one responded. I went into the gym bathroom. The taste of blood was in my mouth, and my lips were bleeding, so it couldn't be over yet!

Brian was sitting on the bleachers with a broom handle in his hand, half-way out of breath. I went into the mop closet, broke a mop in half, wet it down good for stability , made sure it wouldn't break as quick, and whipped him with it until it broke into small pieces like tooth picks. He fought back until the bitter end, blow for blow. I tripped him up and dove on top of him, choked him with my left hand, and beat him with the right until the bones in my pinkie finger broke. He scratched me across the eyes. I gripped his vocal cord and pulled on it until he squealed like a pig "eeeee! eeee eee!" His eyes rolled back into his head. I applied more pressure with all my strength. It wasn't enough to stop him from breathing completely, so I spit in his face and cursed him out.

This was probably one of the best fights I've ever had in my life. I released 24 years of built up anger and hostility. Brian was a good fighter. He was 5'9, 220 pounds, overweight and out of shape. We shook hands afterwards and agreed not to get the police involved. I made my way to the cell without an officer noticing me.

As I looked into the mirror, my face was scarred awfully bad and tears came to my eyes. I couldn't let him get away like that. The next morning I tried to buy me a knife or a pair of scissors. No one had a knife and the inmates in the hobby craft shop refused to sell me a pair of scissors. I walked the plantation hard looking for a weapon. If I could have gotten a cup of gas, I'd be satisfied. But nothing was found to fight with.

For the next few weeks, Brian and I watched one another closely, in the cells, the gym, and even in the chow hall trying to figure out what was on the next person's mind. The thought of killing him kind of settled down. Brian was walking around with a box cutter in his pockets at all times that an officer had given him. We talked and he said it was over, but words didn't mean much to me.

Afterwards, due to my hands still being in pain, I couldn't pump weights. I would just strictly work out with a 25 pound weight bar, practicing swinging it, knocking down invisible men when they ran up to the weight bar head first. A lot of times Brian and several officers come to mind. I even lost weight so I could be fighting size. Late one night, after I'd departed from the gym, Upshaw was joking around with Brian about the outcome of our fight. Brian exchanged words with him.

They exchanged words back and forth. Brian went into his pocket and cut Upshaw up pretty bad, about 5 or 6 different times. Upshaw had to be taken to a free-world hospital for stitches in the head and back. Brian was placed in solitary confinement, which eliminated one of my problems. It was revealed that Brian had been incarcerated at Bullock for approximately 8 years longer than most of the officers had been working there. They made sure he didn't get a free-world charge for the stabbing.

Reva began to talk with me again, "Ain't you glad Brian didn't stab you up?" I listened to this stupid shit because if I didn't talk to her she would probably spread even worse rumors this time around. Women are vicious, especially police.

She was having problems beyond her control, constantly worrying about her son. She was a single mother and the job was affecting her attitude toward her son. It was several inmates at Bullock who were only 16 and 17 years old. She saw their character in her son. She knew if she didn't be extra careful she would be the overseer of her own son.

It was a few females who already had sons in prison or waiting to come to prison. These people are getting paid to police the prison but neglect their very own household. They hadn't realized the plot. Reva had enough intellect left to realize how this prison system was punishing black men because she was supporting them by inflicting punishment herself.

Eventually she gave the white man his job back (resigned). I love her for that particular reason, if nothing else. She was a woman and mother first, police secondly. We continued to correspond for a while but she still had that police mentality. I was trying to shake her from it but the way the prison authorities brain-washed their new pigs, it's pig for life regardless of what other type of occupations the ex-pig may attempt to pursue. This was really our falling-out point.

She sent me a Valentine Day card with two ugly-ass white people on it kissing. Now why do I need a card with something so disgusting on it? I thought I had taught her better. Immediately, I ripped the card up and threw it in the trash and wrote her a raw, uncensored letter, closing it by saying, "Your communication has become a bore, I'd highly appreciate it if you didn't write to me anymore." Who needs a mouse in a lion's den? Not Champ!!! Ha! Ha!

She probably regrets ever meeting me. The lesson learned from this ordeal is that any female who might want to enjoy my company must let me deprogram her from Western ways or no relationship. The insanity inside of prison, as well as on the outside, was increasing.

My homeboy Mitch stabbed an inmate over a domino game. The inmate accused him of cheating and then it was a hostile exchange of words. Mitch got slapped and ran for his knife and came back to serve the steal effectively.

Unrighteous people have taken over the Alabama prison system. Power fell off into the hands of an absolute fool. The prison commissioners have gone all the way off ordering that all educational and rehabilitative programs be cut in half. They are eliminating all academic college courses and cutting the food allowance in half. Coffee and milk is no longer seen around breakfast time, no more free mail, and shorting inmates visiting times.

The prison's administration has reinstated the chain gang, chopping weeds and busting up rocks with a sledgehammer along the Alabama interstate from 5 A.M. until 5 P.M., taking Alabama prison rehabilitation process further and further behind.

Later, the commissioner ordered that all inmates who were found guilty of masturbation disciplinary be forced to wear a hot-pink prison uniform. This didn't stop their sexually deviant behavior. They claim they were tired of wearing white anyway.

Kevin O. Washington was a prisoner at the Cattle Ranch Honor Camp in northern Alabama, where inmates are allowed 8-hour passes due to having minimum custody status. Kevin was one of the few black prisoners there. There were mostly rich white inmates being assigned to this prison camp. He was being discriminated against badly due to his age. He was 29 years old and black, along with the nature of his case. He was trying to endure the racism. Something happened and he couldn't take it any longer.

One Sunday, the warden denied his 8-hour pass and asked Kevin to come to his house to pick pecans. Anyone who believes in reincarnation, this brother was a modern day Nat Turner. He killed the warden, the warden's wife, and two rich white inmates. The rich white men had special privileges. After the slaughtering, state investigators found unloaded pump shotguns in the white men's locker boxes with gun shells. They were using the guns for duck hunting on the weekends and taking hunting trips with the warden to places like Mississippi. The prison system turned Kevin into a monster. He was one of the many black men I've encountered who have been brutalized by the environment. Kevin was later sentenced to life without parole for the crime.

The prison authorities began to screen inmates with violent crimes files real careful after this incident before they were placed at a minimum security camp. I knew it was over with for me, with the nature of my case, my age, and skin complexion. I'd eventually die in prison. Late at night, I'd sit up in the cell after all the rest of the slaves went to sleep. I'd think about life and cry myself to sleep, thinking that my life is completely over. Never will I get the opportunity to prove my positive worth.

While I was asleep, I'd dream that my family and old associates were standing over me at my funeral crying, telling me good-bye. Just as the first shovel of dirt is put on the casket, I would jump up from my nightmare, sweating like a madman. Immediately, I'd write my family and remaining friends and share my horrible experience with them and warn everyone not to let the white folks downtown get them, because I was doing enough time for everybody in the family. It's enough black men trapped inside of the Alabama prison system serving more time for every black person in the United States. Over ninety-eight percent of my letters remained unanswered.

CHAPTER 15
INTELLECTUAL GIANT!

"Let there arise out of you a band of people inviting to all that is good. Enjoying what is right, and forbidding what is wrong: They are the ones to attain felicity."
Holy Quran 3:104

THE MUSLIM COMMUNITIES at Bullock Prison are a bunch of self-righteous, passive, sanctimonious hypocrites. They are some niggers with Islam. In spite of that, we had formed a conscious think-tank coalition. We had the finest minds on the mental plantation: Wise, Hard-Core, Tim, Kenyatta, Brother Derrick, and me. All of us were under twenty-five years old and had been incarcerated from anywhere from four to seven years, and were from different geographic locations in the state of Alabama.

We had a no-religion agenda. Our objective was to produce young, conscious soldiers and to defeat Pharaoh in his evil plan and help us prepare a solution that would better equip us to deal with our enemies.

Our worst enemies were those that kidnapped and enslaved us and brought us over here to the country that they stole from the Indians. They put us on plantations and put the Indians on reservations. Then they took us off of the plantations and put us in the projects and prison.

That's our enemy, the one who's gotten rich off the sweat and blood of our people. They haven't given us anything in return but hell and jail.

Every Saturday evening we'd all meet up in one of the classrooms, which was assigned to us for study purposes to complete dialogue study. We could never come to common terms on anything except that white folks were our enemies.

Brother Derrick had the fiery spirit of Malcolm X; he just wanted to be a leader. Wise felt he was the smartest, so he wanted to lead. Tim wanted to write a newspaper for outside support, which was good, but how are we going to get outside support when we can't support one another. Kenyatta just wanted to spread the message through a rap song. Hard-Core and I just wanted to support the movement.

After several weeks of mind wrestling with one another, I politely suggested that we get together and order at least a book or two a month to help us build our thoughts. Everyone agreed but no one ordered. So I went ahead and ordered "Vision for Black Men" and "From Mis-Education to Education" by Dr. Naomi Akbar and "Black Man's Guide to Understand the Black Woman" written by the highly controversial Sis. Shiard Ali. These wonderful and brilliant black writers have devoted their lives to raising up black people from the mental dead.

Once I realized that the coalition wasn't making the type of progressive satisfaction which I'd expected, I politely asked the slaves to stay away from around me. These slaves just continued to beg me for my books but would not ever order any books of their own. But every store day they would have bags full of cookies, candy bars, and drinks. I was striving for some real knowledge, wisdom, and understanding. Food only satisfies your physical desire temporarily and good books have more value to respectfully cultivate the mind. Therefore, as a student of life I made individual sacrifices to gain great progress.

This was my changing point and divine intervention for me.

Fateem was transferred to Bullock, the brother I'd observed from a distance while in "The Bottom." This brother really was beautiful, a real intellectual giant. He was strong in his faith and determined in his will to conquer all obstacles, which he received many. He'd been incarcerated since he was 14 years old and was 23 years old at this particular time. He had already served 8-and-a-half years on a 10-year sentence for robbery and kidnapping. Over those years he had been confined to the most dangerous prisons in the State Of Alabama, where he'd been stabbed twice, had his tooth knocked out, a piece of his ear bit off, and almost had to kill someone.

Regardless of the opposition he received, he was still a scholar and had learned to measure his demonstration by the amount of opposition he received; and he received plenty and stayed determined to survive through the vicious years of prison. He survived his manhood and survived most importantly his sanity. Fateem had a quality character. Everything he did was done with perfection, and he never graduated from high school. He's done more time in prison than he has done in school! (No GED or Trade), so white folks can't lie and brag like they taught him.

Allah blessed him with a hundred and fourteen degrees which consisted of the Holy Quran. He was very studious. He was always studying and concentrating hard all the time. He was also a walking, talking encyclopedia. If a book has been written on the inclination of the black race, he has read it.

His character, personality, and the way he does things was a perfect manifestation of his relationship with Allah (God!). I learned a lot from this brother. His knowledge was unquestionable. This is my mentor, my alter ego, and an influential factor in me becoming the person I am today. The only man I've ever trusted and, believe me, trust is a very difficult thing to achieve among young black men being raised under Anglo-Saxons. This is a true friend, one who won't betray my trust. The most unselfish person I've ever had the opportunity to meet. He always wanted for his brother what he wanted for himself, and that was freedom in all aspects of life. He wanted me to have freedom from sin, ignorance, fear, freedom from having a slave mentality, and freedom from being a stranger to Allah.

Daily we met up on the prison yard or gym to pump weights. Fateem was like me in many ways. He didn't trust anyone, especially those who were afraid to fight. He'd always stress the importance of cardiovascular exercise. This led me to begin jogging.

During our exercises, we had many good constructive debates from basically everything in the world—from religion to politics. The other brothers kind of stayed away from us. We would get strange stares from inmates as well as the administration. There was an astonishing resemblance in our character. Fateem was tall, broad shouldered, slim waisted, and muscled; in intellect he had no equal, extremely articulate, arrogant and opinionated, a real arrogant stride, angry, and no smile. We both possessed the vernacular of businessmen and could easily exchange our roles to black militants. This really is flesh of my flesh, bone of my bones.

It didn't take very long before Fateem realized that the Muslims there were moving at a slow pace and displaying a lackadaisical attitude towards brotherhood. Within a few months of his arrival, he went to work reconstructing the community, putting brothers in place where they would be more effective.

I didn't revert to Islam right then but my attendance of service began regularly. The Muslim brothers would be seated on the carpet, very disciplined, and quiet. After the Adhan had been called, each would make a short prayer and sit back down. Fateem would emerge to the podium, softly reading from the Holy Quran. "Say! He is Allah, The one! The eternal and absolute. He begeth not, nor is he begotten; and there is none like unto him."

Fateem would always lecture the community on concentrating on inner development, not to focus on the things around you and teach us how to use the word of Allah (God) to transform our miserable lives.

"Brother we must by all means apply our maximum potential to harmonize our spiritual, mental, and physical self to be in tune with God's." These words rocked my mind tremendously. Mentally and physically I had done a beautiful job, but neglected my duties of incorporating spirituality into my life. Spiritually I was a deaf, dumb, and blind pagan Negro. Satan was preparing the hell-fire for my soul.

Fateem gave me a Holy Quran and I studied it intensively, along with the Bible. I actually felt the words of Allah vibrating off the pages. My entire burden had quickly been removed. The borderline agnostic concept I'd developed was gone, the metamorphosis I was going through was pushing me to redefine my life.

The Holy Quran is my book of guidance. I am not the type to be intoxicated off of title or infatuated with idol or engraved images. I became fascinated by the Holy Quran's presentation. It taught me to respect and honor all Prophets of God, from Adam, David, Moses, Jesus, and Muhammad (May Allah's blessing be with them all). I made a 360-degree transformation turn from polytheism to monotheism (polytheism is a paganism system where people believe in more than one God). Monotheism is belief in the one eternal God who has power over all things.

The Holy Quran teaches that Allah (God) is closer to us than our jugular vein. The jugular vein is a very important part of the human body; that particular vein transports oxygen from the heart to the mind. The word of God is just like oxygen to live. Do we need the words of God to balance out our life, so we can live right? Spiritually and morally, Fateem was right! Islam is our beautiful way of life.

Around the beginning of 1996, nearing within three years of my parole date, the administration called me up front and gave me minimum custody and put me in for work release placement. The work release placement was denied. They knew with my mind, with three years on work release placement before beginning release from the belly of the beast, I'd never ever be a part of their system again.

However, I was assigned to a minimum custody squad, which did free labor work in Tuskegee, Alabama. I was excited to see the city again, some civilized humans, and one of the prestigious black cities in Alabama. It was eight prisoners assigned to this squad. We got on the van and I sat in the front in memory of Sis. Rosa Parks. The rest of the slaves ran to the back of the van. I can't lie, I felt a sense of freedom again. The job assignment gave me a sign of hope.

Tuskegee was located just thirty-five miles from the prison. Seeing the city was a big disappointment to me. My expectation was greater based on what I had read. The city was straight ghetto action, drug infested, and trashy.

Every morning the officers would drive through the college campus. The college was really the only clean area in the city. Many beautiful black sisters were strutting their stuff, half-nude on their way to class. These sisters' minds had been poisoned terribly. They wanted to be like Daisy Duke. I can imagine their boyfriends are riding around in the projects acting like Bo and Luke Duke. It's very few black men on college campuses.

Our main work site for the minimum squad was a food bank where a minister had established to distribute food to the needy within the area. We had to sort all the food out, place it in boxes, and put it on trucks to be delivered to homeless people around the Tuskegee and Montgomery area.

On the mental plantation, Fateem was busy observing the environment. In the observation, he quickly realized that too much of black talent was going to waste. After I began to explain to him what I was seeing on the work crew in the city of Tuskegee, he asked me to pause briefly. He went into deep thoughts and spoke. "Brother, inferior minds form opinions, superior minds form solutions."

Right then, he immediately went to work collecting all available talents for a play he had in mind. The play was written from a religious perspective in nature to send out an anti-gang, anti-drug, and a positive message to elevate humanity back to its proper place. My job was to handle the public relations since I was getting a little exposure to the free world. Kenyatta was going to play the main character. We had several other undisciplined brothers who spoiled it.

My homeboy Stonewall was very talented with music and art, so he agreed to make the props and provide the music. A lot of brothers didn't want to participate simply on the grounds that a Muslim had orchestrated the entire process.

It was an administrative figure, Sgt. Nettles, who was wise enough to realize quality intellectually when he saw it. We approached him and let him read a copy of the play and he instantly fell in love with it. He also agreed to present the play to the warden for approval. The warden gave the green light. Everyone began practicing their roles. Like I said earlier, the brothers we had to deal with were undisciplined and they began to catch minor disciplines.

The warden began to confront us, since none of us had the proper token to put into this token Negro's head. He constantly gave us a hard time. Once he complained that the play needed some white inmates before we were allowed to put it on. Fateem agreed to let two white inmates play the role of the police and the devil. Then the warden wanted the racial makeup to be half and half. "No! No! No!"

Everyone disagreed on the ideal our precious talent was utilized for the play, not theirs. The warden was really just flexing his authority to see how far we would compromise. But the only difference between Fateem, myself, and the warden was that the warden went home daily and wore cheap suits, but we were in prison for kicking ass and not kissing it. This forced us to drop the play ideal temporarily.

The administration had reinstated the "Free-by-choice" program. The program originated in the mid 80s. The free-by-choice program was designed for inmates with minimum custody with drug related cases to go around the state to schools, drug rehabilitation centers, and different civic organizations to share their life stories to possibly prevent others from making the mistakes that led us to the prison gates.

Sgt. Nettles was the coordinator of the program. Therefore, it wasn't a problem getting in. I viewed this as an opportunity to manifest some of the knowledge I had accumulated. For weeks, I practiced the parts of my life story that would be most effective and how to best avoid glorifying violence. Fateem would record it on tape and critique me on some high points.

My very first speaking engagement was at Bullock County Vocational Center. This place was located just miles away from the prison. I wasn't handcuffed, due to my custody level. An officer escorted me and two other inmates there. Never in my life did I think I'd be riding around in a state police car speaking to little kids and adults about drug prevention. The presentation I gave was devastating. I let them know that this was not a game we were playing, that prison was for real, but at the same time, I tried to appeal to intellect.

"Hey, this is not a stage-show prison, it is a reality. That officer there is not my friend; he's getting paid to keep me in prison. I'm in prison for being rebellious and I have been rebellious all my life. All my life I've done what I wanted to do, displaying a very hostile attitude for everything! I hated school and dropped out at age 15. I could not get along with anyone who attempted to get me to do right in life. I stayed suspended or expelled, which eventually led me to being jailed. It was my lack of respect for the laws that gradually led up to the total disrespect for a human life. I'm a murderer, exploiter, and a modern day chump. I'm not proud of it. I feel the consequences of it daily.

"Being in prison is real hell. I've been incarcerated for 6-and-a-half years, have not enjoyed one day of it. I'm here to warn you that street life is not worth it, or you'll end up where I am at. Please don't follow my footsteps, don't look up to the people in the streets with fancy cars or expensive jewelry. If you do, society will look down on you. Respect your father, listen to your mother, your teachers, your preacher, and your days shall be long. Stay in school and out of the street."

The crowd gave me an outstanding applause. During the question and answer session, those kids were very curious. Their questions were centered around my life, my education, and the many different rumors they'd heard about prison. Of course, I explained to them the truth in every aspect. My family and I are almost strangers because the time we've been apart. They allowed me to speak again in two hours. The officer who escorted us there agreed, but first he called the warden to get it approved, and it was. Therefore, I spoke at another program. The head supervisor was impressed. She immediately called the warden and informed him on the good job I did.

Back at the prison, the warden viewed this program as an opportunity for him to win favors with the community and citizens of Bullock County. He immediately called Fateem up to his office and told him to put the play on.

Fateem met me in the hallway with the news. Fateem had a smile of satisfaction on his face. This was the first time I'd seen him smile in our seven months of association. He shook my hand firmly. "Brother, I've already heard you've done well. The warden already spoke to me about it. Let's keep in mind all we do in prison is only theoretical until we get out putting it to practical use." His words were true. We walked down to the Islamic prayer room and reworked the structure of the play. This time it was going to be beautiful.

Kenyatta was transferred to a minimum security camp. Brother Derrick let a wicked female manipulate him to masturbate off of her. Therefore, he was transferred to be placed on a special punishment chain gang crew. Some more well-disciplined Muslim brothers were with us. All of a sudden people wanted to jump on the bandwagon.

Other free-by-choice speaking engagements where I spoke were drug rehabilitation centers in Dothan, Alabama; Ozark Court House (AA Meeting); and Spectra Care in Dothan, Alabama. The Haven was located around the affluent section of town. Many rich white people were in treatment there, which had a drug or alcohol addiction. Several were court ordered due to many DUI charges.

Their families were going to the extreme, spending big money trying to get them to maintain sobriety. They had all different types of materials to use, big books, 12 step, pills, etc., the basic things I've run across in prison drug programs. After I spoke about my experiment with drugs, alcohol, and the repercussion involved death, jail, insane asylum, loss of memory, and my favorite example was the drug commercial where the egg is frying, "This is your brain on drugs." My brain was almost gone.

During the question and answer period, this little fine, white, blonde-headed female stood up, tears were in her eyes. This display was a sign of sincerity. She went on speaking about how she was in treatment for spending close to $15,000 of her family's money, up getting high on crack. Afterward she asked "Can I please hug your neck?" Not wanting to show my racist side, I extended her privilege and allowed her to hug me; then all the women in the treatment center lined up to do the same. Most of them were getting in line for a second to hug me. They had been away from men for almost eight weeks.

This was strange. These were white women carrying on like this. Thirty years ago their fathers were probably standing around a black man waiting to put a rope around his neck. I had broken out in sweat. It should've been obvious to them that I did not want to touch them. Some offered to exchange addresses but I declined. I did not have time for writing letters. My mind was strictly on learning.

Between speaking arrangements and working on the outside on the minimum custody crew around Tuskegee, Alabama or Lake Eufaula, days went by quick. Then to top it all off, with six hours of intense study a day and two hours of working out, months began to roll by without me worrying about the frustration of being confined forever.

The chumps didn't want to see the righteous men prevail. Envy was coming toward us from all ends, inmates and authorities. As we strived to make progress, we could feel the tension in the air. This was because our actions and deeds reflected righteousness. We'd be asked by onlookers, "Who in the hell y'all think y'all are?" When the question came my way, I'd respond, "We are two of the trinity."

This is what kicked it off late one night in seventeen dorm. One of the Muslim brothers was talking to his family on the phone. The noise level was very high, so he asked a few young slaves to hold the noise down so that he could hear. The slaves didn't respect it. He went and got some more of his gang-banging homeboys from Montgomery, Alabama, and they jumped the brother while he was on the phone. About twenty of the brothers ran out of the dorm to get Fateem and a few other brothers. They ran back to seventeen dorm to fight all the gang members and slaves out of Montgomery, approximately fifty of them.

While this was taking place I was asleep. It was normal for me to be asleep before 8 o'clock. Around 12 midnight or 1:00 AM an officer, whom I had been striving to teach, came and woke me up, "Your brother is down the hallway fighting and don't look like he's winning; he needs help bad."

Immediately, I jumped up and put my Timberland boots on. The gates were locked and the hallway was crowded with pigs and inmates. I stayed awake the rest of the morning waiting on the bars to be rolled back so I could get down the hallway. Around breakfast time, I went straight to check on Fateem. They were in the prayer room plotting. All Muslims know that retribution goes to the Muslims. I looked around the room as we were seeing what we had to work with and about ten of them had fear and terror in their eyes. They had me scared. Fateem saw it as well.

I spoke "Brothers, I don't know who's a Muslim or a gang member in here to protect Fateem. Whoever get close to him, I will make sure their head get busted." Fateem wouldn't have it any other way. He had realized that I'd die right next to him if necessary. It served as a warning to the brothers who were still straddling the fence, living the life as a gang member and a Muslim. Fateem agreed that all the brothers didn't need to fight. It was good for all to come to support, but fought only if it's extremely called for. We marched down to seventeen dorm but the gang members weren't where we expected them to be.

When we found the person we were looking for, they were nowhere in sight. They had cliqued up about a hundred deep. We stood in the center and told them the person we wanted. He wasn't among the crowd. So we left that evening. In the softball field, about a couple of hundred of the fools were out claiming that they was going to beat up either Fateem or the first Muslim they catch. They even had the nerve to take the bats from the people who were playing the game.

Before we were able to make our way to the baseball field, the warden, the assistant warden, the captain, and 10 more pigs had come from home and different locations to put the prison on mandatory lockdown. During the lockdown process, they attempted to jump an elderly Muslim who refused to support us. He stabbed him in the eye with an ink pen before the other ones ran. We were convinced that we were next. Fateem gave strict orders that the brothers rotate together in groups of four for several days. We stood side by side. We didn't need anyone else.

Combined, we had the courage of a thousand lions. The only mistake that was made was Fateem went to a Muslim brother and asked for a pair of scissors or knife. The Muslim denied him and ran to the warden and told everything. They locked the brother up, then the snitching began and the transferring of brothers. I had advised Fateem on many occasions that there were brothers with slave mentalities working with the administration, but he was just as stubborn as I was and didn't listen. All the responsibility went to Fateem. Therefore, it could be a docile Islamic community.

Fateem was transferred two days later; the people who initiated the fight were just placed in lock-up.

The morning Fateem was transferred, I walked to the transfer area. We both had too much pride to embrace each other and the sadness was in the air. Both of us were lost for words. All of a sudden we shook hands and I said, "Brother Fateem, you was right for what you did and I wasn't wrong either; just stay strong and don't show any signs of emotions."

He smiled shyly and responded, "Champ! We have both experienced some hard times, but remember a lesson hard taught is a lesson well learned. I would be released in eighteen months. I won't rest until you're free."

He lifted my spirit up and provided me with intellectual stimulation. I love the brother as I love myself. If I'm blessed with the privilege of residing in paradise, I pray to Allah that we are both worthy.

One morning during check-out, as the squad I was assigned to began exiting the back gate, the assistant warden saw me getting on the van. He snatched his head around like he was about to break his neck. As he saw me, right then and there he had me back into the prison. "This one ain't checking out." They had signed me out through his snitches.

Over the following weeks to come, I was assigned to approximately three or four different minimum custody squads, including working at the back gate; none lasted over a few days. They were trying to test my reaction to see if I would blow. All of a sudden my name was taken off the list for the free-by-choice program. Shaft would step down on a few officers demanding an explanation; after he realized it was the warden, he stepped back. This was my punishment for being a strong young black man. Harassment was directed towards me daily.

Then, I was finally assigned to a punishment for nothing. We were only allowed to work around on state property painting walls, cutting grass, and anything that justifies slavery. Pharaoh was in full form now. This big sissy was really slave driven.

The squad was cutting grass around the plantation and the sissy threatened to slap me because I wasn't pushing or working fast enough to satisfy him. After he continued to speak evil words of profanity to me about what he should do, I just stopped working and looked Pharaoh directly in the eyes, warning him before he fully perceived the thought of hitting me, he'll be dead. My expression was read perfectly.

He got quiet; this was my last day of working on the plantation, period. Pharaoh didn't want to let me go. I began to write the prison's commissioner, the governor, the warden, the local newspapers, and the state, that I had been rehabilitated and rejuvenated and I was waiting to be relocated back into society.

My family wrote letters and called and visited the commissioner to reinforce our letters daily. I was prepared for whatever problem came my way; temporarily I turned to the scripture for inspiration.

"I am forgotten as a dead man out of mind: I am like a broken vessel. For I have heard the slander of many; fear was on every side: while they took counsel together against me, they devised to take away my life. But I trusted in thee, O Lord

I said, thou art my God, my times are in thy hand: deliver me from the hand of mine enemies and from them that persecute me."

Psalm 31:12-15.

CHAPTER 16
POLITICAL PRISONER

"This camp brings out the very best in brothers or destroys them entirely, but none are unaffected, none who leave here are normal. If I leave here alive, I'll leave nothing behind. They'll never count me among the broken men...I've gotten angry too often. I've been lied to and insulted to many times. They've pushed me over the line from which there can be no retreat. I know that they will not be satisfied until they've pushed me out of this existence altogether."
Comrade George Jackson, 1970 A.D.

EARLY MORNING IN mid-October 1996, while asleep a uniform officer awakens me, "Pack your bags, you're transferring." A strong feeling of apprehension came across me because I wasn't expecting a transfer. As I began to pack my property, the officer questioned me on what I had done to be transferred to a maximum security prison. The letters I'd written to the prison's commissioner immediately came to mind. I spoke out against injustice. I was mentally preparing myself to face the consequences.

The officer escorted me to the back gate. I was then placed inside of a cage, along with eight other prisoners. All had caused serious trouble in one area or another. Out of the nine inmates, there were only two whites. They were really nervous and constantly pacing the floor, chain smoking, faces red. This made me relax.

Around daybreak, a few Muslims and a few comrades came to the back gate asking questions. "Why are they sending you to a Max Camp?" The response I gave was, "They couldn't kill me here, now they're sending me to a max prison to give somebody else a try." They laughed and encouraged me to stay strong. In the background it was many complaints and excuses of why we were being transferred. All of us had minimum custody.

One brother I'll never forget, "Bowleg" stood up shaking his head as he spoke, "Y'all heard the black man tell the truth. These crackers trying to kill us." Bowleg was in his mid-thirties. He was bowlegged, bald headed, cross-eyed, and crazy as hell. He came in front of me and introduced himself as "Black Man." We shook hands and we talked briefly. Bowleg mainly dominated the conversation, "You're alive, brother, you know them crackers are murderous." Over the next hour he said this approximately a hundred times.

The transit officer came to pick us up. Before we were placed on the van, he wrapped us up in so many chains (leg irons, belly chains and handcuffs) that it was impossible to move. I couldn't believe this was taking place. Bowleg was clowning like a real slave. "Yes, Sir, Brother! This how those bastards brought us over here. We are going to have to die in chains until we fight back. Look at them white boys; they are not used to being chained up. They were born free. They are not going to make it in a Max Camp. They'd be killed the first week." He was speaking so strong against them. They were looking as if they wanted to jump off the van.

During the ride, Bowleg and I got better acquainted. He schooled me to the rules of a max camp, because he served time in them before over his many years of incarceration. He'd been in prison for 17-and-a-half years, been raised in a very dysfunctional family, been raised in the custody of the state since he was eight years old, foster care home, juvenile detention home, jails, and then graduating to prison. Before it was all over, he did twenty years, day for day, on a twenty-year sentence.

After nearly a three-hour ride, the van stopped at the back gate of St. Clair Prison, just fifty miles northeast of Birmingham, Alabama. One of the most deadly prison riots of the 80s happened here.

The prison is a big dungeon. Half of the prison cells are built underground. The outside of the prison looks like a very large project with red brick buildings. The filth populates the air.

All the prisoners who arrived along with me were assigned to the R-1 Building; this was an isolated unit of the maximum security prison. It supposedly had been the best housing accommodations. This was only done to pacify us; a therapeutic community program was also being run in the R-1 building. A bunch of zany activities were involved and humiliation was involved. There's nothing to commensurate towards rehabilitation at St. Clair.

The building houses 190 prisoners. Nearly 40 percent of them had life without sentences. The majority were all good brothers with petty crimes under the three-strike law. Brothers like Kenny G and Big Ed all were serving life without parole.

The first night there, I only slept for about an hour. My mind was occupied with other things such as surviving and why I was there in the beginning. Out of the nine of us, I was the only one with a four-year clear prison record.

Early the next morning the warden sent for all of us. The reason we were given to justify their reason for transferring us was they needed some slaves with minimum custody that they could trust to work around their plantation.

The wardens, who were both certified Uncle Toms, selected a white boy called Butch to be the warden runner to work around the administrative office. This is one of the so-called elite prison jobs. Out of seven blacks this cracker got the better job and ended up having more power than a lot of the correctional officers. The wardens granted it with ease.

Butch was a serial killer serving three life sentences. He was skinny and probably weighed 100 pounds with bricks in his pockets. He was afraid of the general population. Over nearly two years he went up on the G yard twice. The G yard was filled with gator type niggers, gangsters, and gays. Every time Butch went up there they screamed so many sexual remarks at him that he refused to even go to the chow hall. All his meals consisted of snacks, which were purchased from the canteen.

Maximum security prisons are very dangerous places. Generally they hold prisoners serving life without parole sentences or other long sentences. Approximately five hundred prisoners are serving life without parole sentences for heinous murder acts, robberies, and kidnappings. Surrounding the prison is a double chain link fence with electronic detection devices running in between, along with guard towers with high-powered rifles, and a police car constantly circling the perimeter. This still didn't stop the many escape attempts.

Once, a group of white boys built a wooden ladder and attempted to escape. They didn't make it over the gate. The motion sensor warned the authorities and they were caught.

Stabbings and murders occurred frequently. A long dark tunnel is in the center of the prison. All prisoners must walk through the tunnel in order to exchange clothes, go to the trade school, or work in the industry where prisoners are paid $40 a month to produce dry chemicals and cleaning supplies.

After they feed chow, gangs are ganged up along the walls waiting to rob or stab a victim.

Every time I walked through the tunnel, I felt as if I was approaching the valley of death. The many stabbings that I heard of always reminded me of the fact that any day I could be next. Over a hundred stabbings took place a year here, including a couple of murders. For weeks I'd walk the prison yard trying to get a feel of the dangerous environment. The prison activities were wild. The illegal acts were constant, including prisoners who knew me from other mental plantations along with old homies greeted me. Mostly I watched everything from a distance.

By St. Clair being close to Birmingham, Alabama, they basically ruled everything on the yard. It was a handful of inmates from the Mobile area. All of a sudden they've lost their voice and heart. Lil Pop was the one who used to hang with my sorry uncle Redbird years ago. He had a posse of crazy niggers who struck terror in anyone's heart who got wrong. Normally he stabbed someone once a year or had someone stabbed. The inmates had nicknamed him "Heart Attack."

When it came to violence, he was serious as a heart attack and he carried the weight of everyone from Prichard on his shoulder. We hadn't seen each other since I was young but he let me know if I needed any type of help, he had my back, which I never did doubt for one second. My own murder conviction reassured me that I'd survive when not caught up into prison life. We'd walk the yard and talk about life on the other side of the gates. It wasn't very much to talk about due to the fact that over the last twenty years he'd only spent 18 months on the streets over three different time spans.

On the weight yard, I was introduced to Shahid. He was like my mentor Fateem in many ways. He had also served as one of Fateem's teachers. Fateem gave me the Holy Quran and Shahid taught it to me, as well as he introduced me to the etymology of words. This enhanced my understanding of the Holy Quran.

Once, things were going sort of bad for me, so I went to Shahid for advice, which I've done on a few occasions. After he listened to my situation clearly, he gave me a Sura out of the Holy Quran to read for inspiration, which became one of my favorites especially when I learned to apply it to my daily life.

Sura 113 says, "I seek refuge with the Lord of the dawn, from the mischief of created things, from the mischief of darkness as it over spreads, from the mischief of those who blow on knots: and from the mischief of the envious one as he practices envy."

This Sura and many more that Imam Shahid taught me were very instrumental in clearing my mind from fear, ignorance, and superstition. May Allah reward Brother Shahid for his good. Brothers like this are the finest of our kind, but are being held captive by our oppressors.

My new job was to be the administration runner. From a slave's perspective, this was considered one of the best prison jobs. Working around the administrative office, I was given multi-tasks, running off papers for the staff, running errands for them, and a variety of other bitch related duties.

There were several white women working around this area. They suspected negativity from me when I passed by their office. They looked at me out of the corner of their eyes. When they passed me in the hallway, they brushed up closely against the walls. I'd laugh to myself to their actions because when I touch a white woman it is going to be to choke her.

Once, a few state correctional officers got killed in a car wreck after work. The administrative figure was falling out with emotional tears and crying out of stupidity. One of them asked me how I felt about the situation. My response was that I wished they were car pooling. They claim I was wrong for thinking this away. These people don't care about me; therefore my feelings are the same for them. When I have to explain to my baby sisters why I can't come home with them, no police officers cry for me.

These people's minds have been programmed to respond to prisoners a certain way. There was an advance training class around the administration office where all officers attended annually to learn how to become better oppressors and how to keep the inmates divided. Often I'd spend time eavesdropping and getting a good hearing on why the police are so stupid. During training they are taught to view all prisoners as manipulative, dumb, and undercover homosexuals. Working around these fools was very educational for me.

Mrs. Jemison was the warden's secretary, full-figured, blonde-headed with blue eyes. Regardless of some of my distorted teachings that this fit the perfect description of a devil, Mrs. Jemison is the nicest white woman I've met in my life.

At first we didn't agree with each other. Every morning she'd come to work with a smile on her face, greeting with a jolly "Good Morning." Sometimes she'd attempt to talk with me. It was my intention of avoiding all forms of communication with anyone who was employed with the state. Mrs. Jemison helped me get the free-by-choice program reinstated at St. Clair. I spoke at Minor Junior High School, Northside Church of God, and Kennedy Alternative School in Birmingham, Alabama.

A letter came to me from out of the segregation unit wanting to know if I was the same Champ from Prichard. If so, they needed my help to bounce from lock-up. The letter was from my old partner Arthur McFadden. Immediately, I sent him some things and began to work hard towards getting him out of lock-up. This was going to be a hard job due to his disciplinary history.

Arthur had been locked down in close solitary confinement for nearly two-and–a-half years with only a half-hour for recreation and twenty-three-and-a-half hours in a small cell measuring six by eight. He had to eat, sleep, and defecate there. Visitation was limited to once a month, during which the handcuffs and shackles wouldn't be removed. His family hadn't seen him in years due to the long drive.

This condition had forced him into a serious mind of regression, loss of memory, and attitude problems. It took me almost two months to convince the administration to free him from the hell-hole.

One Wednesday evening, he was waiting on me by the gym. We embraced. He was looking rough. We hadn't seen one another in the last seven-and-a-half years. We attempted to catch up on the misery of each other's lives. It was difficult to do so because so much had changed behind us that I didn't even feel comfortable talking to him in that manner in which we were talking. His body language told me basically the same thing.

We walked around the yard; he couldn't much because his muscle tone was gone. We sat on the ground and talked briefly until it was time for me to attend Islamic class. I offered for him to come out to hear the truth. He said, "Maybe later on. I need to get myself together. I have three months before I kill my sentence." We shook hands and I went to class.

Friday morning he was back in lock-up for cursing out a female officer because she accused him of looking between her legs. Out of embarrassment and respect for me, the remainder of his time he didn't send word to me until a few days before his release date (April 17, 1997).

I was down around the warden's office working when they escorted Arthur down the stairs. We hugged and promised to keep in touch. I watched as his sister drove away from the prison parking lot. It felt really good to see my original homeboy being released. The sad part was that by September of the same year he was back in jail, this time for murder and robbery.

The State of Alabama's prison system made a mad man out of him. Now he's just an unfortunate product of the state with life sentences; examples like this always forced me to tighten myself even more.

On the prison level, things weren't going too good. Every day I became a victim of harassment from the authority due to jealousy and the environment. They wanted to know why there were not any white inmates participating in the free-by-choice program. They were assuming that I was having my way in prison.

I became a victim of false accusation. They began to say that I'm probably smuggling drugs in because I never beg to shine their shoes or ask them for anything. Almost daily they were searching me down and holding my money orders that my family was sending me. Nothing was ever proven, just rumors constantly. I'd explained to these fools that it was not right to participate in the things which they were accusing me of. It was clear that they weren't going to lighten up until they had something to prove that I was not a good person.

See, this is how Satan works. Satan will attack his victim from all aspects of life. Surely anyone who put on a uniform to become a correctional officer has taken on the role of Satan.

As I was leaving, a female officer who had been trying to flirt with me for the last few months caught me on a bad day.

She attempted to carry on a conversation but my mind was on something else. Therefore, I dismissed the unattractive smile she had on her face. She started calling me all types of sexually explicit names. This bitch was acting like she had lost her mind.

Champ does not care if a bitch has on an officer uniform. Nobody disrespects Champ and gets away with it. My responses to her insults were so negative that I'm embarrassed to have them printed. She was an advocate of Satan and forced me to reveal my other side. The following morning the warden had gotten a poor report of the incident. She had lied and said that I had some contraband and refused to give it to her. After I explained what really took place, the warden looked into it through several other officers. They were not aware of the argument, only what she had told them. This is how I was crossed out.

Daily I focused on a better way to reconstruct my life using Islamic teachings. All praise due to Allah. The Holy month of Ramadan is the sacred month which the Holy Quran was revealed to Prophet Muhammad by the angel Gabriel. During this sacred month Muslims all over the world fast for thirty days and that Muslims read the entire Holy Quran during this month. Fasting is one of the most important preparations for spiritual life.

The fast is ended with an Eid feast. The feast was held on the visitation yard. The Imam from Masjid Al Quran in Birmingham provided the food for the feast. We started off with a prayer. Twenty of us brothers stood for prayer together. We were shoulder to shoulder and toe-to-toe in order to keep Satan out of the midst. All while the prayer was recited in Arabic, the sound of "Allahu-Akbar!" was heard.

After each motion was a beautiful intoxicating sound, after each recital hands to our ears, then bend over to place hands on knees for a brief moment, then all of us stood up together, genuflecting and prostrating our faces on the prayer rugs in total submission to disciplined sincerity. The perfect sound of "Allahu-Akbar!" coincided with each moment. The prayer was ended with a chant of Takbeer! Allahu-Akbar! It is said three times. The spiritual high I was enjoying almost killed my taste for food. All praise due to Allah for a wonderful experience.

Over the next five years of my incarceration, I was locked up in Atmore, the same frustrated environment. The same slaves I met in 1990 were there. I mainly stayed to myself. Prison life wasn't for me. Therefore, I was waiting for the Alabama Parole Board to be convinced of that fact.

With the help of Allah, I was able to elevate myself by conscious endeavors.

Have we not expanded thee thy breast? And removed from thee thy burden. The which did gall Thy back? And raised high the esteem (in which) thou (art held). So, verily with every difficulty, there is relief; verily, with every difficulty there is relief. Therefore, when thou art free (from thine immediate task), still labour hard and to thy Lord, turn all thy attention.

Sura 94 (Holy Quran)

157061

NEARLY SEVEN MONTHS BEFORE I was to appear before the Alabama Parole Board for the third time, I had gotten into a fight that the administration viewed as a potential riot situation. Therefore, after spending nearly a month in solitary confinement, I was transferred to Stanton Correctional Facility in Elmore, Alabama. Stanton prison served as a blessing in disguise for me.

The first week in August, the parole officer came to interview me. This was my blessing—Mr. Lane, who was once a correctional officer while I was confined at St. Clair, was now a parole officer. He reminded me of my recent fight and wanted to know the details. He informed me of the fact that I had never been recommended before and that he really believed that there are only a few model inmates inside Alabama prisons, and that I was one of them.

He recommended me for parole that day and stated nine times out of ten I would be free, and closed by saying, "Tell your family to get your clothes ready and stay out of Prichard!!!"

Over the next couple of weeks, I moved in silence, not allowing anyone or anything to come in between my freedom. Truly, I trusted that Allah had total control over my affairs.

Nevertheless, I could not forget the vicious rumors of prisoners being so excited that they had a heart attack in their sleep, or other inmates who are so evil that they gang up and stab the prisoner before their release date. Prayer haters had regressed to when they hear an inmate celebrate, "I'm out this B," they will have family members call Montgomery to protest my freedom. It was none of their business—it was between me and Allah!

My uncle was in the same prison with me. I didn't tell him until after ten p.m. when the phone was off. The officers had gotten the news of my freedom. I was called to the cubicle. They commented they weren't aware that I had been locked up for nearly fifteen years. I politely reminded the officers that I was like Jesus: in the prison world, but not of it.

One prisoner, "Dre," who had a good relationship with the officer, had served nearly thirty years in Alabama prisons, found out, came to give congrats on my freedom. "Baby Boy, you said some good prayers. I heard you going home."

The morning of my release, breakfast was fed at 4:30 a.m. I was reading when the inmates went to eat. I took my last prison shower. I couldn't focus. I had been up all night. I began to cry due to being overexcited.

My good comrade, Malik Shahid, we prayed together, read some Quran, promised to stay in touch. Malik had five months before his release date. We still talk monthly now.

By 7:45 I was dressed in a charcoal linen suit, black Stacy Adams shoes. The administration offered me a thirty-dollar check to remind me of how much they hated me, along with a don't-come-back speech.

Other inmates and officers were commenting on how I looked. I can't lie. All that was going on was completely irrelevant. My mind was on "Get out of here and don't look back." Those in power want to keep us in bondage. My mind was made up. I had to let Pharaoh go!

My family was waiting on the other side of the gate. Favorite cousin Tiffany and Kimmy were there. I hugged everybody real quick. No time for pictures. No small talk. "Get out of here and don't look back" is what was on my heart and mind. We jumped into separate cars. I needed to be as far from prison as possible.

Tiffany and I rode in her Ford Explorer. She was putting me on the latest rappers. It was shocking that the majority of them went by "Lil" or "Young." We stopped in Montgomery at Shoney's to eat breakfast. It felt good to be free. A feeling I can't describe now or never. For nearly fifteen years I was inmate 157061; that number had become a bigger part of my life than I realized for the first five years of freedom. I would mistakenly write that number when I applied for jobs.

All praises due to Allah for freedom.

My first stop once I arrived in Mobile was the Islamic Center in Prichard. I needed to pray for more protection and strength from the evils of this world. Praying was going to be a new chapter in my life. From there, we rode through the city of Prichard. Everything appeared to be small and strange.

Technology was a strange thing to me. My imprisonment was before cellular phones became popular. As I entered a battlefield of information warfare, it was imperative that I became familiar with multi-media, writing, broadcasting, electronics, etc. My first major purchase was the Dell computer. I had no idea of what I was getting into. But it came in handy. All major employers require that a person apply for a job online; therefore, patience was going to be a mandatory part of my life. Early mornings I would get up, pray. Read!!! Study on patience, from there play around on the internet.

My mother had moved out of the hood. Living in Mobile was strange land to me. The first night of freedom, my closest family members came to my momma's house for a shrimp boil and to eat pizza. It was so funny because Tiffany had to introduce me to my cousins, who were now grown.

Over the next few days I was like a tourist in my home town. Tiffany made sure I was taken care of. Labor Day cookout at my momma's house, a total of three welcome-home parties in two weeks.

Tiffany, Kimmy, Jr., Iris and Marcy and all cousins from my daddy's side of the family wanted to throw me a surprise hood party in Prichard at my aunt Jean's house. Tiffany let me know how to act surprised, what to say, what to do, etc. A real live hood affair—family and friends I had never met were there. My homies, *all* the hoods. My time eating snow crabs. I'm addicted.

Tiffany and Iris put together a black shoe box and took up money for me. Nearly a thousand dollars was collected. When everybody was drunk, Tiffany grabbed the microphone and collected more money. The following morning I opened up a bank account and thought I'd never be broke again a day in my life.

My exes were attempting to regain a spot in my life, but I was on a total different mission. Plus, they were too old. Malcom X stated that Muslim men should choose a female half their age plus seven. I was now thirty-four, therefore needed a female twenty-five years old or younger. A lot of females who were lined up outside of my mother's house like it was about to be a parade, left in tears. Only a few I allowed myself to fall weak for.

During this stage of my developing, surviving was more important than sex. Far too many of my associates had left prison with great intentions only to return within three. My personal mentor Fateem El-Bey had been recaptured and sentenced to thirty-five years in federal prison for numerous bank robbers. Therefore Fateem's demise was a conscious reminder to be patient. As people were judging and making false assumptions, I was looking for ways to make it beyond their limited expectations.

A month after being released from the "Belly of the Beast," I was working for All Clean Janitor Service. This was a job my family had secured for me by way of a church member; to have a job is a part of parole stipulation. My arrangement was to clean up Ben May Library on Government Street downtown. As usual, a group of blacks assigned to clean a big white building.

I did not mind doing the work. It was the supervisor's attitude that was difficult to deal with. After three hours of working, she'd go on a smoke break and expect for me to sit and listen to her lies. Once I refused, the misunderstanding took place. This heifer starting changing the time of lunch breaks. Anything to have a negative attitude for, she found it.

I was doing everything to exercise my practice of patience, and this witch was pushing it to the limits. Our breaking point was when she drew out a chart of my duties which was eight percent of the cleaning. I didn't complain, just asked her do she think she is being fair. She thought it was okay. Therefore I went on to fulfill my duties.

So when I went into the supply closet, I realized she had locked the gloves and cleaning supplies up. When I approached her, she began to holler something stupid. I walked away because I didn't need that charge. Quitting this job was the best feeling I had felt in a very, very long time. Being harassed was not for me. As I walked down Government Street, I felt free.

Knowing, accepting and appreciating who you are will gain you the respect of others. My family was concerned that since I quit the job, I would self-destruct. That was the least of my thoughts. Old foolish associates of mine had been suggesting that I needed to hustle, but I knew I could not be the man that I was designed to be there. Anybody who thought negative of what I wanted to accomplish, I considered an enemy to my cause.

Fall of 2015 I enrolled in Bishop State Community College with plans on getting an associate degree. On the side I was selling clothes out the trunk of my car, and working through a temp agency when time allowed. I was getting it.

Shortly afterwards, Hurricane Katrina hit Mobile. It was a major upset to the Gulf Coast. FEMA checks were a blessing to most. Whenever black folks get money, they spend like crazy. They was buying anything to justify being broke again.

For the next eighteen months I worked, attended classes, sold clothes, power-washed houses, basically everything to earn an honest dollar. I had two bank accounts, nice clothes to wear. Whenever I stepped out, people knew I had made it. People never would believe that I had just been released. If they did not know me, I didn't tell. It was so many things going on in my life.

I woke up one morning, couldn't decide what I needed to do, go to school, work, or go hustle. Therefore, I packed my clothes and jumped on the airplane and flew to Cleveland, Ohio. The trip to Cleveland was a confirmation of my freedom.

Although this was my first time flying, I felt relaxed and free. I was in total amazement when I saw the snow land on the wings of the plane. It was snowing so badly the pilot had to fly over the snow storm.

Aunt Minnie came to get me from the airport. This was my time meeting her. She was in her seventies, but full of life. During my stay in Cleveland, she and the entire family showed a lot of love. Even the meals were full of love, and it was highly appreciated. I realize their understanding was on a whole different level.

The majority of the people I meet in Ohio left the South to progress and their lifestyle is a reflection of it: decent job, bigger homes and fancy cars. The Ohio lifestyle is a reflection of freedom.

During my stay in Cleveland, I discovered that I had a baby brother. My father had gotten a lady pregnant while he was on the run. When my dad was killed, she was almost four months, therefore my li'l brother.

Lamar never had met our dad. Hearing about him was a big surprise. Seeing him in person was an astonishing event. All my life people told me I looked like our dad. But meeting Lamar, he made me cry. We bonded over the next week and partied hard. All his life he wanted to meet his big brother, Champ! And when he finally did, he could not believe it happened. We had very similar backgrounds: drugs, jail, prison and love to chase women, etc. We talk often now.

Although I was free and working to accomplish greatness, my faith didn't change. I still hold on strongly to the rope of Allah. A lot of people had my transformation misunderstood. Becoming Muslim is a part of my life forever.

I attend several Islamic communities in Mobile. My closest friends share the same faith as I do (Zack, Saleem, Abdullah and Makil Shahid).

This way of life, marriage is half of faith. Due to my personal belief, it was hard for me to say I do! I need a female to help me master my environment, not judge me as an ex-drug dealer and murderer. Although a lot of them had adopted that mentality that I was an ex always.

Kay and I had been seeing each other for nearly two years. She looked beyond my imperfections.

Kay had just completed her master's in education, was twenty-six-years old, didn't smoke, drink and didn't have kids, and she was crazy about Champ! When people see us together, they always inquire how did she end up with someone like Champ! I always answer "She got lucky."

I could not adjust to the Hollywood style of proposing. The only time I get on my knees is to pray. For her twenty-seventh birthday I went to the mall, bought a ring and said, "Let's get married." To be honest, I had bad thoughts about spending three thousand dollars.

We had a simple ceremony at the Mobile Masjid of Islam, Imam Ronald Ali conducted. I refused to let a preacher marry me. She agreed to do it my way so we jumped the broom in front of family and friends and had a wonderful reception at Café Royale downtown Mobile. We rented the entire restaurant and had a seated dinner where our guests were greeted by hosts wearing tuxes and offering hors d'oeuvres.

While they waited, we did not have a D.J., so we rented a live jazz band. She knew I loved the saxophone, so we had *Hot Sax* play for us. Immediately afterwards, she moved into my one-bedroom apartment.

I was so tired of looking at a nearly three-hundred-dollar pair of women's shoes, I thought I would lose my mind. My only solution was to find a bigger apartment. But every time we did a joint application, we got denied due to my conviction. Damn! How much longer should this hinder my progress. I had a job, a side hustle and good credit.

But 15761 still haunted me.

Instead of getting depressed about my post, I went into deep thought. So one day we were out having lunch, we decided to go house shopping. It was hard to find something to fit our rich desires.

After three or four months without any luck, I just went to the bank and asked how could I borrow $200,000 in order to build what I wanted. Everybody thought I was crazy, but I let them run my credit. I presented the floor plan and got approved. Six months later, we moved into a brand-new custom-built nineteen-hundred-square-foot house with twelve foot ceilings and a three-car garage. This was her reward for tolerating me during my difficult times.

Some of the greatest challenges I have experienced upon my release are not being able to obtain gainful and stable employment due to my convictions. Corporate individuals don't feel as if I am educated and polished enough. Nevertheless, my inspiration comes from the creator of the heavens and the earth. I use opposition as a force to strengthen my drive.

Pardoned.

Returning citizens who are on parole are still faced with the responsibility of reporting monthly or yearly, including parole fees of forty dollars a month. Being on parole is certainly a big business. A blessing in my behalf was that my parole officer was a very good Christian-hearted man who felt that I was a changed person who had a terrible upbringing, and had used all the oppositional forces that life had thrown my way as a way to reform myself, and that I shouldn't be on parole for the rest of my life due to a crime I committed as a teenager.

Therefore, silently, before my fifth year of being on parole, he called me into his office and informed me that I met the requirements for a pardon. But it had one stipulation— that I needed to pay $888.00 court cost, four dollars for restitution, and one hundred eighty-seven dollars to Prichard for minor possession of alcohol (when I was a teenager I was arrested for drinking a beer on my grandmama's front porch). Immediately, I took care of my fines. The next day my paperwork was signed and sent to Montgomery for consideration.

July 14, 2015, I appeared personally before the Alabama Parole Board and Pardon Unit, five respectable people I had bonded with over the years to write letters of recommendations in my behalf. Pastor Arran McKinnis attended with me. This had been a long wait. I was ready. My name was called. Christopher Napier! The board chairperson immediately began to speak about my unfortunate lifestyle and how I had been working with the prison system since 1966 and that they have never ever given a convicted murderer or a drug dealer a pardon. They asked why did I think my situation was so different? This was meant to crush my spirit and to throw me all the way off.

Without hesitation, I looked this hillbilly in his eyes and politely replied, "When Moses went before Pharaoh, Pharaoh had a hard heart. But God will touch the hardest heart and make people do things they don't normally do. Besides, a pardon will only help me at helping others." The entire panel nodded their heads in agreement. My pardon was granted.

Many progressive developments have taken place since my pardon. I filmed a documentary, *Redemption Beyond My Past.* I was inspired to write this revision of *Poverty and Prison. Frustrations of My Past.*

But the challenge of finding decent employment still is affecting me. Twice, the Mobile Country Personnel Board has denied me employment due to my past conviction. Soon those issues shall be exposed as the enemy of righteousness.

As I promote myself, misfortunes still are appearing. For some events I would even have to borrow gas money to make it to main meaningful connections. I am a firm believer that the good I do in life outweighs the bad.

I am free, no longer a slave to the system.

So I press forward!

Champ loves to speak to groups, large and small. You can get in touch with Chris 'Champ' Napier for further information and speaking opportunities at:

E-mail: Champmypast1967@gmail.com or via facebook at Chris "Champ" Napier

Web Site: www.PovertyAndPrison.com

22946423R00174

Made in the USA
Columbia, SC
06 August 2018